St. Simons
Memoir

Books by EUGENIA PRICE

St. Simons
—Memoir—

The Personal Story of Finding the Island and
Writing the St. Simons Trilogy of Novels

EUGENIA PRICE

TURNER
PUBLISHING COMPANY

Turner Publishing Company
Nashville, Tennessee
www.turnerpublishing.com

St. Simons Memoir

Cover design: Bruce Gore

Library of Congress Cataloging-in-Publication Data Upon Request

9781684427123 paperback
9781684427130 hardback
9781684427147 ebook

For the Goulds of St. Simons,
with love and gratitude

Contents

Photograph sections follow pages 64 and 160.

PART ONE

The First Six

"GENIE is only half here," I heard Joyce Blackburn tell someone in the crowd around the table where I was autographing in a Tampa, Florida, bookstore on December 1, 1961. "Don't get me wrong. She's enjoying all this, but her mind is back on an island we've just found off the coast of Georgia. She believes she may have found the idea for a novel to be laid there."

I heard a man ask which island.

"St. Simons," Joyce said, her voice showing her own excitement. "It's the most beautiful and romantic spot either of us has ever seen!"

Without turning around, I smiled to myself as I went on signing my new 1961 title and talking to those in the line before my table. St. Simons Island was probably not really the most beautiful, romantic spot either of us had ever seen, but something *had* happened there to us both.

At that point, some old friends greeted me and I lost the remainder of Joyce's conversation with the unseen gentleman, except to hear her exclaim, "She'll be beside herself when I give her the names you've written down. We do thank you!"

Joyce Blackburn, also a writer, is my best friend and housemate. My then current title, *Beloved World: The Story of God and People,* was just out, and my publisher had retained Joyce to travel with me during a promotion tour that had stretched from Friday, November 3, where it began in a store near our home in Chicago, on to Iowa, Ohio, and West Virginia, and south into Florida.

For the first time in the seven years during which I'd done autographing parties, I began wishing that this one would end or that I could escape long enough to steal a few words with Joyce. Having

11

overheard that scrap of talk about St. Simons Island, my heart raced. The crowd didn't diminish for at least another hour, and when the afternoon finally ended, the nice people who ran the store escorted us to our car and stood talking for a while about the obvious success of the new book and the party, so that we were en route back to our motel before I had a chance to question her. "What, what, what! What did that man say about St. Simons Island? Who is he? What does he know about it? What names did he give you?"

Joyce is normally a controlled person—a good thing, since I tend to soar at the slightest provocation. "His name," she said, "is Mr. Mort Funkhouser, and he grew up on St. Simons or spent vacations there as a child—I was so surprised when he told me, I'm not sure which. But he loves it too and he told me about two ladies he said could really help us with research for your novel—Mrs. N. C. Young and another lady whose name he couldn't remember, but she's the postmistress."

It was the sixties—their beginning. Tension was mounting in the United States between North and South. For a moment, I felt a touch of panic. "Georgia is different from Florida, isn't it? Do they hate Yankees in Georgia?"

I was born into a state, West Virginia, formed out of the violence of the Civil War—formed to fight proudly, as my history teachers had drummed into me—with the Northern cause. For more than thirty years, I'd lived and worked in Chicago, with a time in New York during World War II, and yet suddenly my heart was on St. Simons Island, a part of a state I'd never seen before that trip. A state I'd never thought about, really; at that point, I hadn't even read *Gone with the Wind!* Anyway, according to our press in Chicago, cars with northern license plates were suspect in some southern states. If the people of St. Simons turned us away, I felt as though my heart would break! Joyce had lived as a teenager in Virginia, and her parents lived there long after she began to work in Chicago radio. She gave me a knowing smile and said nothing. What did she know about Southerners that I didn't know? Did she honestly believe these two ladies would receive us and help with our otherwise blind research for a novel already tormenting my imagination? I had felt completely accepted by the shadowy woods of St. Simons, by the little white church under its sheltering oaks at the north end of the Island. I had felt—strangely at home. But what about those two ladies who might hold the key to my story? What if they resented questions? What if they thought of us as invaders?

In the few days since finding St. Simons, we had done a party at Effie Sutton's bookstore in Jacksonville, Florida, and another with our friends the Constables in Ft. Lauderdale. Now the Tampa party, too, was behind us, and we looked forward to several days of rest before we were due in Charlotte, North Carolina, then Statesville the following week. No matter how we would be received, we were free to head my white 1959 Pontiac Bonneville back across Florida to the simple, shadow-streaked, light-filled Island I already loved.

"Don't worry about how we'll be received," Joyce said when we reached our Tampa motel. "Southern hospitality is no myth. That I know. Get a good sleep now, so that we can start early."

She was right, of course. No point in worrying. We *were* going back for four or five days—time enough to learn how the Island people took to us and whether or not they would cooperate in research for the novel I wanted so much to write. The novel about an island which was about to change both our lives.

But I, who normally fall asleep within a minute or two after I've closed whatever book I'm reading, lay awake a long time that night trying to evaluate what might be happening to us. The nearest description I could find for the inner excitement I was experiencing in what I considered a rather orderly life was that it was very like falling in love. Not just my writer's brain but my emotions, too, were transported. Wasn't that a somewhat foolish way to feel about a mere place? And why this particular place? I had crisscrossed the entire country numerous times, I had loved many other spots I'd seen, but the spell of St. Simons Island did not let me go.

Since finding the Island, I'd done three busy autographing parties, along with their accompanying TV, radio, and press interviews. I felt I had expressed myself adequately about my new title, *Beloved World*. My passion for St. Simons Island had in no way dimmed my enthusiasm for the new book, in which I'd written all the way through the Bible—had told the story of God and people—somewhat in the style of a novel. Without a doubt, it had been the most challenging work I'd undertaken to date. I had seemed compelled to do it. The Bible is a collection of books, but the strong cord of God's love for people binds them together into the most engrossing narrative of all time. Had that piece of writing turned my mind once more to novels? Was that at least part of the reason for this inner excitement? Writing these lines as I am in 1977, I know that it was. Plainly, an old dream was stirring.

In my teens, I had longed to become a novelist. During the years between, that dream had faded. It was once more vivid as I lay awake in the Tampa motel. No two ways about it, I meant to find out if I *could* become a novelist. There is a wide world of difference between writing nonfiction, as I had done in all my books to date, and actually constructing a novel—even with historical records to follow. I was then contracted for two more nonfiction books. I could, of course, write them while handling research for the Island novel. Joyce had already agreed to put aside her own work for whatever time was required to help me dig out the facts I'd need. The facts to fill out a story we had learned sketchily only a week ago! Incredible as it seems, we had spent but a day and a half on the Island. When we awakened eight days ago, neither of us had ever heard of St. Simons Island, Georgia.

This is the way we found out about it. On November 24, the day after Thanksgiving, we had been eating a delicious barbecue at a drive-in called Bootles' Barbecue in Charleston, South Carolina. We were tired. The tour had been fun and highly successful, but public appearances exhaust us both and we longed for the whole thing to end. The high point had been a visit with Mother in my hometown of Charleston, West Virginia, where I'd miscalculated our driving time to Jacksonville, Florida, the next stop, by two full days. Two days to spare. (Had I learned arithmetic in school, we would, of course, have stayed with Mother for those two extra days. Now—eight days later—in my bed in the Tampa motel, I was giving thanks that my grammar-school teachers had allowed me to skip the lower grades where one learned the basics of arithmetic.)

Sitting in the car that day at Bootles' Barbecue, we wondered how to spend our unexpected bonus of time. We'd already toured the historic sites of Charleston, South Carolina, and anyway, tired as we were, we wanted privacy and simple surroundings.

"How about the coast of Georgia?" I asked. "I've never even spoken there. No one will recognize me. I can just . . . be me. We can find a beach to walk on—maybe even pick up some shells. At least, we can sleep."

Idly, Joyce unfolded the Southeastern Triple A map and began to follow Route 17 out of Charleston south into Georgia. A short distance, some seventy miles or so south of Savannah, her finger stopped on St. Simons Island. "Ever hear of it?" she asked.

"Nope."

"Sea Island looks to be the adjoining island. Some friends of mine went there on their honeymoon. Kinda posh, from what they told me."

I shook my head. "Not for me. I want a place where I don't have to dress up for a change."

"Then how about St. Simons Island?"

"Okay. See if the Triple A guidebook offers any clues."

Joyce found the paragraph about St. Simons Island and began to read aloud, her voice showing more and more interest. She read first that the Wesleys had preached there when General James Oglethorpe had founded the colony of Georgia; that Aaron Burr had hidden out there after his duel with Alexander Hamilton; that long-staple Sea Island cotton had been grown there on Island plantations during the antebellum days; and that—here it came—*in 1884, Anson Greene Phelps Dodge, Jr., had rebuilt Christ Church Frederica in memory of his bride, Ellen, who died on their honeymoon; he then had taken Holy Orders and become its rector.*

She stopped reading.

"Wow," I breathed. "What a story!" Then, after a long moment, I said aloud, but almost to myself, "Anson Dodge lived out what I've been writing about for years from all angles I could think of!"

It was true. For years, I had studied and thought and written about the concept that if God *is* a Redeemer, He must be able to redeem far more than sin. He allows tragedies to happen, so He *must* have a way to redeem them. A way to shine up, to make useful even our heartache and weeping. Surely, if we stay open to His intentions, *if* we allow it—He will find a way not to waste a single tear.

And here were a few bare facts in a guidebook telling me a story that bore out this concept dramatically. No greater tragedy, it seemed to me, could strike a young man's life than to lose his beloved on their honeymoon. In his grief, he could have fallen into self-pity. He could have become an alcoholic. He could have killed himself. Instead, he had seemingly allowed God to make creative, redemptive *use* of his tragedy. He had rebuilt Christ Church in his bride's memory and had then given himself to the people of the Island. His grief had not been wasted!

I think the excitement had already begun in me as we drove away from Bootles' Barbecue in Charleston to head for the first time toward

St. Simons Island. There was no formal agreement between us that St. Simons was where we wanted to go. We simply paid for our sandwiches, refolded the map, and started. As though we had no choice.

We reached the Island in the early winter darkness, and the traffic circle at the end of the causeway, which has since been well lighted, was eerie with fog on that black night. We could scarcely read the signs. The air was heavy and warm and nauseous with a foul, billowing odor which to my city nostrils smelled like rotting fish. (We discovered later that it was from a Brunswick industry.) I drove uneasily through the dense night until we reached the blurred outlines of a little, dimly lighted airstrip on our left. Reassured, we crept along between arching trees, their ghostly strands of gray Spanish moss waving visibly and then invisibly in the low clouds. I drove under the Island's one traffic light past the village section and on toward Craft's Ocean Court, which we had also picked out of the AAA book. We could see so little in the pea-soup murk, we hoped our sense of direction was holding. It was. The neon lights of the motel blinked feebly at us, and we turned into the driveway, weak with relief and sheer exhaustion.

We checked in, carried a few things from the car, and, at the direction of Mrs. Mobley, the nice lady who owned the motel, found a restaurant back in the village. We ate a huge plate of boiled local shrimp and a salad and returned to fall into bed early. As we showered, we thought only of sleep induced by the ocean's steady roar, of the warm winter sun tomorrow, and of a sandy beach right outside.

We had no sooner turned out our lights than chaos erupted in the motel driveway. Young people carrying blaring transistors drove and ran up and down, singing, shouting, and dancing. After two hours of it, I dressed and confronted Mr. Mobley in the front office.

"I'm just as sorry as I can be, Miss Price, and we'll certainly never do it again, but before you called, I'd rented a whole section to a high-school sorority! I'll see what I can do to calm them down. We can't sleep either."

Gentle Mr. Mobley was no match for their thoughtless youthful exuberance. The young people went on raising the roof until about 6 A.M. Then at last the Island silence we were to come to love settled over our rumpled beds, and for two whole hours we slept soundly.

In fact, Joyce was still asleep at eight o'clock, when I could stand it no longer. "Joyce," I whispered. Why I whispered, I have no idea —I was plainly waking her. "I've *got* to see that church! Could we go soon? I can make a quick cup of coffee."

In her usual courteous way she turned over, rubbed her eyes, and gave me a smile. "Of course. I'm ready—*after* the coffee."

Again we followed Mrs. Mobley's directions: "Just keep bearing right till you see the church sign." In a few minutes after we set out, we were driving up narrow, picturesque Frederica Road toward the north end of the Island and Frederica, the site of General Oglethorpe's colonial settlement. *And* toward Christ Church, which Anson Dodge had rebuilt in the time of his deep grief.

That day back in 1961, not a single development or golf course or tennis complex or shopping center interrupted the enchantment of the tree-shaded, sun- and shadow-struck road. It was truly autumn on St. Simons, and sunny yellow grapevines spiraled up through the tall oaks and pines and red-leafed black gums and sweet gums until our eyes and our spirits reeled with the beauty. Every half mile or so, I stopped the car while Joyce got out to point her camera into the wild tangles and wonder. After an hour of exclamations, long, awed silences, and many stops for picture after picture, we rounded the bend in Frederica Road that brings one within sight of the white cross atop Anson Dodge's little church, nestled in the hush of its natural setting under the protective oaks.

Neither of us spoke while I parked under the trees across from the handsome old wooden gateway. We just sat there in the beauty and the silence, until one and then the other got quietly out of the car and began the walk up the long brick path toward the small, elegant, white Victorian building.

We walked a few steps, then stopped. A few more steps and we stopped again, to touch the smooth, silvery bark of an ancient crepe myrtle leaning away from the path. It must have been during one of those pauses that I caught my first glimpse of the thick green masses of resurrection ferns growing along the gnarled limbs of the enormous live oaks. We didn't know their name then, but I was so drawn to them that I kept looking for more, and on the churchyard brick wall I saw them again—sprouting full of life along the moss-covered bricks. During a dry spell, we now know, resurrection ferns curl and appear brown and dead. Three hours of Island rain and they spring to life, green and undaunted—resurrected!

Off in one corner of the spacious church grounds, we could see a lone man burning a pile of brush. The sweet, acrid scent of leaf smoke reached us on the golden December air. Otherwise, the sun- and shadow-filled place was deserted. Oh, a squirrel chattered high and out

17

of sight in an old hickory, and what I now know to have been the broken-whistle call of a red-winged blackbird broke the silence now and then, but there was no one else in the churchyard except the man, obviously the sexton, and the two of us. We were alone—and yet not alone.

"No trouble believing in Eternity here," I whispered.

"None. It's—a happy place, isn't it?"

"Yes."

It was. We were sure the man had seen us, but so far we were being ignored. The little white church was locked. We fully intended to go to where he was raking and ask to see inside, but not yet. For nearly two hours, we walked around in near silence among the fern- and lichen-covered tombstones, reading names, trying to imagine the people. In the novel about Anson Dodge, I used our first sight of the lovely churchyard as a pattern for the first time he showed it all to Ellen, his beloved, on her only visit there.

Joyce and I found the Dodge plot, of course, surrounded by its low, elegantly designed stone wall—also fern-covered and undisturbed in those days. We learned later that Ellen Dodge, who died on their honeymoon, lay in a joint grave with Anson. That Anna Gould Dodge, his conscientious second wife, had followed his instructions—instructions set down in his will as a result of a pact made between him and Ellen that they should be buried together. Beside the joint grave, we found the stone marked Rebecca Grew Dodge—Anson's mother—and here, we also learned later, Anna had not followed Anson's will. Rather, she had buried Rebecca in the spot Anson had directed that she, Anna, be buried—next to him and Ellen. This struck me as an unselfish act and made me more curious about Anna. Beside Rebecca Dodge, that day, we saw the tiny stone cross marking the grave of Anson Greene Phelps Dodge III—the only child of Anson and Anna, killed, we now know, as a little boy in a runaway-horse accident. It was much later that Mr. Watson Glissom, the sexton, told us these things, when finally we broke down his resistance to tourists. But this day, we stood for a long time, I remember, at the far corner of the plot with its encircling wall, looking at Anna's stone—wondering. Wondering about them all.

I remember also our looking at the strange brick-covered grave of a Colonel Wardrobe nearby. (I mentioned that, too, in the early novel churchyard scene.) We laughed at the colonel's name because Joyce and I have never been able not to laugh at funny names. Colonel

Wardrobe did not figure in any of the novels, but I pictured him that first day in his Revolutionary uniform, sporting a fancy white wig.

We backtracked a little to the Stevens plot, reading epitaphs, with no idea, of course, that the Stevens descendants would ever become our friends—our neighbors—that a few years later we would buy our own four acres from a Stevens.

Farther on, across a little pine-straw path, we found the Couper stones, beautifully carved and proportioned. We read with special interest about John Couper (later to be a main character in my third novel, *Lighthouse*). Both Joyce and I have Scottish ancestors, and his inscription struck us memorably: *John Couper, born at Lochwinnoch, Scotland, 9 March, 1759 . . . died at Hopeton, Georgia, 24 March, 1850. Endowed with a fine intellect, a cheerful and amiable disposition, and most liberal and benevolent feelings, his long life was devoted to the duty of rendering himself most acceptable to his Creator by doing the most good for His creatures.*

We tried and tried to figure out why young John Wylly was buried under a broken granite column, we carefully read markers in the Armstrong and Postell plots, and we wondered about them all.

Finally, after examining the set-apart and imposing King plot, we walked toward the little church, wanting desperately by then to see inside.

The sexton was nowhere to be found. We had stayed in the churchyard most of the morning; it was a few minutes after noon. Obviously, he had gone to lunch. Or maybe he was having lunch in the car we'd glimpsed parked on the shoulder of the narrow road behind the cemetery. The car was gone. Our hearts sank.

"We'll find a place to eat," Joyce comforted me, "and come right back. Maybe he works in the afternoon too. If he doesn't, we don't have to start for Jacksonville early tomorrow. We can come back here first."

I grinned at her. "You're as crazy as I am, aren't you?"

We did go back that afternoon, and Watson Glissom was working, all right. But we didn't see inside the church. Watson Glissom's opinion of tourists had not yet been altered. He was to become our good friend, but it would take time. Halfheartedly, he promised to show us the church the next morning. We overthanked him for his courtesy. Praise for his work turned out to be what he wanted and deserved.

When we returned about nine the next day, he kept us waiting only half an hour before he slowly finished raking and entered upon the ritual—it *was* ritual—of finding just the right key. Then, ceremoniously, he inserted the key into the lock of the wooden double doors of the dark little church. We begged him—he liked that too—to come inside and tell us all about it. After all, he was the only person we knew with any knowledge of the enchanted spot which had so captured us both.

The doors creaked a little as he eased them open. Watson Glissom fractured our mood a touch by mumbling, "Got to oil that hinge." A touch, but no more. He snapped on some lights and my eyes followed the aged, varnished pine walls and ceiling beams all the way to the simple altar. We stood in silence, allowing the mellow wood and stained-glass windows to embrace us. The little church does that. Retaining its own dignity, it still embraces anyone who walks into it. A welcome embrace: timeless, warm, holy. And blessedly simple.

"Two fellers named Stevens built it," Watson Glissom began with the terse self-confidence of a professor. "By hand. Every beam and plank in here is hand-sawed and planed. They don't build 'em this way no more." And then he went into his "tourist spiel," as he later told us he called it. One stained-glass window, it seemed, had a flaw in it. "Hunt till you find it," he said. "I ain't tellin' ya where it is."

We hunted, searching the group of figures in the window, our minds anywhere but on a possible flaw in the lovely old work. We found nothing. Our hearts and minds were racing too fast with curiosity about what mattered most to us to play his games.

"You ain't found it yet?"

"No," I said. "We give up."

He took a slow minute to chuckle at our stupidity, then pointed to a disciple's finger with an extra knuckle in it! We tried to laugh with him at the absurd irrelevance. We didn't know him well enough yet to have caught on that with this splendid, rocklike character, such nonsense was not irrelevant.

"What do you know about the man who rebuilt this church back in 1884? Is he really buried out there in the same grave with his bride, who died on their honeymoon?"

"I reckon he is," Mr. Glissom said, "unless they lied when they cut them initials A.G.P.D. for Anson Greene Phelps Dodge and E.A.P.D. for his wife, Ellen Ada Phelps Dodge. They wuz first cousins, ya know." He chuckled again. Then behind his glasses we could see his eyes begin to twinkle as he rubbed his work-worn hands together in anticipation. "Now, when you've looked around here a few more minutes, we'll walk down the path to the gate."

Of course, we weren't finished looking at the church, and except for having caught sight of a magnificent window down front, to the left of the altar, dedicated to Ellen Dodge, we'd found out little of value to a novelist. But we obliged, hurrying along beside the sexton down the path. We didn't want to hurry, but the farther we walked, the more he chuckled. We were about to get the real tourist treatment. He told us later, after our firm bond of friendship had been established, that he especially liked to pull this fast one on Methodists who came hunting the tree under which John Wesley was supposed to have preached.

The three of us left the churchyard and walked out into the middle of Frederica Road—lightly traveled in those days—and he pointed to a spot high up in an oak tree on the far side.

"You see that big old rusty ring growin' up there in the trunk of that tree?" We said we did. He looked us straight in the eye, the corners of his mouth twitching with sly laughter, and paused to ensure the full effect of what he was about to say: "Well, you was askin' about Mr. Dodge. This is what I know about him. He used to tie John Wesley to that hitching ring!"

I glanced at Joyce, who was glancing at me. We both knew that we were being had by this prank-loving gentleman, but for a moment I could sense Joyce wondering, as was I, just how to respond without spoiling his fun or drying up what was then our only source of information about Anson Dodge.

Finally, with a charming smile, Joyce said, "I predict the three of us are going to be friends. We all like a good joke and that's a good one. We do thank you for giving us our first piece of information about Mr. Dodge—obviously he rode a horse named John Wesley."

Watson Glissom's puckish smile vanished. He stood for a long moment looking at the ground and scratching his gray head. " 'Pon my honor, you caught me, didn'tcha? Do you know you're the first ones? The Methodists just turn on their heels and walk off when I tell 'em that one!" After a beat, he said, "I'm a Baptist myself."

"Good. My father's a Baptist preacher." Joyce laughed, extending her hand. "We are going to be friends, you know. Miss Price is going to write a novel about your churchyard and the people buried in it. We'd better be friends, or you're going to have to ask Baptist forgiveness for feeling about us the way you feel about other tourists. We'll be back often. Next week, after a short trip to Florida, and as often as we can get back after that. We won't be one of your here-today-and-gone-tomorrow variety of tourist."

When Watson Glissom had shuffled on back up the walk toward the church to "lock 'er up," Joyce touched my arm. "You are going to write a novel about this place, aren't you?"

"Yes. I'm kind of scared of the idea, but I'm going to *try.*" (And in the novel, I did name one of the Dodge horses John Wesley.)

––––––••••••––––––

That was the way we found the Island, and that was the story of our first visit to the churchyard. I relived it the night of December 1, lying awake in the Tampa motel. I was afraid I might not be able to do it, but I had no doubt whatever that I was going to try.

I turned over in the bed, struggling for sleep. We were going back —the very next day—but if I didn't get some rest soon, I wouldn't have sense enough to ask the right questions of the two ladies Mr. Mort Funkhouser had recommended.

Effie Sutton, the bookstore lady in Jacksonville who had started it all, crossed my mind. We liked her. She'd brought off an excellent party for me in spite of the fact that I'd never before made an appearance in Jacksonville. The thought struck concerning how much I owed Effie Sutton! If she hadn't signed me up for a party long before *Beloved World* had been published, I would never have come south. Without Effie Sutton, I would surely never have found St. Simons Island! Someday, I'd be sure to thank her. To thank her and thank her and thank her.

At 4 A.M. I was still not sleeping. I was admitting something to myself which, as long as we'd been friends, I wouldn't have yet dared mention to Joyce. In my secret heart, I wanted suddenly to get out of Chicago and live forever on the sandy little strip of land which had so captivated me. The whole idea was insane, of course. We had just moved into a fine old Chicago town house which we'd remodeled with enormous daring and expense. We loved it. Our garden had flourished that first year, even in the sour city soil, and we were already planning new landscaping for the next spring. Until I'd been on St. Simons Island for those few golden hours, it had seemed that the city we'd both loved for so many years would be my home for as long as I needed an earthly abode. Life without the conveniences of a big city had never occurred to me. I had never even bothered to wonder how people got along in small communities without telephone deliveries, curb taxis, subways, and international airports.

And yet there I lay, wishing the morning would come, so that we could head back to the bright-dark wonder of our new discovery. How large was St. Simons? We didn't know. How long? How wide? How many people lived there? Had most of the present residents been born there, or across the marshes and salt creeks in Brunswick on the mainland? Who else had found the Island and had succumbed to its beauty and stayed as I already longed to do? Had anyone else ever found St. Simons by accident as we had? Was it really an accident? An accident of mere circumstance and time? If so, I would insist upon a capital A in Accident.

Without sleep I'm a zombie, so I dozed most of the way through the grazing land and pine barrens as Joyce drove as fast as possible back across Florida to the Georgia line. There was no 55-mph speed limit in those days, thank goodness. Every hour counted. Since Charlotte, North Carolina, was scheduled for December 8, we would have to leave St. Simons on the seventh, and today was Saturday, the second. We would have not more than four or perhaps four and a half days. I, at least, meant to pretend that those days would never end. I would live them only in the Now of being back in the magic and the green of our Island.

I was already thinking of it as *our* Island, and we knew only the Mobleys at the motel and Mr. Glissom at the churchyard. But it was, as it becomes now to the thousands who come here. I know they feel that way; they tell me so over and over in letters, and I believe it. Until that memorable autumn, I had reveled in the awesome grandeur of the Western mountains, had loved the very thought of New England since childhood, and most of all in the whole country, where natural beauty was concerned, I'd favored northern California and Oregon. But now I had found St. Simons Island, and all else faded. Something missing deep within me had seemingly been restored. Why? The warming Island sun? The light dimming and growing bright in the "dear dark woods" about which Sidney Lanier wrote so long ago? Light that does dim and grow bright right while one watches, as though a giant lamp were being turned up and then down. I have lived here since 1963 and spent most of my time here, and I still don't know the explanation for St. Simons' gift to charm the visitor. I simply still receive the gift daily.

The thought of the light coming and going among those yellow, twining grapevines and the scarlet creeper—the wonder of the tender, wild tangle everywhere—kept Joyce's foot heavy on the accelerator as we hurried back. We would arrive late that day, Saturday. Our reservations had already been made at Craft's Ocean Court, but beyond knowing that we had a place to put our heads, we had no plans except to look up the postmistress and Mrs. N. C. Young.

We slept soundly that night minus the sorority, and while the surf helped, I'm sure, we were also—in some unexplainable way—back home. Early on Sunday morning, we walked far along the then wide, silvery sands of East Beach down the path from our motel, which was near the gleaming white Coast Guard station. We'd thought of going to church in Anson Dodge's sanctuary under its sheltering oaks at Frederica, but as yet, neither of us wanted to see it with other people present. Assuming Mrs. N. C. Young would be at church, we looked up her number in the thin little St. Simons directory and planned to call after one o'clock to find out if she would receive us. The old chill passed over me. What if she wouldn't? I marvel now at *my* provincialism. But I actually feared that she might not approve of Yankees. Mr. Funkhouser had told Joyce that Mrs. Young was elderly. Her mother could well have lost her girlhood home at the hands of Sherman's men!

We called Mrs. Young's number until two o'clock. No answer.

"Let's go back to the church," I urged. "We're just wasting time. My story is up there—at Frederica. We can't see the postmistress, whoever she is, until tomorrow."

The Episcopal services were over and the churchyard empty by the time we parked once more under the trees across the road. The building was locked. Mr. Glissom was nowhere to be seen. Obviously, he had the day off to attend his Baptist church. We were glad in a way, although both of us teemed to ask a million questions of someone. The nice Mobleys at the motel seemed to know little about the secluded church at the north end of the Island, but they told us that St. Simons was roughly ten or twelve miles long and about four miles wide, although much of it was marshland. "About the size of Manhattan Island," Mr. Mobley offered casually. His statement stunned us.

"How many people?" Joyce asked.

"Oh, something under three thousand." He smiled. "That's why it always surprises folks when we mention Manhattan Island, I guess. Our Island is almost empty of people."

They did tell us about Frederica National Park and that there were three or four isolated houses nearby above Christ Church. A lady from New York named Mrs. Agnes Holt, who owned an antique shop, lived up there in a handsome home built on the site of one of the old Hazzard plantations. An elderly lady named Mrs. Plemmons lived alone nearby in the woods. There was also the old Dodge Home across the road from her house, although it was no longer a home for boys. The mere mention of the Dodge Home excited us. We'd have to find someone to ask about that, too.

Once more we roamed among the gravestones, this time finding another family plot filled with Goulds. In the years to come, the name would become magic to me and to my readers, but as with the other plots, we found this one merely beautiful that day, somewhat over-grown and mysterious. In particular, one handsome stone bearing the name James Gould said, several lines down, "He was a native of Gran-ville, Mass." How did he happen to be buried on this remote little coastal Island? How and why? *How and why?*

In her typically careful way, Joyce had brought along a small notebook with a list of questions. A look at it now makes us both laugh. It is certainly true that in order to get the right answer one must ask the right question. Some of ours were ludicrous, but we learned. By trial and error, we learned.

Late in the afternoon, with the early sunset backlighting the giant oaks and pines and hickories, we started once more down Frederica Road. We'd have an early dinner and go early to bed to hasten the morning, when the red-brick post office would be open for business and, we hoped, for talk with the postmistress. As for the N. C. Youngs, even if we'd approved of dropping in unannounced on anyone, we had no idea where on Frederica Road they lived. We would wait. Surely in such a small place the postmistress would know everyone.

———◆———

"Oh, you want to see Mrs. Everett—Mary Everett. She isn't here anymore. She retired on Friday." The pleasant gentleman at the post office must have noticed our crestfallen faces. "Are you friends of hers?"

"No. We don't even know her. But—" A wave of rare timidity

enveloped me. I'd never written a novel before. I all but revered it as a literary form, and had no idea whether I could actually write one. Now I was having trouble even using the word. "Well, you see, I'm doing a—a *book* on St. Simons Island, and over in Tampa, a gentleman told us that the postmistress might be able to help with our research."

"Oh." The expression on the man's face fairly shouted that people doing books on St. Simons Island were an old story to him—not, he was sure, that any of the books would ever come to fruition. "Well, you can see Mrs. Everett easily enough. She lives right across the street in the white house."

"Do you have a telephone so we could call her?" Joyce asked.

He laughed. "Call her? When you can walk right across the road and knock on her door?"

"That man knows we're Yankees," I said grimly when we were back in the car thinking over what to do. "I felt he was almost laughing at us."

"You've got to forget that Yankee-Southern thing," Joyce said firmly. "I've heard you speak from platforms a hundred times about not prejudging anyone. Mrs. Everett is probably a lovely, generous Southern lady who will help us all she can."

I frowned, because I was downright nervous. Tourists now aren't at all nervous about finding prejudice, I notice, but that was sixteen years ago and the troubled sixties were just beginning. Anyway, I *was* guilty of prejudging, I saw later—I was downright prejudiced against white Southerners, but it was all mixed up with expecting them to be prejudiced against me.

"All right," I said finally. "Let's knock on her door. If I don't find out something about Anson Greene Phelps Dodge soon, I'll explode."

A white trellis arched the gate to the Everett home, a frail trellis covered by an enormous small-leafed vine whose thick trunk looked as though it had grown there for half a century or more. (I later learned that the vine is called a Confederate jasmine and has the most heavenly-scented flower on earth. Clouds of its delicate white blossoms fill the air with their fragrance and beauty in the front and back of my own house now, but it's probably just as well that I didn't know it was called *Confederate* jasmine that day!)

We pulled my Bonneville into the parking area—sand, of course —in front of the Everett home, combed our hair, freshened our makeup a little, and went bravely to knock on the front door, Joyce smiling at me, I uneasy.

Before we were halfway up the front steps, the screen door flew open and a woman in her late sixties, wearing a sweater which matched her blue eyes, came across the porch literally beaming.

"How do you do?" she said. "Were you ladies looking for someone?"

"Yes," I answered. "Mrs. Everett, who until recently was the postmistress."

Her arms opened. Yes, they did. I know, and Joyce backs me up, that my memory is not playing tricks in retrospect. "Well, just come on in the house and sit down. I'm Mary Everett!"

"We apologize for not calling first," I mumbled, but she didn't even seem to hear me. She was calling to someone at the back of the house.

"Dutch! Dutch, come here. We've got the nicest company!"

From the parlor of the modest coastal house that was to become our "headquarters" for all the remaining years of both their lives, we saw Dutch (L. W.) Everett appear in the kitchen doorway just beyond the dining room, a smile lighting his lean, sensitive face. Dutch walked like a rancher even though he was born in Brunswick across the creeks and marshes on the mainland and had lived for much of his life on St. Simons.

"Well, hello, ladies," he said, his hand out. "Welcome to our house. Mama here's got to be glad to see you. She just retired from the post office after eighty years, you know"—a chuckle and wink came on that exaggeration—"and she needs somebody to talk to besides me!"

"Hush, Dutch," Mary said in the sharp, affectionate voice we would come to love and expect—the voice she always fell into when his teasing got a rise out of her. "Sit down, ladies. This is my husband, Dutch Everett—and Dutch, these ladies are—" She broke off and we all laughed.

It was the first chance Joyce and I'd had to introduce ourselves.

"Sit down, sit down," Mary said right after we gave our names. I took note that not a shadow had crossed their faces when I said we were from Chicago—"up in Yankeeland."

"Genie is bent on writing the story of Mr. Anson Dodge and Christ Church," Joyce began. "And in Tampa, Florida, a man told me that you might be able to help us find out what we need to know, Mrs. Everett."

"Christ Church?" Dutch's face glowed. "Mary and I haven't

missed early Communion in that little church in—how many years, Mama?"

"Never mind, Dutch. They don't care how long we've been going. They want to know about Mr. Dodge."

My hopes soared. "The Florida man thought you could help, and also a lady named Mrs. N. C. Young," I said.

"Oh, yes, we know Mrs. Young," Mary Everett said. "She's a member of the little Catholic church, St. Williams. We've been friends for years."

"Captain Young used to run the boat for Mr. Coffin up on Sapelo Island," Dutch offered. "That's the neighboring island to the north. Coffin's the fellow from up North who developed Sea Island back in the twenties. He was a fine man. So is Captain Young."

"Dutch." Mary frowned, but not crossly. "These ladies want to know about *Mr. Dodge.*"

"Oh, there are certain things I desperately want to find out for my book, but"—I laughed at myself—"we love this place so much already, we're dying to know everything about—oh, just everybody, really!"

They laughed with me, and Dutch said, "Well, darlin', that's what our little Island does to folks who come here from away. We know what you mean."

"Yes, we do," Mary chimed in. "Now, what is it you want to know? I've been so busy in the post office for so many years, I may have forgotten what I did know about Mr. Dodge." She promptly went off on a tangent—but I really did want to know *everything.* "You know, my father was the rural postman here since time began! My sister Berta helped him. We all did. In fact, the story goes that when Oglethorpe stepped off the boat at Gascoigne Bluff, he was met by a Gould and said, 'I want you to be my postmaster!' "

If Mary was a Gould, she'd be the first one we'd encountered outside the churchyard.

"Did a Gould come with Oglethorpe?" I asked.

Dutch laughed again. "No, darlin'. That's one of Mama's little jokes." He scratched his handsome silvery head. "When *did* the Goulds first come to S'n Simons, Mama?"

"How would I know, Dutch? You know how busy I've been with the post office all these years."

"You must miss it terribly," Joyce offered.

Mary's light, gray-blue eyes—the eyes we've come to call Gould eyes—misted. "I do miss it. I declare I do! I guess what I miss is having the people to talk to." Her smile came quickly. "But now, I've got you two girls. I tell you, the Lord's good, isn't He?"

"Well, how'll we find out for them about Mr. Dodge, Mama?"

"Why, Berta, Dutch," Mary answered his question. "You know my sister Berta knows all about everything! My sister Berta wrote a fine history of Christ Church once," she finished proudly.

Our hearts leaped. Something actually down on paper! "Oh, marvelous! Could we see what she wrote? Do you have a copy? Was it printed anywhere?"

"Yes." Mary glowed. "I'm sure it was printed somewhere once a long time ago, but I don't have a copy. Berta has it, though, and that's the first thing we have to do, visit Berta. She'll be glad to see you both, I know."

Joyce and I exchanged glances. "Uh—is it too much to hope that we might see her this afternoon? Could you go with us, Mrs. Everett?"

"Well, I tell you the truth, ladies, I can't go today. I've got a meeting to attend."

Dutch twinkled. "This is Mama's new bridge day. She's just been waitin' to retire so she could go to those afternoon bridge games."

Mary flashed him a warning look. A "meeting" had sounded more important, and we could already sense that she truly wanted to help us—or at least, to let us down easily if she couldn't.

"But I tell you what," Mary went on. "You girls check by anytime you want to tomorrow. I'll let Berta know we're coming so she can get out her paper on the church, and we'll just find out everything you need to know about the whole situation!"

We doubted that. There was no way this gracious, warmhearted lady could have known the multiple research needs for a novel that would cover such a long period of time. But our hearts rested. The Everetts had welcomed us as though the four of us had always been friends; and now they told us how to find the Youngs' residence on Frederica Road.

Mary and Dutch went with us out to the car—this became their habit—and it was decided that we'd pick Mary up at ten the next morning. Without a suggestion of self-consciousness or strain, we hugged all around, and Mary told us again how glad she was that we'd come.

For the remainder of the day, after finding the Youngs away, we used up a full tank of gasoline wandering slowly up and down Frederica Road and into every mysterious sandy side lane not marked Private. We drove across another causeway to fashionable Sea Island and cruised the length of its one through street, admiring the impressively landscaped quality homes, the prestigious Cloister Hotel, and the River House. Sea Island was like another world: affluent and man-made. We thought it unique, but it was not our place. The beauty on St. Simons was wild then, untended, random—primitive by comparison, its roadways choked with wildflowers, its grapevines and smilax free to go their liberated ways.

At the motel when early dark came, we were both unusually quiet. Finally, I said, "How about keeping it a secret that I've ever written a book before? With all my heart I want to know that *these* people—Islanders—love me for myself. Not because I happen to write books for a living."

"I don't think it would make a bit of difference," Joyce said. "Certainly not to the Everetts. But whatever you say."

We went to bed early again, hoping that would bring the morning sooner.

———————

Mary Gould Everett was ready and waiting when we pulled up in front of her house across from the post office on Beach View Drive, in what she informed us was the pier section, pronounced "pay-ah." By ten thirty, we had turned off Frederica Road at Mary's direction and were headed out a secondary road called Lawrence.

"There's a fishing camp out here," Mary told us. "Owned by the Taylors. Mrs. Banford Taylor—lovely lady."

"Your sister's name is Berta Taylor, isn't it?"

"Yes. Her husband is Captain Douglas. His brother, Captain Reginald, married Mrs. Banford."

"Is Captain Douglas Taylor a military man?"

Mary laughed. "Doug? No, darlin'. A lot of men here on the coast are called Captain. Captain Doug still does run the boat over to Little S'n Simons Island every day, though—and he's in his eighties. He's looked after Little S'n Simons for years for a nice family from the North."

We remembered Dutch Everett telling us that Captain N. C.

Young once piloted a boat for Mr. Coffin, the man who developed Sea Island. We'd picked up the fact that if a man could expertly navigate the tricky coastal waters, he was likely to be called Captain. It was a title of respect. It meant that he knew the tides and currents, understood the erratic weather patterns, could take soundings. Captains were undoubtedly men of enviable skills. The idea appealed to us.

"The Youngs must be visiting one of her sisters," Mary said. "They don't leave their place much, but I've tried to call several times. Mrs. Young was born at Doboy Island and grew up in Darien, I believe it was. They may be up there or in Savannah, where I think one or two of her sisters live."

Dear Mary was free with everything she knew, but at times she was pretty vague. All the same, she had completely charmed us and seemed to enjoy telling us about the Island as much as we loved listening. Happy as kids at Christmas, the three of us drove along the bumpy two-lane Lawrence Road, which ran straight between acres of dense, high-colored woods. Mary was taking us to Berta; at last we were going to find out something definite about Anson Greene Phelps Dodge, Jr. In less than two weeks' time, that had come to be of prime urgency to us both. We loved using his entire, impressive string of names and did it at the drop of a hat.

Of course, I did have a niggling hope that Berta might be a touch more definite than Mary, but if she turned out to be half as lovable, I could be patient. Joyce had warned me repeatedly that I'd have to let everyone we saw set the tempo of our conversations. Understanding how Southerners made an art of conversation, she urged me to relax and not press for quick answers—not an easy thing for me yet. I tend to press, wanting everything finished yesterday.

Mary told Joyce to slow down as we drove beside a cleared area of pasture land, and at a picturesque old Georgia farm gate she announced triumphantly, "Here we are! This is Oatlands Plantation. It used to belong to a man named Dr. Grant before the War Between the States."

My heart quickened. We had one more scrap of information.

"Now, you two just sit still," Mary said when Joyce pulled up at the closed gate. "Let me open it—I know how. Captain Doug has to keep it closed to hold his stock in."

Back in the car with us, after we'd pulled through the gate and Mary had closed it, she sighed and laughed at herself. "I declare, I'd come to see Berta more often if it weren't for that frazzlin' gate of Douglas's. I hate to open it." We vowed inwardly, of course, that we'd never let her do it again. "But," she went on, "isn't it beautiful in here, girls?"

It was. We drove back over the sandy lane into woods, and our history-hungry hearts leaped as we came in sight of the first authentic ruin we'd seen (except for that of the King slave hospital, preserved on the golf course, which was located at the site of the King family's Retreat Plantation). We know now that St. Simons ruins are few and far between. During the years after the Civil War and well into this century, the tabby rubble of plantation houses and outbuildings, along with the ruins of the entire town of Frederica—which colonizer Oglethorpe had laid out—were carted off so that the thick tabby chunks could be reused to build new houses.

To our question "What is tabby?" Mary said with an airy wave of her hand, "We'll get Berta to explain that whole situation." We were to find that Mary was fond of using the word "situation" in just that airy way.

Joyce parked beside another car under a giant oak tree and turned off the motor. We were in the cleared area in front of a modest frame house similar to Mary Everett's home.

"Look! There's Berta now. I declare," Mary said, laughing, "she's already been down to the store. Berta? Berta!"

A somewhat heavy-set, graying lady was limping along toward the front steps with the help of a cane, a large bag of groceries in one arm. Her back was to us. She didn't miss a beat or even look up until she had reached the steps, tossed her cane to the ground, and laboriously but gamely pulled herself and her load up the steps by means of a pipe railing. Then she set down the groceries, turned, and gave us a beautiful smile and a big wave.

Joyce and I got the remainder of her load of supplies from her car and followed on back through the large, low-ceilinged living and dining rooms to Berta Gould Taylor's kitchen. After much talking and laughing between the two sisters—never, however, excluding us—we settled in the living room around Berta, who seemed tired from her shopping trip and somewhat distracted when Mary told her what we wanted.

She and Mary were as different as two sisters can be. Berta took long pauses before she began to speak—always. She was the older, but not by much. The slow, thoughtful speech was merely Berta's way, we learned during a dozen more such sessions at her house. She conducted herself at all times in the manner of the matriarch of the family, well accustomed to letting the chatter go on until she had something truly important to add.

"Tabby? Why, Mary, couldn't you tell them what tabby is?"

"Why, of course I could, darlin'." Mary laughed. "But you're the family historian. I wanted you to tell them."

Berta then explained that tabby is made from a mixture of lime and oyster shells, sand and water, poured into wooden molds to make thick, strong walls and floors. "Back in Oglethorpe's time," she went on, "they'd pile up big heaps of oyster shells out there near the Frederica River, set the shells afire, and celebrate." Her laugh was low and musical. "They even portioned out just so much beer and ale to the Frederica townspeople, and all night long, while the lime was burning out of those shells, the folks had a good time. Then, after the fires burned out, they had their shells ready to mix into the lime and sand. Of course, here on the coast we never have a shortage of sand." Her eyes twinkled. "They say that once you get S'n Simons sand in your shoes, you'll always come back."

Joyce wrote feverishly in her notebook. I dared not. My handwriting would have told us nothing by sundown.

"Yes, I did write a short history of Christ Church a long time ago," Berta allowed casually. "But, my goodness, I don't know where it is."

"Oh, yes, you do. You said yesterday you did," Mary insisted. "Think a minute. Let me help you hunt."

"No." Berta cut her sister off short. Then, with a good laugh— "You're the last person I'd want to help hunt for anything, Mary! You girls come back in a few days and I'll see if I can turn it up."

Our hopes sank. What did she mean by "a few days"?

"Tomorrow, maybe?" I ventured.

"Oh, I can't say right now. I'll have to wait till it comes to me. Would you like some coffee? I can make some. Douglas drank it all before he left for Little S'n Simons this morning."

We'd grown somewhat accustomed to their British pronunciation of Saint as S'n and liked it. I felt the interview was coming to an enforced end, but I tried one more question: "Is Little St. Simons a nearby island?"

Berta nodded. "Right out there across the Hampton River.

33

Owned by some mighty nice Yankees, the Berolzheimers." Her smile was genuine and beautiful. "Nice Yankees like you girls. Coffee?"

"Thank you," I said, more for the "nice Yankees" than for the offer of coffee. "We'd better go. I'm sure you're tired from your shopping trip, Mrs. Taylor. Uh—could we come back tomorrow—just in case you've found that church history? We'd call first."

"Make it day after tomorrow. Give me a little more time to look." Berta struggled slowly to her feet. "I'm not crippled up like this by nature." She laughed. "I fell and broke my leg not long ago." Then, without changing her matter-of-fact tone one bit, she dropped a bomb-shell of information: "You see, as to that history, Mr. Dodge, who built the present church, married our aunt. She was his second wife—Anna Gould."

We had been there for almost two hours. Two pleasant but almost fruitless hours until that moment! Joyce and I could only stare at these congenial ladies, and then I hugged them both. I hug when I grow suddenly elated. At that moment, I was more than elated—I was elevated. A rich vein had been struck, courtesy of the ex-postmistress of St. Simons, who had neglected to mention that our mystery man, Anson Greene Phelps Dodge, Jr., had been married to a member of her own family! The Gould sisters, who had interested us mainly as friends until then, suddenly became a key—perhaps *the* key—to unraveling the story of Anson Dodge.

We drove Mary Gould Everett back down to her house and with very little urging stayed for "dinner" at noon with her and Dutch and her late sister Julia's daughter—tall, strikingly beautiful Julie Shelfer, whom we were urged to call Ju-ju. Penny, the Everetts' tiny, shy cook, served us "Penny's biscuits and fried chicken"—both delicacies we were to revel in for years to come—diet or no diet. Diet "situations" bored Mary Everett even more than they bored us.

Finding the Youngs' house still closed and silent, we headed that afternoon for Fort Frederica National Park, just above Christ Church and facing out onto the winding Frederica River and Sidney Lanier's marshes of Glynn. Oglethorpe's colonial period had little or nothing to do with the years in which Anson Dodge lived and worked on St. Simons Island, but we were eager to learn about any period on the Island.

"If you ladies like history, you need to see Margaret Davis Cate's material," a park attendant told us in the small Frederica museum.

"Who is Margaret Davis Cate?"

"Well, she's been the postmistress at Sea Island for years, and she's a historian of note," he said proudly. "She brought this whole National Park project here into being. The Federal archaeologists dug where Mrs. Cate said to dig and every time—*every time*—they found the foundation of just the house here at old Frederica she said they'd find!"

"Does Mrs. Cate live on the Island?"

"Yes. But she's just about at death's door, I guess. Stroke. Pretty bad one, they tell us."

Our hopes, raised so quickly, once more fell.

"Anybody wanting to do a book on anything that has to do with the history of this Island needs to talk to Margaret Davis Cate."

"Well, is her material available anywhere?"

He nodded. "We'll have it here, according to her will. But it'll be packed away in big cardboard boxes till the new building is finished to house it."

"Then it's really not available."

"Not for a long time. Only Mrs. Cate could sort it out easily, and she's one sick lady right now."

We expressed our sympathy and left the museum to stroll out across the area where the old town of Frederica once stood. There were well-documented markers along its central street, and we also saw that the tabby foundations had been exposed and preserved. But it all interested us only mildly; our history books in school had scarcely mentioned Georgia and its founder. We did examine a section of tabby carefully—a substance looking much like concrete, but containing whole and broken oyster shells. Joyce learned years later, as she did her own research for her fine biography of General James Oglethorpe, that the Indians had called it *tapi* when they taught the white man how to mix it.

That day, Oglethorpe interested us very little because his name was not Anson Greene Phelps Dodge, Jr. We wandered off the lane marked Broad Street and out under the tall trees beside the Frederica River, which we knew had sparkled its way through the marshes under a similar autumn sun when Anson had lived at Frederica—where he must have lived in order to be near his church.

The man inside the museum had been pleasant, but he'd also informed us that he was from the North and knew little about St.

Simons Island outside the history he was required to know at the fort site. We longed so to have access to the Margaret Davis Cate material, we were still groaning over her illness. Suddenly, Joyce stopped walking and looked at me.

"Did he say Margaret Davis Cate had been the postmistress at *Sea* Island for years?"

I stared back at her, the truth dawning on me too. "Yes. Yes, he did. Do you suppose—?"

We left it unsaid. Without a doubt, Mr. Mort Funkhouser in Tampa had meant to refer us to the postmistress at Sea Island—a *historian.* Already, to us, there was only one Island, St. Simons, and therefore only one post office. Joyce began to laugh first, and we both laughed so hard we had to lean up against an old cannon—which had been set up more than two hundred years ago to fire broadside at Spanish ships that might have dared venture into what Oglethorpe considered *his* waters.

Laughing is one of our favorite means of communication—natural to us both. Finally, I said, "I'm glad! No matter how informed Mrs. Cate is about Oglethorpe and his Indians and settlers, Mary Gould Everett's Aunt Anna was *married* to Anson Greene Phelps Dodge, Jr., and *he's* my man. Do you suppose Mr. Mort Funkhouser knew about Aunt Anna?"

"Oh, probably not, and I don't think there's any doubt that he meant for us to see Mrs. Cate!" Joyce patted my hand, resting on the battered old iron cannon. "We're being looked after. God led us to the right postmistress. He never makes mistakes! I have no question about our being exactly in the right 'situation.'"

"Maybe it's all really God's idea for me to do this novel," I ventured some time later.

"No 'maybe' about it. He's got to be for anything creative that's going to fulfill you."

Bemused by the fascinating case of the mistaken postmistress, we wandered along the Frederica River, soaking in the beauty of the high, open-domed sky that lent such a vastness to the marshy landscape. Sidney Lanier's Victorian poem, "The Marshes of Glynn," which we'd both known since school days, no longer seemed quaint and exaggerated to us. Between us, we recalled the first stanza, chanting it:

"Glooms of the live-oaks, beautiful-braided and woven
With intricate shades of the vines that myriad-cloven
   Clamber the forks of the multiform boughs,—
      Emerald twilights,—
      Virginal shy lights,
Wrought of the leaves to allure to the whisper of vows,
When lovers pace timidly down through the green colonnades
Of the dim sweet woods, of the dear dark woods,
   Of the heavenly woods and glades,
That run to the radiant marginal sand-beach within
   The wide sea-marshes of Glynn. . . ."

"Do you love the marshes?" Joyce asked.

"Oh, yes. Far more than the beach. Marshes are like the desert —changing color with a changing light."

The day was what we came to call a bright-dark Island day. The great lamp in the "dear dark woods" was turned up and down with the passing of every plumy cloud across the sun. We stopped outside the restored ruins of the old fort to watch a fellow maneuver his riding mower skillfully up, and then down, an embankment. Finally, he turned off the motor, got off the machine, and strolled amiably toward us.

"Mighty pretty day," he called with a pleasant smile.

"It's beautiful! How long have you lived on St. Simons Island?"

Joyce gave me a fleeting look. There I was, jumping right into questions again. "You let Southerners tell you what they choose," she whispered.

"Oh, okay."

"I was born here," the youngish man said, and his brown, weather-lined face and wind-bleached hair showed that he'd spent most of his years under the Island sun. "You ladies from off?"

"Yes. Chicago."

"Come all that way to see Fort Frederica?"

"Well, frankly, no. You see, I'm writing a book about Mr. Anson Dodge, who was once rector of Christ Church. I'm hunting people who might know about him. Or even remember him. Know anyone that old?"

The man laughed. "Sure do. Don't know that she actually remembers Mr. Dodge, but she's old enough. I'm sure of how well she knew his second wife, Mrs. Anna Dodge. Wasn't anybody knew her better.

You should talk to Mrs. Lorah Plemmons. When you leave the park, turn left. She just lives around the bend in the road—the road to West Point. West Point was an old plantation owned by a man named Hazzard back before the war with the Yankees."

Joyce had her notebook out. "What's the lady's name again?"

"Mrs. Lorah Plemmons. Lives by herself in a little white house her twin daughters built for her—mostly with their own hands. They teach school up in New England now. Mrs. Plemmons will be glad to talk to you. She's like a mother to me. Tell her Billy Osborn sent you."

"Do you know her number so we could call her first?"

He laughed quietly. "Call her? She doesn't have a phone, but even if she did, you wouldn't need to call. That lady's door is always open to anybody. Never knew a stranger. Smartest woman you'll ever meet, too."

"Well, should we just go—knock on her door?"

"Sure! Tell her Billy Osborn sent you. We're good friends."

We drove north around the bend in Frederica Road, and there across the road from a one-storied brick house sat the little white cottage under its tall trees—a place that would become one of the most familiar and dearest places on the Island to us over the next several years of our lives. That day, we were simply following another good lead. We got out of the car and knocked on the screen door of the small back porch. No one answered. We knocked again, more sharply. No response. At the front of the house, two new rooms were under construction, but no one was working on them. We walked toward the backyard, where some towels and a pair of lavender bloomers snapped on a line in the breeze from the rising tide.

"Mrs. Plemmons? Anyone at home? Mrs. Plemmons?"

A wren in a persimmon tree shouted and another answered from far in the woods. Cardinals flew as thick as Chicago sparrows about numerous bird feeders. I glanced at the ground, and there under my feet were the most beautifully colored leaves I'd ever seen. Red, shaded to brown and chartreuse and yellow and salmon—heart-shaped. Leathery, I discovered when I picked one up to show Joyce. Something in the happy silence made me whisper with excitement as though we were about to discover a shining secret. "Look! Look at this."

"Pear leaves," Joyce said.

"How do you know that?"

Without waiting for an answer, I called for Mrs. Plemmons again. My shout sounded too loud.

"I'm acomin'!"

The cheerful, reedy voice came from inside a little building to the rear of the yard. And then came the chuckle we can both still hear anytime we tune our ears to heaven.

"That is," she called, "I'm acomin' if I can get myself outa this corner!"

We hurried toward the outbuilding, through the double open doors, and there, penned in behind several sacks of cement and fertilizer and a bookcase filled with paint cans, her white hair flying, smudges on her merry face, stood a bent, elderly lady—bent from the weight of many years and from the big joke on herself that she had worked her way into a corner with company there and couldn't get out.

Between us, we moved her barricade, everybody laughing, as she refused Joyce's offer of help in climbing over.

"Never mind. I can make it now. Don't know how I boxed myself in like that, but this garage got to be too much for me. Had to clean it up a little." Wiping her hands on her flowered apron, she laughed again. "A fine how-de-do, company findin' me in such a fix."

Those first few minutes together, the three of us simply stood there and laughed like teenagers. A thing Joyce and Lorah Plemmons would do at the drop of a hat for all the years in which we had her to love. They could just look at each other and laugh, over nothing except the sheer joy of being together.

She had called the outbuilding a garage, but there was no sign of a car. (We learned only recently from her daughters that she had long ago owned a Ford touring car and had learned to drive it—her way.)

As we left the garage together that day, we told her who we were and what we wanted. She was quite stooped, her old legs stiff with rheumatism, but when she shook our hands, her grip was as strong as steel. The strength in those work-worn fingers put an immediate end to our wondering how in the world she had managed to haul those bags of cement and that loaded bookcase. That she would have managed to extricate herself sooner or later even if we had not come, we had no doubt whatever. She had just temporarily lacked leverage. Meanwhile, her special concept of time—eternal time—with which we became familiar through the years, would have guarded her from either panic or surrender at being penned in the garage alone. ("Worry about only one thing today," she used to tell us. "There's plenty of time tomorrow to add to the list.")

Inside her spotless, comfortable cottage, she puttered around "fixing" us a Coke, and then, after she had politely excused herself to wash her face and comb and repin her long, snow-white hair, we settled in her shadowy little parlor to talk. She had to be as old as Billy Osborn said, and in order to have done all she'd obviously done in the garage that day, she had been working since early morning. But she insisted that we stay and talk as long as we wanted.

Seated face to face, an unexpected shyness came over her—unlike our merry carrying-on outside—but I tried being patient and she tried to remember, and we learned that she had been brought by Anna Gould Dodge to the Dodge Home for Boys back in 1919, when her twin daughters, Sarah and Mary, were three years old. They would be almost exactly my age now, I thought irrelevantly—forty-five. Trying harder than ever to remember Joyce's admonition to go slowly and wait for answers, I decided to settle that day for finding out as much as I could about Anna Dodge, Mary and Berta's aunt, who had married Anson Dodge some time after his first bride had died on their honeymoon.

Mrs. Plemmons took a long time to think through each answer —not that her mind was slow. It was as fast as quicksilver. She was merely trying to be accurate. The shyness came and went as we talked, but I'll never forget the look on her intelligent, gentle face when she took a deep breath and said deliberately, "Yes, I remember Mrs. Dodge. I reckon I do. She was *good.* Me and her were *friends.* She called me Old Faithful. She was my boss, but we were friends. I'd get up about four thirty of a morning and milk the cows and feed the other stock and the chickens and maybe hoe a little in the Home garden, and then I'd come in and fix breakfast for all the boys—we had fifty at times —and then when they'd all gone out to play or to school, I'd hear Mrs. Dodge acomin' down the steps from her room upstairs. It was a big old house over where the park is now—and I'd know she was acomin' so we could have our morning coffee together."

Without explanation, Mrs. Plemmons got to her feet, went slowly to the kitchen, and returned with a small ironstone pitcher. It looked old. She handed it to Joyce to examine. "That's the pitcher we always had our cream in for our morning coffee. After the big house burned,

I dug around in the ashes for a keepsake. I found—*our pitcher.*"

"When did the Dodge Home burn?" Joyce asked.

"Back in 1927, just about two years after Mrs. Dodge died. I'm glad she didn't live to see it go up like it did. Built all of heart pine. Went up like a tinderbox. I was workin' in the garden when I saw it start. They built a makeshift house out there where the park is now until the one across the road could be finished."

"Were your daughters living in the Home too when it burned?"

"Yes. We were all there. Mary and Sarah wasn't but eleven."

"Did Mr. Anson Dodge die before you came here?"

"Yes. He died back in 1898. Mrs. Dodge lived there by herself with the homeless boys, except for a little help, till I got here in 1919 or near there somewhere."

Joyce was writing furiously in her notebook, and it seemed to increase Mrs. Plemmons's shyness—perhaps reticence is the word. Or perhaps she was still sizing us up, being as cautious about what she said as we later learned her to be.

"I suppose the Home was opened before Mr. Dodge died," Joyce said.

Mrs. Plemmons nodded. "Yes. After they lost their own little boy."

"Oh, they had a child?" I was pushing her; we'd seen the child's grave.

She nodded again. "Killed in a runaway-horse accident when he was about three. I could show you the exact spot where he was thrown outa the buggy. I wasn't here then, of course, but Mrs. Dodge told me the story a hundred times, I guess. The baby's little head struck a catalpa tree. The tree's still there."

———◆———

"I thought I'd die when you mentioned leaving," I said as we drove slowly back down Frederica Road past the little white church. I was under its spell more deeply now than ever. "Oh, I know she was tired. But what a gold mine she's going to be! Doors are opening all over the place, aren't they? And don't you *love* Mrs. Plemmons to pieces?" I was perched on the edge of the car seat. "How can you look so calm?"

"I'm not calm. I'm driving. You should take my pulse. And yes, I feel as though we've—just met a rare soul."

"She even asked us to come back tomorrow. Anytime." After a moment, I said more quietly, "And so did Mary Everett. I was dead wrong about Southerners, wasn't I? These people, at least the three or four we've met, don't seem to hold grudges against Yankees . . . we're just like anyone else . . . just people together."

"You've never lived in a small place where everyone is known to everyone else," Joyce said. "But life has stayed so simple and open on this Island, even I find it hard to believe. And I was born in a small place."

"It's like they've forgotten the Civil War by now. Funny, that's what I've always thought of when I bothered to think about the South."

"I doubt anyone's forgotten. Maybe they've just had to learn to live with—essentials."

"Or, maybe they're just genuinely polite." We rode in silence for a while down the road through the light-filled trees. "Have you ever met anyone like Lorah Plemmons?" I asked Joyce.

"No. I don't think there's ever been anyone quite like her. She almost makes me believe in reincarnation—as though we knew her before—a long, long time ago. In a perfect garden."

We "checked in" at the Everetts' about midmorning the next day. (Mary, still in the mental environment of her post office, asked us to "check in" with her every day. As though she needed to ask!) Our talk this time began with Mrs. Lorah Plemmons.

"Oh, my, yes," Mary said. "I tell you, she's one of the sweetest women I ever met. Aunt Anna couldn't have made it without her, could she, Dutch?"

"There's never been a finer woman anywhere," Dutch said. "Mama's right. Why, some of those boys she raised in the Dodge Home—grown men now—will drive as far as five hundred miles just to get to spend a little time with her." He laughed. "I guess she's got more sons than any woman alive!"

"As old as she is," I said, "and as hard as she seems to work, do you know she asked us to come back again today?"

"Doesn't surprise me." Dutch grinned.

"Now, what about Mrs. Young?" Mary asked. "Have you been by again?"

"Yesterday. They still weren't at home."

"Well, I declare. They must have been visiting one of her sisters. Seems funny for them to be gone overnight, doesn't it, Dutch?"

"Well, I guess it does." The happy-natured man laughed again. "But how long's it been since you and Mrs. Young have seen each other, Mama?"

"Oh, not long. I don't just remember when. Still, I always know the Youngs are there back under their big trees." She turned to us. "You'll like them. Of course, dear Mrs. Young *is*—what you might call a talker. But always interesting. And they tell me she knows a lot about that whole situation at the Mills."

"The Mills?" We were all ears.

"Yes, darlin'. Mr. Dodge's father was one of the lumber-mill Dodges from up North. His uncle too. I don't know what would have happened to the Islanders after the War Between the States if it hadn't been for those Mills. My Uncle Horace Gould—Horace Abbott Gould —worked as bookkeeper at the Mills all his life, didn't he, Dutch?"

"That's what Berta always said. And Captain Young might have been born at the Mills. I know I've heard Mr. Dodge baptized him when he was just a baby."

"You'll like them both," Mary went on. "Why don't we call them again, Dutch? Maybe they're home today."

While she was looking up the number in the thin little directory, Joyce and I, I'm sure, reached the same conclusion. It might seem that we weren't going to get very far with our research except by spending time and more time with these dear people—there was certainly going to be a lot of extraneous conversation!—but, as with our first clue about the Mill days on the Island, great, golden nuggets did turn up—even though almost unnoticed by those who were being so generous with their time.

"Hello, Mrs. Young?" Mary rather shouted on the telephone. "This is Mary Everett. How are you and Captain Young?" A hand over the mouthpiece, while she talked in a stage whisper to us: "They're home. She's tellin' me all about where they've been. I was right— visiting her sister. Just hold on. I'll get a word in here in a minute. Mrs. Young's awfully nice." Then, hand away from the mouthpiece and talking into the instrument, "Well, I'm so glad you had such a good time. Say, Mrs. Young, there are a couple of lovely girls here from Chicago and they're writing a book about our beautiful Island! Yes.

Isn't that wonderful? What? They're from Chicago, Illinois. Just the sweetest, nicest people you'll ever meet, and they've been trying to find you for I don't know how long. They'd like to talk to you—ask you some questions. A man in Tampa, I believe it was, told them to be sure to see you and me. Well, he didn't know my name, but he mentioned the postmistress." Laugh. "Yes, that's right. I retired, I guess while you were away." After another period of listening to Mrs. N. C. Young, Mary broke in. "Well, what I called for is this. They'd like to stop by as soon as you can see them. Will it rush you too much with your unpacking if they come by, say, late this afternoon?" More listening. Then, "Well, that's just wonderful. Four o'clock. I know they'll be tickled. And oh, you and Captain Nix are going to love them. Dutch and I do. It's like we've known each other all our lives, and we only met day before yesterday!"

Promptly at four o'clock, we were greeted in the sandy lane that wound in and around the Young house from Frederica Road by Captain N. C. Young himself. He stood under his giant oaks—tall, spare, erect, his handsome face in a half smile, his thick white hair glinting in the afternoon sun, his hand raised. The picture is still sharp in my mind, not only because it became familiar with the passing years as the Youngs grew dearer and dearer to us, but because the serenity and strength of the keen mind in the aging body—the keen mind as evident as his good looks—came to typify the quality of all the older folk on St. Simons Island. In Nix Young, in Edith, his wife, in Lorah Plemmons and the Everetts, in Berta Taylor and her Captain Doug (the only one still here at this writing), we not only *saw* quality and inner strength and wisdom and daily good humor, we experienced it with them. They were all so much older, they referred to us as "the girls." And yet their perpetual good humor and the childlike pleasure they took in their Island made them seem, not the oldest group of people I'd ever known at one time, but the most spirited and resilient.

With natural gallantry, Captain Young opened the car doors and bowed to each of us. In all the years in which we arrived at and departed from their home, called Youngwood, Nix *gave* us his little bow. It was a gift we never took for granted.

Standing with him under his big, prized live oak, we introduced ourselves, and immediately, especially between Joyce and Nix, there occurred a genuine love relationship.

"Now, my lady is inside," he said, gesturing gracefully toward the front steps. "She awaits you."

And she did. We saw her as we climbed the steps, sitting like a grand duchess in "her" chair by the window off the wide front porch. The house, with its attractive steep roof, was spotless and airy. Mrs. Young did not get up, but extended her hand to me and then to Joyce as her husband made introductions.

"Sit down, ladies," Mrs. Young said, turning her rather large, handsome body in the chair so as to face us where we sat on the sofa between "her" chair and "his." Once we were all seated—Captain Young too—the striking-looking lady began a monologue delivered with a soft, coastal accent, beautifully phrased and enunciated and spoken as though she were taking up where she'd left off with a carefully prepared lecture.

From the monologue, we learned that they had visited her sisters Pearl and Madge in Savannah, and that there was another sister, Bess, who lived in Albany, and still another, Mildred, who lived on St. Simons. That she, Edith Young, had been born on Doboy Island and Captain Young in Darien, but that his father, who was in the lumbering business, had moved his family to the Dodge Mills on St. Simons when Nix Young was only a year old. That we should run by the local St. Simons Library and ask to see Abbie Fuller Graham's Scrap Book on the mill days. That Abbie Graham, whose father had been mill superintendent, was Edith Young's best friend, and that Mrs. Graham had not only begun the St. Simons Library, but had spent years assembling the rare old material in the Scrap Book which now belonged to the library. Almost in the same tone of voice, she added that they were extremely sorry we'd failed to find them at home when we called, but that she knew we'd both enjoy knowing their two daughters some day, Lucy, who lived in Sparks, Nevada, and Elizabeth, who lived in Columbia, South Carolina. (We were sure both daughters were too young to be of any research help, but the fact that she wanted us to meet them spelled acceptance, and for this we gave thanks.) The monologue ended with, "So—you're writing a book on S'n Simons Island?"

We said we were, and also that we'd just found out about the Dodge Mills and hoped they'd both be able to help us with its history, once we'd formed some questions.

"I grew up at the Mills," the Captain interjected softly, "but my lady's the encyclopedia in this family."

And she was. For over an hour, without a single question from us, her lively mind and speech kept us listening intently as she went into the history of the Dodge Lumber Mills, which were at Gascoigne Bluff at the lower end of the Island (where the causeway to the mainland begins now). The information poured out so readily that all Joyce could do was jot down possible further questions for our next visit. There was no break for questions then, and anyway, we were too fascinated by Edith Young herself to interrupt. Her wealth of knowledge and perspective on that period of the Island's history was astounding, though I'm sure she hadn't thought about it all in a long time.

Mostly, as she talked, she looked out the front window across the porch and onto the wide yard which, Captain Young had told us before we came inside, was so neat because he kept it mowed himself. "I built my own riding mower," he boasted simply.

Finally we had the chance to interrupt and offer to return the next day, since they'd just had a long, tiring drive. Edith Young had been generous with her information, but for a moment or two we weren't sure we'd be invited back. We were wrong. The seemingly sharp looks she sent us only now and then, as though sizing us up for worth, we learned later were merely a mannerism. Oh, she did size us up. She sized up everyone in a flash. Her brain was phenomenal, her instincts sure. But those glances were just to make sure we were listening. And although she admitted to being a bit weary, she kept total control of the visit by insisting that the Captain serve us a spot of his homemade scuppernong wine before we left.

"You may indeed come back tomorrow. At four o'clock," she announced as we said good-bye.

The others had said, "Anytime." One visited Edith Young by appointment. The Youngs rested from two to three; by four, they were "receiving."

But from that first somewhat awesome visit on, Joyce and I were the receivers. There was nothing we could ever give our friends the Youngs compared to what they gave us.

When Captain Nix escorted us to our car, we slipped in a question just for him: "If you lived at the Mills when you were a little boy, did you ever see Anson Dodge?"

"I not only saw him, I was scared to death of him!"

"Scared of him?" Oh, dear—I didn't want to do a novel about an ogre who frightened little boys!

Nix Young laughed with his eyes. "He scared me half out of my wits! Oh, I guess he was just a young man then, but he was a preacher and he had a black beard and wore a round hat—and he baptized me. I didn't care for any of it!"

———————

By the end of our third day back on St. Simons, we had met our first six. The six elderly folk who would not only grow to be dearer to us than most of our own relatives, but who would come to love us, too. These six, in their eagerness and willingness to help, would in their separate ways make possible my three novels laid on St. Simons Island, *The Beloved Invader, New Moon Rising,* and *Lighthouse,* the trilogy of books which of necessity—a necessity that will be more understandable as this book goes on—I wrote backward in time, so that, chronologically, they should be read in the reverse order.

Not that we were anywhere near finding the first novel's title, that early December of 1961. Suffice it to say, in nostalgic retrospect, that *we* were the invaders, and were made to feel beloved, on that Island which had belonged to them for so long and where we were discovering a whole new world. The thought of having to drive away from it in just a day and a half made us almost ill. When would we find a way to come back? That we would come back, neither of us doubted, but *when?*

A strangely suspended, work-filled year stretched ahead before we could even think of returning. We didn't speak of it. There had been no decision made to come back; we simply knew. I was going to write the book, but Joyce and I were too close for me not to be aware that she was as deeply involved with the Island and its people as I. I took encouragement from her enthusiasm. I tend to make quick decisions and jump; she is more thoughtful and cautious, but she was *not* cautious about St. Simons Island! And because I value her judgment so highly, I was relieved and was able to trust my own instincts about the place more than ever.

The first thing next morning, we turned into the winding driveway that led under more big trees to the St. Simons Library. Mrs. Fraser Ledbetter and Mrs. Lillian Knight greeted us politely but with somewhat the same skeptical expressions we'd seen on the face of the man at the post office. Still, they were good librarians and so, after a momentary plunge into a back room, Fraser Ledbetter brought out Abbie Fuller Graham's old Scrap Book. It was a treasury of information that went far beyond the Mills! For nearly two hours, Joyce copied article after article and page after page. Much of what we found that day was never needed, of course, but in the old, yellowed newspaper story of Anson Dodge's death and funeral, we learned the basic facts of the romance found in *The Beloved Invader.*

Fraser Ledbetter and Lillian Knight were to become two of our favorite Island people in the years ahead, but that day, although they were courteous and helpful, both women were too busy with a flower show about to be held in the library to notice much when we returned Abbie's Scrap Book and took our leave.

In the car outside, I said, "Wouldn't you love to know Abbie Fuller Graham?"

"Yes," Joyce said. "That woman would understand how we love this Island—for sure."

Later, at Edith Young's urging, I began a correspondence with Abbie Graham, who in her older years lived in Wellesley, Massachusetts. This kept little cheerful shafts of love and Island lore coming our way for all the years in which I worked on the St. Simons trilogy. For instance, she could still "see" and describe for me the breathtaking Island sunsets over the Frederica River.

———————

We spent the remaining time going like excited children from Lorah Plemmons at Frederica to the Everetts, to Berta Taylor, to the Youngs, picking up a small fact here and a large one there. The dear folk seemed not to realize when they gave us something useful or when they didn't. It was all the same—all lovingly given and all fascinating to us. There would be an hour, two hours of talk about seeming irrelevancies, and then a jewel would be dropped in the same conversational tones—and their eyes would light up when Joyce dived for her notebook as we both exclaimed with delight.

Whether it was during these early visits or later, I cannot now remember, but my writer's imagination was set winging the day Lorah Plemmons quietly mentioned that a large framed photograph of beautiful Ellen, Anson's beloved, lost bride, still hung in the big front hall of the Dodge Home even when Lorah came, some twenty years after Anson's death! Lorah didn't know it, but that gave me two excellent leads: first, Lorah had thought Ellen to be extremely beautiful; second, I was able to deduce that Anna Gould Dodge, Anson's second wife and

Lorah's friend and employer, must have been inordinately unselfish to have permitted him to leave his first wife's picture hanging—and even more so to have continued to leave it so long after his death.

Joyce and I discussed the two women—Ellen and Anna—for hours on end. "We need to see a picture of Anna," Joyce said, and I agreed. If only there'd been time to remember to ask Mary Everett. Of course, it always took time to hunt up old photographs, but I fully intended to keep in touch with Mary and Dutch by mail, and the Youngs too. And Joyce wrote that down in her notebook: *Ask them all to hunt up pictures.* They did, and some of those pictures appear in this book.

Another possibility came to me: Could Anna Dodge have permitted Ellen's picture to remain in the hallway of her home out of regard for Ellen herself as well as for love of her deceased husband? By any chance, could Anna and Ellen have met and become friends? In other words, had Anson ever brought Ellen to the Island—whether before they were married or before, as bride and groom, they left the country on their fateful wedding trip? On the eve of our leaving the Island, Ruth Backus, a dear friend of Lorah Plemmons, allowed us to look through one of her treasures—a rare copy of a privately printed little white book containing the writings of Ellen Ada Phelps Dodge! There, we not only saw her photograph—which was indeed beautiful—but read a poem she had written about St. Simons Island.

So she *had* been there!

I was never able to find out through either the Island people or the living descendants of the Dodge family about a possible friendship between Anna and Ellen, but I "gave" them one just the same. It seemed so right to me. In a novel based on fact it is, of course, up to the author to supply the always missing pieces. The small crystal gull which Ellen gave Anna was suggested by a cherished piece which Joyce owned. My conviction that Anna was remarkably unselfish had ample basis in fact—the picture still adorning her home after Anson's death and the selfless way in which she had buried his mother, Rebecca, next to him, reserving the far corner of the stone-walled Dodge plot in Christ Church cemetery for herself.

After all these years, it's impossible for us to recall the exact day when Berta Taylor dropped the "ending" of *The Beloved Invader* into my hands. Joyce and I both remember that it was at the end of a long session of talk, at a point when reluctantly we were leaving because

Berta seemed tired. For certain, it was the same day that Berta had told us at length how her mother, Maimie, had been Anson Dodge's staunch supporter in the church, and how she had always decorated it at Christmastime.

"Mothah used ropes of smilax and sprays of holly and cassina berries—some powdahed with lime to look like snow . . ." My Yankee ears were still having trouble understanding the slurred, soft, coastal speech . . . "She would powdah the smilax and the holly and the cassina with lime and blend them in with big old cedah gahlans."

Joyce says I sat frowning and when Berta went right on, I stopped her. "I'm sorry, but what was that last item you mentioned? I don't know what that meant."

Berta looked a touch impatient at being interrupted, but more perplexed that I hadn't understood. Joyce came to the rescue. "Cedar garlands, Genie!"

"Oh."

After we'd all had a good laugh—at me, certainly not at Berta Taylor—she went on with the story that gave me the ending for my novel—always the most difficult part of any novel for me, next to its beginning.

By the circuitous route that was becoming familiar, Berta had moved from her mother, Anson Dodge, and the church at Christmas back to her Aunt Anna, Anson's second wife.

"Oh, yes, Aunt Anna told me about her heartbreak at Mr. Dodge's death. Told me many times when I was a girl. She adored that man with everything she had. Loved him with all her heart and being."

Mary Everett, sitting that day across the room from her sister, beamed with pride and injected one of her frequent "You see, girls? I'm just too young to remember, but I told you Berta knew just about everything!"

We were always amused because, in the face of her evident pride in her sister, Mary also never failed to add, "I was just too young to remember!"

"Go on about Anna loving Anson Dodge, please," I urged.

"Well, she did. She loved that man. Do you know she just packed up and left the Island once they buried him . . . out there in the same grave with his first wife?"

In Anna's time almost no one ever left the Island except in an emergency.

"No, no," I prodded. "We didn't know that. Please tell us about it. Where did she go?"

"Well, she and Mr. Dodge, of course, had done a lot of traveling in the years they were married. He had plenty of money and had been all over the world. Anna knew how to travel by then and I'm sure they had friends in lots of places, but she wanted to be alone with her grief. The first boys had come to the Home. Aunt Anna and Mr. Dodge had already opened the Home in memory of their own child. The boys needed Aunt Anna there. She knew that. She loved children. Of course, she had a cook and a housekeeper to help take care of them, but the little fellows needed her too. And yet she couldn't stand it in that big house without Mr. Dodge. So, she just lit out and went from city to city trying to find peace. Finally, she ended up in New Orleans. Then, one night while she was taking a buggy ride with a hired driver, she suddenly caught the smell of steak and onions cooking somewhere in a place they'd passed. Mind you, she'd not been able to eat much since Mr. Dodge died. The steak and onions smelled good. They made her hungry. And she knew, right then, she could face going home to St. Simons!"

Much later on, Joyce and I made a trip to New Orleans just to familiarize me with the streets Anna might have driven through that night when the homey aroma of steak and onions gave her back both her appetite and the courage to deal with reality. It was a real gift from Berta to have an ending that was not only satisfying but had actually happened!

During our last visit with Lorah Plemmons before we left, we tried to keep her talking about the physical look and feel of the old Dodge Home—the same tall, Victorian house Anson Dodge had had under construction while he and Ellen were honeymooning in Europe and India. We knew by now that India was where Ellen had died. Lorah owned a scarred but handsome nest of Oriental tables which the newly married couple had sent back to Frederica among many other treasures —treasures Ellen would never see again—but which came and were received at the Frederica dock as a favor by Anna Gould. The ornate nest of tables had become a familiar sight in Lorah's parlor, but once she told us their origin, we all but revered them. (They belong to us now. Sarah and Mary Plemmons urged us to accept them when Lorah died early in 1977 at the age of almost one hundred and two.)

The Dodge house as Lorah described it was "big, had three stories with peaks and gables in the roof. There was a big dining room where the boys ate and a small dining room where Mrs. Dodge ate and any friends she might have there." Lorah told us about the handsome carved stairway off the large entrance hall, the big porch that ran around three sides of the house, and the square, high-ceilinged room where Anna kept her "papers"—the room that had been Anson's study. There had been "a lot of fancy woodwork to dust"—a fact about which no one could be more certain than Lorah Plemmons, whose hands had dusted that fancy woodwork for so many years.

Between Mary Everett's telling of it and Lorah's retelling, we pieced together—for our own sakes, not for the book—the story of how Lorah Plemmons had come from the north Georgia mountains with her twin girls to live and work at the Dodge Home. Of course, as Anna grew older, she needed a strong and wise woman to help her at the Home. Anna's sisters had been educated, but Anna had chosen to stay on the Island with her beloved father, Horace Bunch Gould, the main character in my second novel, *New Moon Rising*. From the years spent with her father, an educated man, and from constant reading, she was self-taught, though provincial and somewhat shy when she married Anson Dodge. Once married to him, she grew to love the excitement and broadening influence of his culture and travel. And so, by the year 1919, Anna very much wanted someone she could trust with the supervision of as many as fifty homeless boys. The coming of such a woman would not only free Anna for occasional travel but would relieve her of some of the heavy burden involved in the guidance of the boys' lives.

By some means, she learned from a friend about Lorah Plemmons, a young widow with two infant girls, all needing a home. Anna went to the mountains herself and brought Lorah and Sarah and Mary back to St. Simons. We knew Lorah and have known her daughters now for many years. As far as loyalty is concerned, and love of a place, Lorah came to consider herself a native Islander, and her daughters are Islanders to the core. No one doubts that Lorah was a gift of God to Anna. She was to us also.

Mary Gould Everett *was* too young to have remembered much of what we needed to learn about, but during those first days—and indeed, to the end of Mary's days—she gave us love and stimulation and laughter and support. Mary colored the Island for us as did no one else. Any thought of her, once we were back in Chicago beginning to work our way through that tightly scheduled, busy year that stood between us and a return to St. Simons, transported us right back under the Island sun. Maybe it was because the others were so much older that Mary only seemed to be our spark plug, but I don't think so. She *was* a spark plug. The post office's loss was our gain, and we like to think we helped fill some of the empty days away from the career she'd loved for so long.

One thing we know—the shoe box filled with shrimp sandwiches which Mary handed us when we stopped that December day to say good-bye to her and Dutch helped us through the wrench of leaving the Island. Stopping under trees for lunch—trees too far north to have gay Spanish moss banners waving from their branches—might have made us too "island-sick" to eat, if it hadn't been that no one could make shrimp sandwiches as Mary made them.

There was a love note tucked inside the shoe box too. It read; "We'll miss you girls—hurry back to us."

We fully intended to do just that. At the earliest possible time.

PART TWO

Interim

THE Christmas and New Year holidays of 1961–1962, spent with Mother in my hometown of Charleston, West Virginia, were not as lonely as she and I had expected. This was only our third Christmas season without my father, and Mother had moved shortly before into a handsome old house near the downtown section of the city, leaving forever the dream home on the hill which she and Dad had built with such joy—the carefully planned spot where they would spend their days gloriously together once he'd retired from his dental practice. He had gone to be with God instead, and Mother was starting the second part of her married life alone: giving Dad the most meaningful gift any woman could give a man—her total effort at learning how to live creatively without him. The first two Christmases had been hard for us both. My brother, Joe, and his family were living in Columbus, Ohio, and their 1961 Christmas call helped—we all laughed a lot and repeated goofy childhood sayings, such as shouting "Merry Yule"—but St. Simons Island helped most of all.

Hour after hour I talked to Mother about it, wishing for more facility with words as I tried to describe the yellow grapevines and red creeper decorating the tall pines and gums and oaks more beautifully than she could ever decorate a Christmas tree. She had never seen Spanish moss, and I'd brought along a piece to show her how the coarse, pearl-gray strands were interwoven with mysterious irregularity into veritable banners that waved from tree and telephone wire. Laughing, she reminded me how I'd always said I hated Spanish moss, Southern drawls, and almost anything to do with the South. Hated it all in my snap-judgment way without ever having seen for myself; we'd gone no farther south than Virginia on holidays during my childhood, and as an adult all my traveling had been north to New England and west to California and Oregon and Washington.

I doubt that anyone ever had a more understanding mother than I—considering what I'm like. Not once did she ever urge me to marry and settle down and give her grandchildren. The thought of such a thing seemed as foreign to both her and my handsome, happy-hearted father as it did to me. That I would somehow carve out some kind of career for myself appeared inevitable, even to my more orthodox brother, Joe, who loves me as deeply and steadily as I've always loved him, in spite of our widely divergent interests. He sells guns and could not be less interested in books, but he loves his only sister. I hate guns and spend my life either writing or reading books, but I adore my only brother. The years and the distance have never changed that one iota. Nor has either of us ever tried to remake or even to influence the other to our way of thinking. The women's lib movement has appealed to my sense of fairness, but it took me a while to understand what all the fuss was about, since I've always been as liberated as a human being can be to find my own way, my own life-style, my own pursuits.

I believe my mother to have been the key to my freedom for all the years of my now fairly long life. She always wept a little each time I said good-bye and went back to college or to Chicago or New York —wherever I happened to be living and attempting to find work as a writer—but she also urged me to go. To hie myself to a big city where I'd have what she called "advantages." The "advantages" were there, but so were a lot of other things. Still, Mother's unshakable belief in me as a creative person and my father's equally unshakable belief in me as "my girl" kept me at least no more than a little left of center where my behavior was concerned. They supported me until I was well into my thirties. Oh, not quite every month of that time, but almost. The careless, wasteful side of my nature I tried to keep from them both— although Dad and I were so much alike, I doubt that he was fooled— because I wanted their respect more than anything else.

My first soap opera went on network radio when I was about twenty-two. I seemed destined to be what Mother always believed I would be, but that early triumph ended abruptly with a change in ownership of the network—the old NBC was split into NBC and the Blue Network (now ABC)—and my sudden success went down the drain. My parents only encouraged me and once more began to send my allowance. And through all the high "ups" and the low "downs" of the next decade they remained supportive and cheerful and believing. Then, at a low, low time in my personal life, I met Jesus Christ, and the burden of my happiness and welfare and success shifted from Dr. and Mrs. Walter W. Price to the Lord God. I didn't change in my tastes or my talent—or lack of it—but in my values. The things that once had made me laugh now made me weep, and the things that had once made me weep now made me laugh. Best of all, I had a Polestar by which to set my course. Not merely as a struggling writer who had to prove herself or admit defeat, but as a human being who began to long for balance above all. The story of that conversion at the age of thirty-three can still be read in a book called *The Burden Is Light!* In print after more than twenty years, it now includes in the latest edition an added chapter on those twenty years—the perspective gained from just living them and from my life on St. Simons Island.

In that first holiday season after finding the Island, it was already giving Mother and me a focal point for enjoying ourselves. For hour after hour, day after day, and evening after evening, Mother listened to my excited talk of the Island and its people.

"You've got to see it and meet them all," I kept saying. "I can't wait to take you down! I'm sure Joyce and I have only touched the history there. You created my interest in history when you kept taking Joe and me to all those battlefields and old restored houses when we were children. You've got to love St. Simons! You've got to love it as much as I do."

"I'm ready to go anytime you can take me," she said. Then one night, sitting in her spacious, high-ceilinged living room, surrounded by the familiar furnishings that bore the marks of her exquisite taste, the lights burning on our tiny Christmas tree on the big round marble coffee table, she asked softly, "Will you and Joyce move to St. Simons Island to live?"

My heart went into a spin. I tried to give her a smile—a casual, you've-got-to-be-kidding smile. I didn't make it. "What?"

"Will you and Poddy move there sometime?"

She and Joyce, who share a totally fey brand of humor, had begun for some reason of their own to call each other Poddy years before, when Joyce stopped often to visit Mother and Dad en route from Chicago to her own parents' home, then in Hampton, Virginia. My parents loved her dearly. Mother hadn't asked, "Might you and I move there sometime?" She hadn't even mentioned herself. As usual, she was leaving me free. She was just asking a question prompted by that ESP of hers which had caused her to call me long distance so often during the years—always at just the times when I needed to hear her voice. I really tried to look surprised. "Move to St. Simons—to *live?*" Of course, the thought had crossed my mind a hundred times, but I could honestly tell her that Joyce and I had never discussed it. "We're in debt on the Chicago house, remember? And I've got a year or more of heavy speaking commitments. St. Simons Island is not centrally located, no matter how gorgeous it is."

There was no doubt that the town house we'd loved so in Chicago had lost some of its glow, but we did still love it, still intended to work hard in our garden out back come spring. After all, I'd thrown dollar after dollar into dried blood and nitrogen and every other product advertised to make a compost pile work and had doubly injured my back hauling heavy sacks of peat moss up and down the basement steps. Far more than money had gone into that house and its funny, long, narrow bowling-alley lot.

Mother recalls that I sat there for a long time saying nothing. Finally, I said, "I love the Island too much to talk about . . . moving there, when it's so beyond me to manage."

In a moment, she patted my knee and whispered, "Don't forget —all things are possible with God. If it's His idea, you'll swing it."

———————

My date book for the year 1962 tells me that I returned to Chicago on Monday, January 8, and by January 10 was settled into my third-floor office again, planning the contents of my next contracted book for the Zondervan Publishing House, to be titled *A Woman's Choice.* When I think of that book now, I always remember one chapter in it, toward the end, in which I developed a beautiful and sound premise based on a "light" that came to Joyce on the one night I spoke in Statesville, North Carolina, en route north. We had been talking, of course, about the Island we had just left and our newfound friends there.

"Those people have taught me something already about—creative love," Joyce said. "About God Himself."

"Me too, but what have they taught you?"

"That we're all creators. That participation in God's creativity is the stuff of life. That I'm directly responsible for the kind of world I create around you in our daily lives. We're all responsible for the kind of world we create for those around us just as surely as God was responsible for His created world. Have you ever experienced a more beautiful atmosphere around you than when we sat in Lorah's little living room? In Mary's?"

I've just checked *A Woman's Choice*. That's the gist of what I tried to develop there. I meant to give Joyce credit—in fact, I'm surprised to find I didn't—but then manuscripts are sometimes cut when edited, and such a credit may have been. Never mind. We get our "light" from the same Source, and I know I've told from many platforms what she taught me that night in Statesville, after the Island folk had taught it to her—had *demonstrated* it to us both in the kind of "worlds" they'd created around us on their Island. The bright worlds we'd try to keep around us by some means throughout the long, busy year ahead.

By January 11, I see in my date book, I had written a rough draft of Chapter I of *A Woman's Choice*, and by February 10, a Saturday, I had written eleven chapters and was on an airplane flying to a speaking date in Buffalo, New York. On Tuesday the thirteenth, the date book says, I flew home again, and by February 21, *A Woman's Choice* was finished. On March 2, we celebrated the happy fact that we'd shared a home for a whole year. (We'd been friends since my conversion in 1949.)

"Don't you wish we could celebrate on St. Simons?" I asked.

"Did you have to ask that?"

My schedule said that for the rest of March and right up to the first of April, I'd be flying to the West Coast to speak and autograph books, then to New England and then to Ohio, but although the summer would take me to Washington, D.C., Grand Rapids, Michigan, and lots of places in between—like Wisconsin and Minnesota and Indiana—the month of April, wonder of wonders, was free! *A Woman's Choice* would be published in the late summer of 1962, and I'd be "out" autographing another new book for almost six weeks' time, but there was that lovely shining blank month of April in my date book.

I had planned to spend at least part of April with Mother, and Joyce was going to her parents in Indiana for an extended visit, but— a whole month free?

In minutes I had Mother on long distance and was regaling her with plans which literally evolved as we talked.

"You and I will stop off in Columbia, South Carolina, on our way and pick up Aunt Betty and take her with us to celebrate her April birthday!"

————•◆•————

In my ample 1959 white Bonneville, christened Bonnie, Mother and my Aunt Betty Vaughan and I laughed and acted silly all the way from Columbia, South Carolina, to Savannah, Georgia. I always connected my beautiful Aunt Betty with good times and laughter. Since their childhood, in which they were especially close among a very large family of brothers and sisters, Mother—Anna—and Betty Davidson had always found something funny in about anything that happened. They passed their humor on to me, and just now I could not have been happier—except to wish Joyce could be with us—as we zoomed along old Route 17 toward the Island in the first week of April.

There had been letters and long-distance telephone calls galore moving between our house in Chicago and the Everetts and the Youngs on St. Simons. We longed often to call Lorah Plemmons, but in those days she was still refusing to have her happy life with her cardinals and wrens and painted buntings disturbed by the ring of a telephone. She was complete in herself—her daughters habitually left her enormous freezer stacked, and one longtime Islander friend, Frances Burns, who worked in the post office and whose husband had been one of Lorah's "boys" in the Dodge Home, brought her bread and milk and fresh vegetables. She needed no telephone. But during one excited call to Edith Young, she informed me—she did not merely suggest—she simply informed me that, when I brought my mother down, we were to stay with Mr. and Mrs. Walter Goodwillie at the Ship House on East Beach.

"A charming place built like a big ship—right on the water. They're lovely people and attend St. Williams, my church."

So of course I made reservations at the Ship House. We would stay in what cheery-voiced Mrs. Goodwillie had told me long distance was their largest apartment—overlooking the water and called Quarter Deck. I could stay as long as Mother and Aunt Betty were content to stay too, up to the last week in April. I didn't have to be anywhere else until April 27, when my date book read, "Sign books in Grand Rapids and speak."

Elsie Goodwillie and her sophisticated husband, Walter, and their people-dog, Brenda—all three of whom Joyce later immortalized in her children's book, *Suki and the Magic Sand Dollar*—greeted us in the Ship House driveway, and Walter carried our luggage upstairs to Quarter Deck—a great, airy living room furnished in comfortable wicker, plus two bedrooms, kitchen, and bath. Aunt Betty flew to the floor-to-ceiling windows which enclosed the entire east end of the enormous room and plopped herself down on the cushioned window seat.

"I've found my place," she announced. "No big deal, but you know I can't take the wind in my sinuses, so you dolls do just as you please—I'll sit here and tell the tides when to come in and when to go out."

We bustled around unpacking, all three of us in high good humor. Mother immediately undressed for a shower and was padding around in her altogether when a sharp knock barely preceded the opening door, and there stood Elsie Goodwillie, a stack of fresh towels in her arms. She and Mother stared at each other for a split second, then with the utter aplomb I've come to expect from Elsie, she said cordially, "I hope you ladies are comfortable," deposited the stack of towels on a table, and disappeared before Mother had time even to blush. Mother and Elsie (we later learned that Elsie also had the maiden name of Davidson) have laughed often since over that encounter, which did away forever with any shred of formality between them.

By dinnertime, I had brought in a load of groceries and was hatching another plan. The winter and early spring had been so busy, I had traveled to so many cities, written an entire book, and answered so much mail, I had not yet dared to nail down a date when Joyce and I could come back to St. Simons to stay for any length of time. We both knew we were coming back. A quick look at my date book before I left Chicago showed that my last lecture for the year was at Houghton College in New York on Friday, October 26, but there was also a note in red pencil concerning a short book for young people which I had promised. Any writer knows what disciplines he or she must exert. We don't all consistently follow this self-knowledge, but at least a writer who has worked at a craft professionally for as many years as I have is fully aware of what blocks concentration and what facilitates it. No one needed to tell me that the book for young people *(Find Out for Yourself)* had better be written away from the happy distraction of the upcoming novel and St. Simons Island. Part of me wanted to renege on the book, but as a Christian I knew that was out of the question.

Still, I had reasoned that day as I drove slowly back to the Ship House from the grocery store, there could be no harm in one or two weeks on the Island before the year ended. Once I'd done the lecture at Houghton College, I could begin the promised book, get the feel of it —the sense of renewed confidence needed every time I start another one—and then schedule at least two full weeks on St. Simons before Christmas!

My foot went down hard on the accelerator as the plan grew. Then, remembering where I was, I slowed the car. One thing St. Simons had done for me already was to accentuate by contrast the tensions of my hectic pace. For these few blessed days anyway, I meant to enter into the Island tempo. But I saw no reason why Mother could not fly to me for Christmas in Georgia this year. Joyce would, of course, go to Indiana to her parents, but Mother and I were free. The thought of Christmas on St. Simons Island filled me with a kind of childlike wonder. As I turned into 11th Street on East Beach and headed toward the Ship House, I could almost see the ropes of cassina berries and "cedah gahlans" in candle-lit Christ Church back in the days when Anson Dodge was its rector and Maimie Gould hung the decorations.

Loaded with grocery bags, I climbed the stairway to Quarter Deck singing "Jingle Bells." If Mother and Aunt Betty thought me odd to be singing about one-horse sleighs on a bright, sunny, Island spring day, they didn't show it. Typically, they both entered in with my plans for the Christmas holidays.

"I haven't flown alone in a plane since your father went away," Mother said. "It's time I did. Can't wait, can you?"

"Can't wait, can you?" has, from my childhood, been a familiar litany in the Price house. Both my parents endowed my brother and me with a magnificent sense of play. Even small, daily things could be exciting to anticipate—to wait for.

For four or five days, I took Mother and Aunt Betty, when we could drag her away from that big front window overlooking the ocean, up and down Frederica Road to visit Lorah Plemmons, the Everetts, the Youngs, and Berta Taylor out at Oatlands Plantation. I watched Mother carefully. She was falling in love with my Island too. She became the note-taker this time as, at every opportunity, I popped another question during our visits.

Now that I've done archival research for the first two novels in my St. Augustine trilogy, I do have to laugh at the "visits" which Joyce and I called "research" in those early Island days. I have found the more

Anson Dodge
(The Beloved Invader)

Ellen Dodge
(The Beloved Invader)

Anson Greene Phelps Dodge III, aged three, a few weeks before his tragic death

Horace Bunch Gould as an old man (Invader; New Moon Rising)

Dodge Home a few years before it burned to the ground in 1927

Captain Charles Stevens, Horace's good friend (New Moon Rising)

Black Banks plantation house

James Gould's lighthouse

Marker at grave of James Gould, Christ churchyard

TO OUR FATHER

In memory of

JAMES GOULD

Who died
September 3rd 1852
In the
80th Year of his age

He was a native of
Granville, Mass.

JOYCE NORMAN

orderly research done in archives of various libraries and historical societies to be, in its way, an equally exciting and stimulating experience, but there *is* some order to it. Research for almost all of the St. Simons trilogy was joyful chaos, served up with endless love and endless cups of coffee and tea and homemade wine and cookies and hot biscuits and fried chicken and cornbread and my very first taste of collard greens.

It was a little less difficult, a bit less agonizing than before, to drive across that causeway toward the mainland when Mother and Aunt Betty and I left the Island at the end of our pleasant visit. I *was* coming back. I had called Joyce long distance in Indiana. She was excited too. As early in December as I could clear my desk and get packed, we would head old Bonnie once more south and east toward the Georgia coast.

I kept the promise to myself and wrote several chapters of the book for young people; I kept my remaining speaking engagements; and on December 6—almost exactly one year from the day we first found the Island—we were there again, unloading Bonnie beside an attractive brick seaside cottage we'd rented long distance through Larry and Beth Black, St. Simons realtors. The cottage was called "Go Native." We were ready to do just that.

—————

Go Native, perched on the edge of a sand dune, was extremely attractive from the outside, though contemporary for our taste. But it was on St. Simons Island and so, to us, was a palace. Inside, the two-storied living room with balcony sleeping quarters had an enormous fireplace and comfortable furniture. There was one bedroom, a well-done kitchenette, and an adequate bath. The little house welcomed us on the brisk, bright December afternoon when we arrived under what seemed to our Chicago-tempered bodies a warm sun.

"I'll go out first thing and find a telephone and ask Larry Black how to get a load of wood," I said excitedly as we carried in our things. Naively, I said I hoped it would be cool enough at night on the Island to have a fire.

"I doubt that you have to worry," Joyce said. "You've never lived by the water."

"Oh, yes, I have. I grew up on the Kanawha River. Our house was right across the street."

"A river isn't an ocean."

It isn't. I did manage a load of wood from Johnnie Golden, a tall, spare, courteous black man who was to become far more important in our lives than either of us dreamed possible that late afternoon when he dumped the overwhelmingly large heavy oak logs at our door. (In Chicago our grate took light 12-inch birch logs.)

"I brought some fat pine too," he said proudly. "You didn't order any, but there's no way to start that oak without it."

"Fat pine?"

"Fat pine." Mr. Golden's nod had authority. "Full of resin. Good oak's a little green. No other way to make it burn." He held out a sticky, heavy splinter of pine. "Here. Smell it."

I did and Joyce did, and it's quite possible that that was the exact moment when, unknown even to us, we both became Georgians.

As soon as the car was unpacked, of course, we were back in Bonnie and on our way to "check in" at the Everetts'. Mary had written to us regularly all the time we were away, and more often than we should have, at night, we'd reached the place where we just had to call her long distance. She shouted then, for sure. After all, Chicago was a long way from St. Simons, and she seemed, bless her, always to be as elated to hear our voices as we were to hear hers.

After a good visit with Mary and Dutch, we had dinner out and returned to Go Native for our first long evening before our fine oak-and-fat-pine fire.

In front of the gigantic fireplace, we had noticed (who could help noticing?) a king-sized, overstuffed armchair for two. Joyce, knowing my penchant for large, comfortable chairs, had already "given" it to me. Her generosity turned out to be impractical. The house was so damp and cold when we walked in that evening that even my spirits dropped. Briskly, I went out to select some live-oak logs. That is, I was brisk when I began carrying. But those logs were so heavy I had to bite my lips to keep from giving up.

"I knew to bring big ones," John Golden had boasted. "I've brought wood to lots of folks in this cottage."

Sensible, considering the immense, gaping fireplace. Joyce is the better fire builder of the two of us, but I love to toss on the logs, so I lifted and heaved nobly—one huge live-oak piece I'll never forget! I injured my back permanently, as it turned out, but I hadn't yet discovered that, and nothing could have spoiled our fun at that point. The damage does make my writing days seem longer now that I'm older, but I live with it.

After much experimentation with not enough and then too many fat-pine splinters, we were transformed that night from city dwellers who started lightweight birch logs with newspaper and one or two scraps of kindling to rugged live-oak fire builders. The blaze roared up the chimney, taking most of the heat with it, and the chill clung to the glamorous but clammy cottage. In fact, it clung and settled for the entire duration of our visit, and the big chair which Joyce had so graciously given to me became *our* chair. Mother arrived during a slight warming spell, but almost every night before she came on December 18 found Joyce and me, each wrapped in down comforters, huddled in that chair, fortunately big enough for two. I remember two or three nights after Joyce had gone to Indiana when, with the wind howling off the ocean, Mother and I also had to share it.

Shortly before Mother was due, we bought our first artificial Christmas tree, a tiny one at Maxwell's store in the village, and decorated it with little hand-tied red-velvet bows and one string of tiny white lights. Until then, we'd both pooh-poohed artificial trees, but although the Island roadsides and woods stood thick with real ones, we wouldn't have cut one for any money! Our lives had been treeless in the city for too long.

Mother exclaimed over our pretty tree and the house, and Joyce gave her the balcony bed area and doubled up with me until Mother and I took her to the blessedly small, quiet St. Simons airport to get the old Delta prop plane we'd already named the Bluebird. I tried to imagine Joyce's conflict as the plane roared down the single runway. She would not have enjoyed Christmas away from her parents, and yet she was leaving St. Simons Island for a long, long time. Our schedule was too full of work and speaking engagements for us to think of coming back for almost another year.

Beth Black, of the real estate office, had come with her nice Larry on one of his many trips to Go Native in those early December days when we were still hoping that somehow the one heating unit in my bedroom could be made to work. It never did, but Joyce and I got better acquainted with Beth, and she brought up the name of Agnes Holt, the New York lady who lived alone in the beautiful white-columned house at West Point.

"You'd both love Agnes. Larry and I do. She speaks your language, she has beautiful taste, she loves books—and she's as crazy wild about this Island as you are. Why don't you just stop by her shop, the Tabby

House, and introduce yourselves while you're here? You should see the shop anyway."

We did and, as Beth predicted, we loved Agnes on sight. Her shop became her to a T. Housed in an old slave cabin that was once a part of the Kings' Retreat Plantation (at the crossroads near the airport), the Tabby House itself was a work of folk art. Agnes had papered the interior with old newspapers as the Negroes had done to keep out haunts and bad spirits. The original wide floorboards were scrubbed white, and the stock of antique furniture and silver was exquisite. We not only loved Agnes, with her soft, modulated speech—the elegance of speech of one who was born in the South but has spent years in New York—I also fell in love with an old butternut hutch which stood against one wall of the shop.

"That hutch was here when I bought the shop last year," she explained. "I like it so much I don't care if anyone ever buys it!"

I seldom see a thing which I truly want, but the memory of the grain and color of that soft-toned, worn antique hutch returned again and again during the next long year.

That first December, knowing that Mother and Agnes would hit it off, we invited Agnes for dinner one night at drafty Go Native and were fascinated to learn that she too had rented Go Native during her first weeks on St. Simons. Her mother was visiting her from Jacksonville, and one night the wind blew so hard through a missing louver in the jalousie windows facing 12th Street that her mother's hat—worn to protect her head from the drafts—blew right off!

Beth Black had been right. Our circle of new friends on St. Simons Island would include not only Larry and Beth but Agnes Holt, still dear to this day.

I doubt that two people ever had a merrier Christmas than Mother and I that year. She seemed truly freed to be able to confess to her own delight at *not* having to cook Christmas dinner for once, and giggling like two idiots, we set out for Brooks, my Island grocery store, to buy two frozen turkey pies, a bunch of celery, and a can of cranberry sauce. Joyce and I had tried the turkey pies and liked them. Our giggles only increased when, on the day before Christmas, we discovered at the store that other tourists (there weren't many then, but enough) had had the same idea for Christmas dinner. There were no turkey pies left, and not even one can of cranberry sauce!

"I think a bunch of celery sounds worse than fasting," I said.

"We'll eat out. But before we hunt a place to eat tomorrow, let's drive up Frederica Road and call on the Plemmonses. Lorah's daughters will be there; they're due to drive in tonight. Anyway, I love their mother so much, I *have* to give her a big Christmas hug!"

About three o'clock in the afternoon on Christmas Day, a time when we felt the Plemmonses would be finished with dinner, Mother and I drove slowly up through the sun-shadowed wonder of Frederica Road (as it was then) and parked in the cleared area near the Plemmons cottage where Joyce and I had always parked. The clearing was what was left of a lane that once led to the old Dodge Home—a lane Lorah had told us the children called Pretty Lane. We liked the name and parked there until we began to feel at home enough to drive in the Plemmonses' big yard under Lorah's shiny camphor tree.

The sun was warm; birds shouted their winter calls from the dense woods behind Lorah's cottage. I hadn't once missed a snowflake for Christmas. The Lord God had decorated His trees with sunlight on St. Simons Island for His own birthday that year. Branches hung heavy with red holly and cassina berries, and pale, powdery blue berries adorned every cedar branch. And yes, the yellow grapevines and scarlet creeper still spiraled up and down and around in a wild and holy profusion of light. We took a deep, grateful breath and began the short walk across the road and up Lorah Plemmons's lane.

At the back-porch door, I shouted "Merry Christmas!" and let out the Indian war whoop with which Lorah and Joyce and I had already begun to greet one another. In her high-pitched, vigorous voice, Lorah whooped back as the kitchen door flew open and two red-cheeked gals in blue jeans, with shirttails flying, joined their mother: "Merry Christmas! Merry Christmas! Come on in. Dinner's on the table!"

They had seen us park in Pretty Lane and had hurried to set two extra places at their festive Christmas board in the cheerful kitchen Joyce and I had come to love.

Neither Mother nor I will ever forget the goodness and wholesome joy of that day, or that meal—Sarah's perfect turkey with "gallons of giblet gravy," Mary's yummy candied sweet potatoes, and Lorah's indescribable Southern snap beans and cornbread. Mother and I ate as though eating were going out of style. But most important of all, on the day when we celebrate the coming of incarnate Love into this old world, we had experienced that Love incarnate in our three new friends. Sarah and Mary are like my sisters now, and Lorah, though gone from our sight, will always be close, the merry, wise, strong mother of us all.

I hadn't seen my own courageous mother so happy since my father went away. The Island had given me still another, deeper joy: she might never leave her own home and friends to move there, but she loved St. Simons too.

On a cold, blowy, gray day during the first week in January, Mother and I packed Bonnie and began the long drive north to Charleston. I drove through an ice storm most of the way over the mountains, I remember, but I wasn't nervous and not at all afraid. A new sense of adventure had seized me. I believed in the future as I'd never believed before. Nothing was clear where actual plans were concerned, but St. Simons Island and that first novel were in my future now. Instead of a logical fear of our danger as we crept around those steep Blue Ridge curves, Mother and I simply enjoyed the breathtaking beauty of the ice-covered trees as we rolled over the wet, slushy roads to the foot of the West Virginia Turnpike, less than a hundred miles from Charleston.

"Let's stop here somewhere for the night," I said. "It will make our happy holiday last that much longer."

Mother agreed, and although all we could find was a meager out-of-date motel with no telephone, we cozied in with coffee from our thermos and sandwiches put together from the remaining contents of our ice chest. We thanked God for our Christmas on St. Simons and for the safe trip over the mountains, and just before I crawled into bed, I looked out the motel window to see the road we'd just left iced over solidly.

We'd decided to stop driving just in time. It seemed a good omen in all ways.

After a day or so, I said the always difficult good-bye to Mother and drove back to Chicago in time to meet Joyce's plane from Indiana.

We settled in for a long winter of working and waiting—a winter I think I'll never forget. I finished the promised book for teens and began the next, for which I'd already signed a contract. I traveled through the winter section of my speaking schedule, and at night, when I was at home, we dreamed before our crackling fire of the Island and of Anson and Ellen Dodge and of Anna—of the happy times in Lorah

Plemmons's house and in Mary and Dutch's living room, where, at Mary's command, Joyce and I alternated sitting in the "Black Banks chair."

Black Banks had been the name of the old Gould home. When the flatboat bearing the Gould furniture had overturned in Buttermilk Sound as the family was making its Civil War-time escape from their beloved Island, the graceful platform rocker with its hand-carved spindles had been the only valuable chair saved. We dreamed also of the soft breeze which always seemed to blow through the Youngs' parlor in the tight coastal house which Captain Nix, with an experienced sailor's eye to the weather, had designed and built himself.

I normally read a couple of books a week, and that winter I read and reread a magnificent novel which deepened my own desire to learn how to construct a novel—not a novel as great as this one, naturally, but at least a good one. The book was the late Gladys Schmidt's *Rembrandt*, a biographical novel about the life and the soul of the renowned Dutch artist. I had never before been so moved by a book, nor have I since. It gained neither the critical nor the popular acclaim it deserved, but as much as any other happening in my own life, Gladys Schmidt's *Rembrandt* nurtured my determination. For months I intended to write to tell her a little of what she'd done for me. I'm sorry to say I didn't get to it before she died, a few years ago, but I like to believe that she knows now.

We played Schubert's Quintet in C Major until we wore the record thin because that music, somehow, transported me back—as I would surely need to be transported when I began the novel—into the nineteenth century, when Anson Dodge rode his horse up and down the Island roads. In the third movement I could almost see him making his sick calls and hear him comforting the bereaved of his tiny parish, as he spent his lonely days without Ellen—in the redemptive way which had so attracted me to his story in the first place. In my mind, as the music played, I saw him as a handsome man of medium build, energetic, dark of hair and beard, astride his mount, John Wesley, doffing his round parson's hat here at Mrs. Postell as he passed her place at Kelvin Grove, there at Mrs. Horace Bunch Gould as he passed Black Banks.

Who lived at Frederica then, I wondered? Who were Anson's neighbors at Frederica when at last the dream house he and Ellen had designed was completed so that he could move in—alone? The Stevenses, for one, we'd learned through Berta Taylor. Also her husband's family, the Taylors, headed by Douglas and Reginald's beautiful mother, Belle. Who else? I'd learned of no hostility to Anson; would I need to fictionize a family who could be his enemies in the church? Didn't every minister have troublesome parishioners? I dared not let my own love affair with the Island and its people warp the novel until it turned into a saccharine, jasmine-scented Southern tale without conflict or realism.

Joyce had filled one notebook with questions for research which she would do for me at the Chicago libraries that winter while I finished my current manuscript. She earned her own living in the big city by free-lance acting and production, by writing and directing, but she had willingly—I thought rather eagerly—agreed to suspend her own schedule that winter so as to be free to dig into the more complex archival research for the novel. We could, after all, go only so far with our questions to the Island folk. The book *was* primarily about Anson Dodge. We had everything to learn about his own prominent family in the North. Joyce wrote countless letters to New York and New England libraries where information concerning the Dodge, Phelps, and even the Gould families might be found. Neither Mary nor Berta had seemed to know much about their great-grandfather, James Gould, who had for some reason come south from Massachusetts to St. Simons Island. As it turned out, I needed little or nothing about James Gould until much later, when I wrote *Lighthouse,* but our involvement with all the Goulds of St. Simons was so deep by then that we swam happily and confusedly among both essentials and nonessentials.

And so the days passed with Joyce writing her letters or plowing out in deep snow to one library after another, hoping to find one more small piece of the puzzle so that she'd have some good news for me at the end of the day, when I came down from the third-floor aerie where I wrote. For one stretch of days, we lived on hope that she'd really unearthed something when, at Newberry Library, she found a Gould Family Foundation listed. Our hopes remained high until her letter to the Foundation was answered. There was a Gould Foundation, all right, but it was the wrong Gould! The well-known Jay Gould's wealthy background had nothing whatsoever to do with our dear Goulds of St. Simons. The same excitement flared again in the case of the Dodge family. Anson Dodge's grandfather was indeed a rich and illustrious New York merchant prince, but the Dodge Foundation which Joyce discovered was that of the Dodge automotive family and not of Anson's forebears.

Then one day I was glancing at a magazine to which I once contributed called *Faith at Work,* and there before my eyes was the name of a board member—Mrs. Cleveland E. Dodge of New York. I no longer remember why, but somewhere in the magazine was a notation that her husband was president of Phelps Dodge Company. Our hopes rocketed again, and this time not without result. I wrote at once to Mrs. Dodge in care of the magazine, and back came her letter full of encouragement and the hope of concrete help. Dear Polly Dodge not only reassured me by telling me she had liked my other books for years, but mentioned that she was certain there were—out of print, but perhaps obtainable—books on the life of her husband's ancestor, William E. Dodge, the merchant-philanthropist. And perhaps one on the Phelps Dodge Company itself. Immediately Joyce got out letters to a handful of book finders, and at long last, word came from three different sources informing us that I could indeed buy used copies of several titles: one, *A Merchant Prince of the Nineteenth Century;* another, *William E. Dodge;* still another *A History of the Phelps Dodge Company;* and best of all—at least, at that point, the most exciting—*The Memorials of William E. Dodge,* compiled and edited by D. Stuart Dodge, his son. From somewhere, lost to me now in the current clutter of my memory, we had learned that D. Stuart Dodge was Ellen's own father!

That night, after reading the letters from the book finders, we played Schubert's C Major Quintet so loudly, the manager of the big apartment building next door called in a rage. We apologized and turned down the volume, but there was no way to turn down our excitement. We didn't have the books yet, but they were available. Joyce would place the order the next day, and I would manage to keep on with the other writing until the books came. The book on which I was working during the daylight hours that winter was *God Speaks to Women Today.* He was speaking to me too. Loud and clear. I was, by grace, able to give my full and concentrated attention to its writing and to learn from it, while simultaneously, on another track, I felt more and more assurance that I was doing the right thing to try a novel about this young, heartbroken, redemptive man of God whose Island seemed also mine.

Oddly enough, my date book for that year of 1963 mentions

almost nothing about St. Simons Island or the novel. In fact, I seem only to have noted mail answered, speaking dates, plane departures, and chapters written on the current manuscript for *God Speaks*, so occupied was I in finishing out the schedule. There is nothing written down until August 21, when I scribbled this:

Take a day off and give yourself a treat by trying a résumé of *Dear Dark Woods*, the only title we've come up with yet for the St. Simons novel about Anson Dodge.

("The Beloved Invader" as a title was still a long way off.)

The date-book pages for that summer contain nothing further about the novel except one page during the first week in June which bears a simple notation: Letter from Fred Burk, J. B. Lippincott Company.

This simple scribble says little in itself, but everything to me. It marked the beginning of one of the most important relationships in my entire life.

I was nearing the halfway point in *God Speaks to Women Today* when the letter came from Fred Burk, then religious sales manager for Lippincott. In the letter, he courteously asked me if I would have time and be willing to read and give him a comment on a new novel they were publishing by a fellow writer whom I admired, Agnes Sanford. Now, I often receive letters from publishers asking for the favor of a comment. Or, more often, a publisher will simply fire in a galley or a manuscript with the request tucked in the package. Most authors try to aid other authors in this way, but we're not always free to spend the time required to read an entire book. I comply when possible and when I can give a favorable comment with a clear conscience, but I was uniquely disposed to do it this time. In addition to my admiration for Agnes Sanford, I had two special reasons. First, I had always admired Lippincott books, and so far as I could remember, the house had never before asked me for a blurb. As a child, my favorite textbooks were almost inevitably published by Lippincott, and secretly, in my youth, I had hoped some day to be published by them too. The hope had been forgotten with the years, but the letter from Fred Burk caused me to remember. Second and most important, someone at a publishing house had actually been sensitive enough in his letter to ask if I had the time!

That same day, I dropped a note to Mr. Burk—a rather warm one, as I remember—thanking him for his courtesy and, for want of a better way to wind up the letter, or perhaps for some subconscious reason, I added that I'd be especially interested to see what another Christian writer was doing in the way of fiction, because it so happened that I was clearing my desk to begin my own first novel.

On the day my letter must have reached Fred Burk, now my dear and valued friend, a wire came from him telling me that I'd be hearing from Miss Tay Hohoff, Senior Editor in the trade division of J. B. Lippincott Company, and that Lippincott hoped I hadn't signed to do the novel with anyone else. Before the regular mail was delivered at my Chicago address the following morning, an airmail special delivery letter arrived from Tay Hohoff—a masterpiece of writing, not high-pressuring me, simply giving me *her* qualifications as an editor: she could refer me to Agnes Sanford, with whom she'd worked on several books, and to Harper Lee, the famous author of the highly successful best seller *To Kill a Mockingbird.* She mentioned one or two other outstanding American authors—Zelda Popkin, I remember—and asked if she, Tay Hohoff, could come to Chicago for a consultation. *As soon as I would permit.*

I read her letter aloud to Joyce—then Joyce read it aloud to me. Although I was already an established author in my field, there was in me a sort of inner elevation. In Joyce too. We who talk so freely to each other could find little to say—we just looked and beamed!

Part of this lift sprang from the reputation of J. B. Lippincott as a quality publisher, but there was much, much more. Neither of us could have defined it then. Our excitement over Tay Hohoff's letter went far beyond the reputation of a publishing house. In fact, I'd been at the profession of writing quite long enough for publishers to have lost some of their magic for me. The glamour had been replaced by realism in my attitude toward them. They were—like us—faulty, often warmhearted, sometimes sensitive, usually enjoyable people. Now and then someone special would come along, some relationship with extra meaning, such as the one I'd known with the late Peter deVisser at Zondervan, but I'd developed the needed caution—not skepticism, just caution. The romance of learning that a publisher actually wanted a manuscript hadn't exactly faded for me, but the years do wear away some of the luster. Primarily, the publishing of books is business. Competitive buying and selling, profit and loss. So, our inner elevation was not just because a major publishing house had expressed the hope of getting my first novel. I knew then and I know now, fourteen years later, that the elevation came from the woman herself, Tay Hohoff— from the very tone and authority of her letter.

A postscript asked me to call her collect. I did, and her voice heightened my interest. That it did amuses me now, because during the years of our work together, I learned how she hated talking on the telephone. But that day, her rich, lilting voice with its cultivated accent and her straightforward manner made me feel as though I couldn't wait to meet her. In a short recess from my other writing, I'd experimented just enough with a beginning for the Anson Dodge novel to know that I was going to need editorial guidance and help from someone. I'd written for years in many forms, but never a novel. Not even a short story. I was apprehensive and uncertain, and until we knew exactly when Tay Hohoff was arriving, I hadn't even admitted my apprehension to Joyce.

I really tried to convince Miss Hohoff over the phone that we wanted to meet her at the Chicago airport—she would arrive two days hence—and that was my first encounter with her unshakable authority. She disliked being met by strangers and would much prefer to arrive at my home on her own. Instead of feeling rebuffed by her surprising firmness, I felt relieved. I didn't like being met at airports by strangers, either. I now realized that along with the elevation, I had also felt a kind of deep relief from the moment I first read her letter. I, who had for so long made my own independent decisions in my personal life and my professional life, was experiencing for the first time the sheer relief inherent in finding someone to look up to—to obey, as it were (within reason anyway), where my work was concerned. I could look up to Joyce and to my mother where my inner life was concerned, but I longed for an outside authority in my writing life—someone who would tell me straight without considering my feelings. I might not always agree with this vibrant-voiced Hohoff person, but at least I'd never get trapped within a wrong decision from false praise when honesty would have freed me far more. I respected her that much even before I met her. And I was certainly no young, impressionable kid. I was forty-seven years old and reasonably fond of my own opinions on most things.

Like two excited idiots, Joyce and I prepared for the visitor's arrival. Since she would arrive about one o'clock, I'd asked on long distance what she liked to eat. "Almost nothing," she said. So we made a delicious fresh fruit salad with tender loving care and toasted English muffins. Joyce remembers that Tay asked for tea to drink. This doesn't sound quite right to me, but Joyce's memory outstretches mine.

At any rate, the house was in order and polished, and we were dressed and looking out the big front window a full half hour before Miss Hohoff could possibly arrive.

Finally, a little after one, a taxi pulled up and out of it stepped a slender, gray-haired lady in a smart slouch felt hat and vintage trench coat. She paid the driver, got out her own small piece of luggage, and strode briskly toward our front door.

Before we opened the door, we both loved her.

No matter that this sounds a bit silly. "It all sounds a bit silly, my dear," Tay herself said when we told her our version of that first visit —much later, after the three of us became friends. So be it. It was that way for us both.

I took her bag, Joyce her coat and hat, and as I walked with her toward our living room, she announced with startling abruptness that she was *not* religious!

I laughed and replied, "Good, neither are we. We're Christians, but there's a big difference."

"Oh," she said, and it was a long time before I understood what that enigmatic "Oh" meant.

In fact, she had to explain it to me some years later during one of my extended visits with her (and her lovable husband, Arthur Torrey) in her New York apartment. I remember almost exactly what she said and how she looked. First, she laughed her surprising, girlish, infectious laugh—surprising for one so thoroughly reserved. "I actually said that, did I? Well, I don't suppose I'm surprised that I said it. I abhor religiosos and you'd written a lot of successful religious books. Actually, I was nervous as a cat walking into your place that day. I expected a dowdy Bible-thumper to greet me." She laughed again. "It turned out to be *you*—thank God. And of course, that *dear* Joyce. I love her too, you know."

We knew. There was no way to mistake it. Tay used fewer words for everything—in her own fine writing in her books, in her letters, in her conversation—than almost anyone I'd ever known, but the words she used meant the more for it. There was no false sentiment in her. Mostly I had been praised for my other books for years. By my publishers and by my readers. Music to an author's ears, of course, but I'd developed a kind of immunity. Inside, I longed for someone whose opinion I truly valued to tell it to me straight and in few words. One editor had had this kind of understanding of me, Peter deVisser at Zondervan Publishing House. Now Peter was dead.

But Tay was there that day in my living room, saying, "Will you tell me about this book you're writing? Oh, I must say we're all very pleased that you haven't signed yet with anyone else. We want you as an author."

That last sentence is the first and only compliment she gave me for about two years. It wasn't a compliment, of course. It was Tay stating one of her unadorned facts, as I later learned. The J. B. Lippincott Company did want me as an author—all of them, apparently, including the brass. And including especially the man who was then Chairman of the Board and who became my warm friend and adviser, Mr. Howard K. Bauernfeind.

Without the usual preliminary small talk, I began to tell Tay about St. Simons Island and Anson Dodge. And Ellen, who died on their honeymoon, and Anna Gould, who became his second wife. "The book will have a Christian theme," I said with a smile. "The man *was* a minister, and the story struck me because he *lived* redemption in his short life—in the face of tragedy."

"Of course," she said matter-of-factly. "It wouldn't ring true without a Christian theme. Especially not from you." And then she smiled her sudden and totally disarming smile. "I'm not against God, you know. Not at all."

For about half an hour I talked on about the story—little as I knew it then—without a word from her. When I'd finished, and when Joyce had finished adding her carefully chosen details to my picture of the Island, Tay said, "Well, we want the book. If you can write it half as well as you tell it, splendid. I did not bring a contract. I think it's just as important for an author to want to work with a publisher as for a publisher to want to work with an author. Take your time about deciding. I want some long years ahead for us. I don't want to risk a snap judgment on your part." The smile again as she stood up and we shook hands. I can still see the slender fingers, capable, a little arthritic, the recognizable writer's bump on the middle finger from the ever-present editor's pencil. "Don't make a quick decision, in spite of how well we've hit it off today—the three of us."

She came to mean as much to Joyce as to me. She was never Joyce's editor, more's the pity, but she criticized her manuscripts, and Joyce still rereads one long, constructive letter Tay wrote to her back in 1965—rereads it again and again before she begins any new writing job.

Tay did allow us to drive her back to the airport that day, and although her visit had lasted only about four hours, we felt as though we said good-bye to someone we'd loved for a long time.

It took me a while to come to *know* her, but she was uniquely easy for me to love from the start.

To say that she did not intimidate me, once we began working together, would be to mislead. She did. But the intimidation turned into determination to write—for her—up to my very best, whatever that might be. The determination holds to this day, even though she died in her sleep during the night of January 5, 1974. In my date book on that day, I wrote, "Tay, my 'editor, dear' left me." She left so many of us bereft and yet determined to do—whatever it is we do—up to our best. After the second novel or so, my familiar name for her came to be "editor, dear." She thought it sentimental and snorted at me for a while; then, as a mutual friend in New York used to say, "She loved it! And didn't know how to say she did, except to snort."

In my date book, I find this written on January 1, New Year's Day, 1974: "I'm going to call my 'editor, dear' but she's so ill and frustrated with herself—with her near-blindness, in particular, what will I say? I can't wish her a Happy New Year! But I'll call her. Can't help it."

I called her home number and she put on her best telephone manner, by then not fooling me at all. But we had a cheerful conversation. She had lost her hatred of telephones, evidently; toward the end, she called us almost every evening. Pretending, of course, to be finding out how "her author" was doing with the current book, *Don Juan McQueen*. True in part, of course, but she was lonely—Arthur had died by then—and the glorious courage and independence through all her seventy-five years must have sharpened the awareness, the reality of her rapidly failing health and eyesight. We talked that New Year's Day about this and that—about Don Juan, of course. I told her a funny story and she had a good laugh, and then a strange thing happened. I was, out of deference to her illness, about to hang up, with the promise to call her again soon.

"Wait," she said. "I'm not finished. We laughed together once when you were here at my place about the fact that I never tell an author he or she has done a good job. Remember?" There was an eloquent pause. "Well, I've been thinking. You should have known that when I didn't say it was *bad*, I thought it was *good*. But last night I decided to tell you the next time we talked that . . . I'm downright proud of you. You've done a splendid job on Don Juan—so far as I've read—and Genie, my dear, you've come so far since *The Beloved Invader*. There now—I've said it. And you're going to go still further and write better and better books. All this New Year—and always."

I didn't hear her voice again. And yet, I've "heard" every word of what she said a thousand times.

I've written of Tay's death as she would have me do it, I think, since it had to be done: swiftly, to the point; and now it's behind me. I'm free to write about her as she was—living, far more than she knew, beside my typewriter as I worked hour after hour for the remaining time in Chicago and after we moved to St. Simons. As she still is— her vibrant, prodding, loving spirit with me through the remainder of *Don Juan McQueen*, through the long and difficult novel *Maria*, through these pages as I write now. She very much wanted to edit this book too.

Tay had another author, Gladys Taber, who loved her and whom Tay loved. Gladys, my friend now through letters, is another gift from Tay. Through our mutual devotion to Tay, Gladys and I are drawn together. Of a vanishing breed of editors, Tay was. There are few left who give line-by-line care to an author's manuscript and who, knowing that a writer's life can be lonely, bother to check often on how things are going.

In the Epilogue to *The Beloved Invader*, I wrote, "If I have made the transition from non-fiction to fiction, it is because Miss Tay Hohoff was my patient and wise editor."

I am still trying to write up to my best—because Miss Tay Hohoff was my patient and wise editor.

I was ready—eager—to sign a contract right there, before we took Tay to her plane that June day in 1963. But I didn't say so. All the way back from O'Hare airport, Joyce and I talked. Not about whether I would sign or not, but about the enlarging experience, in such a brief visit, of Tay herself. We'd met someone who knew her profession through and through, whose long years of experience and evident skills (demonstrated surely in the books she had edited) could mean a turning point in my writing career. Not once did I say, "Well, what do you think? Should I sign?"

We both knew I would.

After several long-distance calls during which Tay and I negotiated the contract, I signed for the one novel only, and the option clause was removed because my next manuscript was to be published by Zondervan. I was permitted to set my own deadline for the novel, and Tay and I had a perfect understanding that I couldn't even begin until I'd finished the manuscript for *God Speaks to Women Today*. I have the old contract for "untitled St. Simons novel" beside me as I write. The date is July 17, 1963—the beginning of an entirely new phase in my personal as well as my professional life. They have always been hopelessly intertwined for me, actually. I fail to see how an author without at least one good friend at a publishing house can function creatively. Writing is a solitary, slavish occupation in many ways because it is always intensely personal. *I* go into the pages of my books. Another more erudite or more detached writer might think that childish. So be it. If I'm to arouse emotion in a reader, it must first force its agonizing or humorous or grieving course through me. Tay never permitted me to overdo the evoking of emotion, and because she did not permit it, I truly believe the emotional content of my novels runs deeper.

I know I embarrassed her by telling her that I loved her—at least for a year or so. But not once did she fool me as to the steadiness of her devotion and faith in me. I have dedicated only *Don Juan McQueen* to her, but in a very real way, every book I ever write will be hers. I still catch myself wondering, when in doubt about a line or a scene, "Would Tay buy this?" Often, inevitably, the answer comes —sharply sometimes—"No!" At other times: "Okay, go ahead."

Through the remainder of July and August I wrote feverishly and with renewed self-confidence chapter after chapter of *God Speaks*. Along with the writing, I worked out the remaining dates on my speaking schedule—including a three-day appearance at the Christian Booksellers Association convention in August. By early September, I was the possessor—after nearly fifteen years—of a date book devoid of one single speaking date! I hadn't exactly put the lid down on taking any more, but my conscience was clear of those already committed, and the moment had come when we were talking at night of nothing but our return to St. Simons Island—for the entire winter this time.

When Mother and I had done a stint of house-hunting on St.

Simons the Christmas before, we had rather fancied a plain but sturdy little white-clapboard cottage just down the street from the Ship House, called "White Cap." Mother particularly liked its name, and it seemed comfortable enough. It had a large, airy living room, a dining room, a small enclosed sun porch, and a convenient kitchen; and in a cramped hallway that led to the bath between the two bedrooms, there was a large oil heater.

Besides, it was near the Ship House, and I'd been quite drawn to the Goodwillies during the time Mother and Aunt Betty and I had stayed with them. Walter Goodwillie had already told me that Elsie, his attractive, vivacious wife, was "the best secretary on earth—why, she can take dictation in both French and English, I don't know how many words a minute. You wouldn't have to worry at all about a manuscript typist here on St. Simons. Elsie can handle it." That he turned out to be absolutely right is the understatement of the century! Mother and Elsie had become friends, and it seemed to please Mother to think that we might rent White Cap and live so near the Goodwillies. (No matter how old one becomes, mothers seem never to stop hoping the offspring will live "properly" in a good location.)

One night early in September, Joyce said in her quiet but definite manner, "We're going back. Why don't we just set a date and go? The longer you stay around Chicago, the more certainly you'll be caught up in more speaking dates or other commitments. We're free to go now, both of us. Let's call Larry and Beth Black and see if White Cap is available this winter."

We did and it was. And within three weeks, we'd arranged for our dear Chicago friend, Lorrie Carlson, who'd been typing my manuscripts and helping enormously with my mail for a long time, to live in our house all winter and to handle my considerable mail by answering what she could and forwarding the remainder. We'd packed our works in progress, all of Joyce's archival research, and our St. Simons notebooks (nearly two were filled by then), reams of paper, carbon, both typewriters, our most casual clothes, our favorite pots and pans and skillet, our charcoal broiler, and what seemed like a ton of books. We'd put our garden to bed for the winter and arranged for the monthly bills to be forwarded, we'd notified Tay of our plans, and three days before September ended, we were on our way back to the sandy, tree-shaded little Island whose almost mystical aura had not once dimmed for either of us.

On October 1, we drove up in front of White Cap, and because we knew this time we didn't have to face leaving again until late spring —when the rents doubled on St. Simons Island—we both sat there and looked at each other and grinned before we began unloading the car. I don't cry easily, but I felt like it, and Joyce did shed a few happy tears.

For a week or so, we unpacked and put away and shopped and put away during the morning hours and treated ourselves in the afternoons with visits to all our people. The welcome was ongoing. Mary Everett, entering into our special sense of play as always, kept on shouting "Welcome back" and "Welcome to St. Simons Island" every time we parked in front of her house. Berta Taylor even found the misplaced history of Christ Church, and at night after we'd chased the sunset to our hearts' content, we pored over Berta's pages until I could have quoted them verbatim. Lorah Plemmons, her blue eyes dancing, had a pot of Great Northern beans and cornbread and onions, or chicken and dumplings, ready and waiting—seemingly no matter what time we arrived—now, no longer parked in Pretty Lane like strangers, but up under her big camphor tree like members of her family.

Edith Young began that very week a practice she kept up for years. She would make a big batch of her special barley-vegetable soup, then call the Goodwillies at the Ship House so we'd know to drop by to pick up our jar of it. And of course, daily, or almost daily, we checked in at the Everetts' for dinner at noon with Ju-ju and Dutch and Mary, both of us gaining weight on Penny's superb hot biscuits and fried chicken. After having lived all my life in a city, I was flabbergasted at such kindness. Flabbergasted and thankful that we hadn't brought along our bathroom scale!

Lorrie Carlson, back in Chicago in our house alone, did a magnificent job with my mail. She not only writes beautiful letters; she is sensitive to how much to say and how much not to say to each of the wide variety of people who write to me. My correspondents, because of Lorrie's own loving nature and perceptions, seemed just as happy to hear from her as my assistant as if I'd written myself, and I reveled in the brief respite from the always teetering stack of unanswered letters. I was free to dress as I pleased—in blue jeans even back then, and comfortable old shirts and jackets—and free of speaking engagements for the first time in fourteen years. As for the telephone, Joyce and I had convened a "family" conference en route from Chicago and arrived at the conclusion that, since we had the good Goodwillies just up the road from our cottage, we'd have no telephone that winter. I would call Mother once a week and Joyce her parents, Tay and the people at Zondervan knew how to contact me at the Ship House, and to this day we both marvel at the even-tempered Goodwillies, who never once complained when one or the other of them had to run down the rutty little street to tell us we had a phone call. I can still see Walter and Brenda, their people-dog, loping down 11th Street toward our house.

Those first days before I went back to the final chapters of *God Speaks to Women Today* were the nearest either of us had ever come to heaven. We were delighted that the evenings so near the ocean were cool enough (well, almost) for a fire in our White Cap fireplace. John Golden had arrived once more with an enormous load of heavy oak and fat pine, which he stacked under the carport at the side of our cottage. We slept like babies at night, probably because we were so happy and our minds so uncluttered, but also because we both—although I have always hated to walk—explored the wide, silvery beach by the hour. I picked up shells while Joyce, seemingly bent on recording every sunset and every changing sweep of wet color along the sands, used up countless rolls of film. And I, who as a smugly satisfied urban cliff-dweller for some thirty years had poked the nastiest kind of fun at bird watchers, became one!

Within two days of our return, I had driven down to the village and bought myself the best pair of binoculars I could find. Joyce already had a pair, of course, since she'd watched birds before with her dear friend Isobel Millar in the dunes and forest preserves around Chicago. But in my newfound feverish curiosity about birds of all kinds, I had to have my own glasses. And with my writer's imagination and my pell-mell judgment, I "identified" birds not to be found in our Roger Tory Peterson's *Field Guide to the Birds.* We began a checklist of birds (which we still keep on the same old creased, ragged piece of yellow paper), and I added some amazing "finds." Joyce, tolerant as always of my enthusiasm, let me go wild. Until then, I'd enjoyed nothing in the way of outdoor recreation except picking up shells on a seashore. Now I had a new nature passion, and the writer got into that too. Here is a portion of a corny rhapsody I wrote to Isobel Millar back in Chicago which proves that in those early days of ornithological pursuits, I was in no way hampered by my amateur status:

Truly I have been born again into the world of whistling dove wings, screeching boat-tailed grackles, Bach-analian mockers, savannah sparrows, skimming skimmers, *and* a mind closed to practically everything else in the world but the occupants of the tall pines and the scrub oaks and the oleander bushes. Mine is the single eye. The gate *was* narrow, but I entered in. Where once I was blind, now I see. Instead of the sunset I see the terns and gulls across it. At times I mount up even to believing that I see a penguin sitting placidly in the sun on a warm Georgia beach. My cup runneth over with secondaries and primaries and hooked bills and yellow rumps and white scapulars—lesser and greater coverts, and I am at peace. I may never write another book. I see no prospects of ever reading anything untouched by Audubon's immortal spirit, and *my* spirit soars like a peregrine falcon into the wild blue yonder where willets and pine siskins and yellow throats and flickers shall be followed by me all the days of my life, and I shall dwell in the realm of ornithological wonders forever. . . .

Writing that goofy letter mirrored my carefree mood in those days, but the love of writing—agony and all—plus a deadline spelled out in a signed contract turned my sights eventually back to the completion of *God Speaks to Women.* I had stopped keeping a date book. Schedules had gone out with the ringing of the telephone and the slap of mail through the slot in my front door. But I made my deadline on the book, and by Thanksgiving Day, when we had turkey and trimmings with Lorah in her kitchen, I had begun the novel about Anson Dodge and his little church.

PART THREE

The Beloved Invader

THE writing had gone reasonably well, considering that for me the novel was a brand new genre. It went well, that is, until November 22 blasted me and everyone else in America into a paralyzing limbo.

Joyce and I were buying Christmas wrapping paper in Glynn Stationers, down on Mallery Street in the Village, when the small radio behind Ida Rowe's desk (now Ida Hartmann) blared the unbelievable words. "Just minutes ago, President Kennedy was shot in Dallas as he rode in a motorcade there. He has been rushed to Parkland Hospital and we await word of his condition."

We stopped looking at the bright rolls of paper just to the left of Ida's desk. No one spoke. With the other citizens of our country, we just stood there listening to the solemn bulletins. Waiting. Waiting to hear if the young man on whom so many of us had pinned such enormous hope—had been killed.

After what seemed an eternity, we learned that the President was dead. Ida began to weep.

"I can feel with his widow," she whispered. "I watched my husband die suddenly—not long ago." From that day to now, Joyce, Ida, and I have had a special bond.

The fateful days dragged by. Stunned, we sat helplessly by the radio at White Cap, hearing the drums beat, their relentless roll echoing through the canyons of the capital. The black, riderless horse bucked and reared, but the cortege did not pause; and they buried the President. Through the long hours of that dark day, we heard it all from one distant station and another, and even I—who would like to be able to cry naturally but can't—wept.

After a few days I was back at the typewriter, and by December Elsie Goodwillie had done her first manuscript typing for me—the first four chapters. Rough as those chapters were, I needed Tay Hohoff's approval of what I'd done.

I wasn't recognizably scared anymore, but I was apprehensive. After all, except in school, I'd never done anything even resembling a short story, and at times the very fact that I was doing a novel for an esteemed editor like Tay made me shaky inside. Joyce and I drove to the post office, mailed the manuscript, checked in at Mary and Dutch's, and then, on impulse—and because I needed to have some fun while I waited—dropped in on the Goodwillies at the Ship House. Their hospitality was so easy and warm, that particular visit marked the first of what came to be a habit. We would finish our work each day and walk up 11th Street toward the ocean to join our neighbors for a happy hour of Elsie's energetic, lilting piano and good talk about how deeply the four of us had fallen in love with St. Simons Island. Elsie and Walter had lived in a beautiful home in Pennsylvania, had done all the best golf courses and clubs in the East, but then they, too, had found St. Simons and everything had changed for them. Now they were starting a new life—as innkeepers on the little sandy strip of land which had captivated us all.

I will never be able to thank them for their friendship and support in those happy but suspenseful days of beginning my first novel. And their beloved Brenda had become our one regular and welcome visitor at White Cap. She would scratch on the screen door of our cottage, leap her gladness at being received—as she always was, even in the middle of a paragraph—and then head straight for our kitchen, where she would wait politely and patiently by the refrigerator. Joyce would get the expected weiner or scrap of braunschweiger, whatever our contribution for the day might be; then Brenda would gulp it, lie down —stretching her long, dark-brindle length on our little rag rug—and nap. Never mind that she began leaving her fleas behind, collected from romps on the beach. We just called the exterminator and all was well again. Until the next visit. With both of us, that dog could do no wrong. Brenda is gone now to doggie heaven and is buried under a brilliant red azalea in Elsie's backyard on Bartow Street.

I think only about ten days passed before the letter came from Tay which nearly put me under. It seemed like a month, but it wasn't. She *cared* about her authors' psyches; she was resolute about making her comments at the earliest possible time. In the interim, I had tried to go on with the writing. As I recall, I did write another chapter or so, but the butterflies in my stomach swarmed daily, and I doubt that I'll ever forget opening that letter with the now familiar J. B. Lippincott New York return address. Her brief, to-the-point note said not one word about the first three chapters. Had I known her better then, I'd have been lyrical, because that meant she thought they were fine. But I'd been accustomed to praise from my other editors, and so I froze. Especially when I came to the end of her first paragraph, in which she acknowledged receipt of the chapters and apologized for being a little long in responding.

Now, Genie [she wrote], really! That second section of Chapter 4 is dreadful. You're still writing radio dialogue and by some means we've got to put an end to that. Try it again and perhaps you'd better let me see it again too.

I could feel Joyce trying to rescue my shattered ego, but there would be no real help for me until I had tried it again and received Tay's approval. None of which could be done that afternoon. Just that week I had read Pamela Frankau's book about writing fiction called *Pen to Paper.* That book, along with Tay's letter, convinced me that I knew nothing at all about what I was trying to do. Surely, I would fail. (Do keep in mind also that, until I tried my first novel, I had absolutely no idea of how much more difficult fiction is to write than nonfiction.)

"Maybe we should drive down to the village and call Tay," Joyce suggested. "She might still be in her office. I think it would help if you could talk it over with her."

At that point, I couldn't imagine what there was to talk over, but I agreed to go.

"Just write it again," Tay said, in a voice that sounded as though she could have strangled me for being so naive. "Just keep writing it until you get it right. That's what novels are about."

Years later, after *New Moon Rising,* the second novel in the St. Simons trilogy, had hit the best-seller lists, I told Tay about that dark afternoon. She was dumbfounded.

"You should have known," she snapped, "that I simply loathe telephone conversations. I was feeling very warmly disposed toward you —I was pulling for you, actually."

Of course, I know now that she was—for her own sake as well as mine. She had been assigned my book. It was up to her to see to it that I brought it off. But the quick wind-driven storm that sprang up off the ocean that night matched my turbulent mood. I must have slept—I usually do—but the next morning, when I rolled in another sheet of yellow paper to try it again, I would have sworn that I'd lain awake all night worrying.

For years Joyce and I had both worked in radio drama in Chicago. And so, before I began work, we sat by our fire and tried to figure out why Tay said I'd used radio dialogue. The scene was a toughie at best. I now know. A family seated around a dinner table talking sounds simple. It is not. There was a certain amount of plot advancement I needed, and it still seemed right that it should come through the conversation of the Gould family at dinner.

"You've always been able to depend on actors to bring your words to life," Joyce ventured. "Is there any way you can shift your own responses to the scene and picture a lone reader, reading to himself or herself without benefit of a trained interpretation?"

To this day I can't tell you why that helped, but it did.

I rewrote the scene, we got it off airmail that afternoon—and waited again.

The revised section of manuscript must have reached Tay promptly. (The United States mails were still dependable in those days.) On the third day Walter and Brenda came strolling down 11th Street to tell me that Western Union (we had our own Island office then) had just called to say they had a telegram for me. I could either call them back from the Ship House or drive down to the Kent Hotel on Mallery Street to pick it up.

"Let's go get it," I said. "I can't face what it might say, even in front of Walter Goodwillie!"

Back in the car with Joyce, parked in front of the Western Union office, I opened the yellow envelope—read the brief, brief message, broke into a big smile, and handed the telegram to Joyce. My heart was pounding.

The message read: HURRAY! TAY.

I'd made it. To this day, when anything particularly good happens, Joyce and I say, "Hurray, Tay!"

Joyce flew home to her family for Christmas, and Mother again came to the Island. She and I had another Merry Yule time with the happy Plemmonses three, and that same day, I remember, sexton Watson Glissom dropped in to wish a Merry Christmas to his old friend Mrs. Plemmons and stayed for dinner too.

I had some difficulty convincing Mother that a woman of Lorah's age *still* cleaned Christ Church! But, approaching ninety, she did. Saturday after Saturday, Joyce and I had timed our trip up Frederica Road so as to catch her starting her walk—a half mile at least—from her house to the church, a broom and rake over her shoulder. Of course, we'd pick her up, making a joke of the fact that we just happened along, and then for two or three hours the three of us would make a game of cleaning up the little sanctuary for Sunday morning services. I vacuumed the carpet-covered kneeling benches in Christ Church many, many times before I knelt at one. Joyce would sweep the sand and dust out of the corners while I ran the vacuum cleaner, and Lorah dusted pews and polished the altar rail designed and built by Anson Dodge in his grief. Everyone on the Island, old stock as well as newcomers to Christ Church, knew Lorah and loved her. We still get a good laugh at the memory of certain Altar Guild ladies—heads covered for entering the sanctuary—speaking to Lorah and staring discreetly at the two strange tramps in blue jeans sweeping and dusting with her. Lorah, in her carefree way, didn't bother to introduce us, which only added to our good laughs once we had finished in the church and were outside busily helping her rake up certain grave sites which she was also paid to tend. The only person she introduced us to was Mildred Abbott, her dear brown friend from the Dodge Home days, who also came on Saturdays, to clean the rector's study. Lorah's introduction was recommendation enough for the three of us; self-possessed Mildred became instantly our warm friend and still is. She and her daughter, Pat, and her grandson, Tommy, are our neighbors now, too.

Since there were no bookstores on the Island or in Brunswick in those days, Joyce and I had pledged that for a while, at least, we'd tell no one but the Goodwillies and Agnes Holt that I'd ever written a book. There were eleven published by then, but it meant too much to me that these Island people loved me *for myself.* I didn't want to take a chance of changing a thing. Some persons always seem intent upon keeping authors on pedestals.

On our first Island Christmas, we'd bought music-box bells for Lorah, the Youngs, the Everetts, and the Taylors. When Christmas 1963 found us again on St. Simons, we decided that, since I was by then sure of their love, we'd go ahead and give our friends signed copies of various of my published titles. I remember the look on Mary Everett's face when Joyce handed her a copy of *Share My Pleasant Stones.* She thanked us profusely before she'd looked at the book; then she frowned briefly and said, "Well, I declare! This book's got our Genie's name on it!"

They all seemed merely pleased, not at all surprised, and I went right on feeling loved for myself alone. Quite the same as I'd felt during the previous months when, so far as they knew, I was a somewhat retarded middle-aged writer, hoping to get her first book published.

Real winter came to St. Simons in January of 1964, and for two seasoned Yankees, we were as enthusiastic as kids. There was no snow, but there were the beautiful cascades of ice around everyone's outside faucets—left running to prevent a freeze-up. Now and then a revolving sprinkler in someone's yard made a hanging ice-swirl that fascinated me endlessly. Fortunately for us, Dutch and Mary Everett made a special trip to our house one day to remind us that a hard freeze was due that night and we'd better leave our faucets running.

That brief visit has stayed in my memory both with gratitude to Dutch's thoughtfulness and because it produced a good joke on Mary —a joke I played unintentionally. Her days revolved around the TV serial "As the World Turns." That day, she was genuinely worried about a child in the story who seemed about to die. She was afraid Dutch would take so long to check our faucets that she'd miss that day's episode.

"I tell you," she said, her brow furrowed, "I'm scared they're going to lose that little boy!"

"Don't worry," I said airily. "He won't die. The kid's obviously got a contract."

Mary was dumbfounded. She laughed finally, but for a minute I thought she might let me have it with her purse.

When we checked in the next day, she seemed relieved to tell us that they'd reached home in plenty of time for yesterday's episode and that the boy was better.

94

By March, when the winter-quiet mockingbirds were beginning to sing, Tay had more manuscript, and Joyce and I were beginning to worry about the new baseball season. We worried as only true fans do about spring training for our long-beloved cellar-dwelling Chicago Cubs. Since childhood, we had both been rabid in our love of one sport and one only—baseball. It happened that both our fathers, whom we adored, followed it closely and had taught us not only to love it but to understand at least some of its fine points. To this day, I could almost give you a play-by-play description of the glorious fall of 1944 when, thanks to Gabby Hartnett, the Chicago Cubs won their only World Series in my lifetime. Of course, that was during World War II and most of the good players were off fighting, but never mind—the Cubs took the Series. And because I'd lived in Chicago since I was eighteen —back in the thirties—the Cubs were my world. (My dad had gone to dental school in Cincinnati, so of course the Reds were his club. Doggedly. As doggedly as the Cubs were mine.) What worried Joyce and me about spring training? Ask any real fan. One simply worried, as though each contracted player and each youngster struggling to find a spot on the team were family.

Chicago was fading from our minds as the place we wanted to live; we seldom mentioned it because we were daily more at home on St. Simons Island, but we remained Cub fans. Lorrie Carlson made a point of keeping us up on the Cubbies, and when the news began to break that the Milwaukee Braves might move to Atlanta, we were caught on the horns of a real dilemma. From the clippings Lorrie sent, we could see plainly that anyone who considered himself or herself a midwestern baseball nut should be fighting such a move. We were definitely not fighting it! And we railed for hours at the northern press for doing so. Why shouldn't a growing city like Atlanta have a major-league baseball team? After all, it had been a knowledgeable baseball town for all the years the superior Triple A Atlanta Crackers had been there. Finally, the humor of the whole thing caught up with us: we would undoubtedly have resisted too, if we hadn't had the glorious adventure of finding Georgia.

The Milwaukee Braves were then a far better team than our poor losing Chicago Cubs, but how could we break a habit of a lifetime? Win or lose, the Cubbies had been *our* team. Since my early thirties, I had spent memorable afternoons at Wrigley Field when it was nearly empty, screaming my head off for the young men who made up the Cub team. Never mind the loss column, they were my boys and could do no wrong. Could I possibly change allegiance at this late date? Was I really pulling for the Braves to move to Atlanta? The answer was yes. More clearly than by any other example, our new love affair with Georgia was confirmed by this surprising enthusiasm for the possibility that the Milwaukee Braves might become the Atlanta Braves.

That year, there was no baseball to listen to on our little radio, of course, and only now and then could Joyce even bring in an Atlanta station, but we studied Lorrie's clippings and spent many evenings in profound baseball discussions.

————◆————

My days were spent at the typewriter working on "Dear Dark Woods"—still the working title of my novel. Late in the month, Walter Goodwillie and Brenda brought a message down the street that Fred Burk wanted me to call him. I walked back with Walter and Brenda and placed a collect call from the Ship House. Fred was enthusiastic over plans for early promotion of the St. Simons novel—then more than half written. Without having to wait for galley proofs, he wanted multiple copies of the manuscript to send out to reviewers and especially to a few select catalogue houses. When I told him Elsie Goodwillie had a mimeograph machine, he was lyrical—having no more idea, I'm sure, than I what was involved in such an undertaking for Elsie. But when I informed Elsie, she didn't blink an eye.

"Of course! I'll cut stencils instead of typing it on bond."

That sounded simple enough to me—until I laid eyes on my first stencil. But Elsie had a way of making everything sound easy, and so I blithely told her to go ahead and cut stencils, once I had given her my final version. All through the next weeks, Elsie doggedly and good-naturedly endured cutting stencils for page after page. It is one thing to type stencils for a club program or even for a report; it is quite another to cut them for a manuscript of nearly 400 pages! But Elsie did it, and morning after morning at eight or eight thirty she would appear at our front door, a fat bundle of new waxy stencils in her arms which I corrected before I went on with the writing for the day. It must have been about this time that Elsie's Catholic church began to use a hymnal and Mass book in English, because she was "discovering" one after another of the old hymns that Joyce and I had known since childhood. In her beautifully childlike and delighted way, Elsie appeared on our front stoop each morning with not only her armload of new stencils but her new English hymnal as well.

"Listen to this one," she would say, beaming. "I'll bet you don't know *this* one." Of course we knew them all, but we wouldn't have spoiled her fun for anything. On one morning I will never forget, after announcing that she'd found "another new one," she began singing at the top of her voice, "Holy, holy, holy, Lord God Almighty!"

Joyce and I joined her, and for fully five minutes the three of us stood on the stoop of White Cap and treated the neighbors to lusty, off-key singing, while Brenda ran up and down, her long tail waving. Those were the days when the beauty and the openhearted capacity for joy in Elsie Goodwillie began to dawn on us. She is our dear, dear Island friend, and the years have deepened those early impressions. We love her and we count on her love, with confidence and under all circumstances.

Our routine went something like this: up early, for us; I would make our coffee (Joyce vows it is one of my true talents) while she built the fire in our fireplace, and then just good talk until Elsie and Brenda arrived at the door with more stencils and usually more singing. Then, breakfast and work until lunchtime, with me forging ahead on the novel and Joyce, freed for the time from research for me, beginning a juvenile biography of the explorer-doctor Sir Wilfred Grenfell. Not only had St. Simons Island handed me a new start in my writing life, but Joyce had made the almost unbelievable discovery that the one person who could help her most with the life of Sir Wilfred lived right on the Island. In a seaworthy, silver-shingled house called "Tillandsia," smack on the beach at the south end, we had found Mrs. Vara Majette —unique in all ways.

For weeks, Mary Everett had been telling me that I should call on her friend Mrs. Majette, said to have been one of the first woman lawyers in Georgia. Also, according to Mary, Vara Majette was sagacious in many fields besides the law—"the smartest woman on earth, I guess." It so happened that on the beach one day Joyce and I had run into Mrs. Majette's two interesting daughters, Jenks Bond and Morgan Grant, and learned from them that their elderly mother had accompanied Sir Wilfred Grenfell on his last expedition to Labrador as his attorney. Furthermore, Sir Wilfred had himself lived for a time in his later years right on St. Simons' East Beach, not far from our cottage. Thus was begun another three-way friendship, and the joy and stimulation of being close to the Majettes that we still have. (Morgan and Jenks, despite their married names, are still Majettes to us because of the sheer force of their amazing mother's character.)

Tillandsia has now been sold, and Vara Majette, whose faith in Joyce was an enormous encouragement during the years, is gone. But not our memories of those first special afternoons spent with the three —or alone with Vara when the daughters were traveling—memories of afternoons ventilated by ocean chill under the doors and around the windows but warmed by blazing logs on the fire, glasses of blackberry wine, cups of tea, cakes—and always stimulating conversation.

At the end of each workday, usually about four o'clock, we'd hop in Bonnie and spend the minutes until sunset time with Dutch and Mary or with Lorah at Frederica. Then, with our old friends laughing at us, we'd say good-bye so that we could go chase the spectacular Island sunsets. At night, before our own fire, we read aloud—as is still our custom—what each of us had written that day—each of us reading the other's. That is, if what we had done wasn't so rough we couldn't bear to hear it.

———————

The golden days passed too quickly, and it was late spring, 1964. Always my favorite time of the year, this spring had suddenly become a time of dread. The rent on White Cap doubled when the "season" began in May, and with our place waiting in Chicago, we knew we'd have to go back soon. In fact, Lorrie Carlson had already found an apartment for the summer right next door to our house. Lorrie would share her summer's rent with another friend, Dee, from her hometown in Minnesota, so it all sounded ideal—except for the agony Joyce and I would have to face the day we began to pack to leave the Island.

Through the weeks of late March and April, when azaleas and wisteria make St. Simons Island a garden of color and almost painful beauty, we both kept writing, pushing far back in our minds the fact of the swiftly passing days. Joyce spent long afternoons with Vara Majette, who seemed to like what Joyce was writing about her old friend and client, Sir Wilfred; and Tay seemed to like what I'd done. At least, she wasn't saying one way or another, and I'd learned by then that that meant I was away free. But that day at the end of May when we'd have to load Bonnie and drive across the marshes was coming nearer and nearer.

One day at lunch, I laid down my half-eaten sandwich and said,

"You're as depressed as I am at the thought of leaving, aren't you?"

"Yes. And I'm trying not to be."

"Should we sell the Chicago house and move here forever?"

Joyce looked at me for a long time before she answered. "Oh, there's so much money tied up in all those remodeling costs! Maybe —maybe we'd better see how it feels to be back—not to be here."

I knew she was right, of course. We finished our lunch and returned to our typewriters, she at the dining room table, I on the sun porch.

About three in the afternoon, a sharp knock sounded at our front screen door. We looked up to see our blessed Mary and Dutch standing there with looks of deep concern on their faces.

"Now, you darlin's know how Dutch and I make it a practice never to bother you when you're writing, but something important's come up. I want either one of you to go right now and get out your checkbook!"

I walked obediently to my desk, got my checkbook, and then asked, "All right, Mary, what do you want me to buy?"

"Well, you know that be-eautiful Gould row up there in that gorgeous Christ churchyard? By the back fence?"

We nodded. The entire cemetery was as familiar as our hands to us both.

"And you remember my precious baby sister, Fé? From Albany?" (Pronounced "Al-benny" in south Georgia.)

From one meeting, we certainly did remember Fé Gould Powell —with joy and instant affection.

"Well," Mary went on, "a friend of Jeff's—that was Fé's husband, who died—a friend of his from over in Albany bought a lot right in the center of Gould row some time ago. We don't even know the man, and we want you two to hurry up and buy that lot because he wants to sell it, and we don't want *any outsiders* in there!"

By then we had met Mary's daughter and son-in-law, Mary Jane and Lee Howe, and her son, Bobby, and his family; we had met Berta's husband, Captain Douglas Taylor, and their daughter, dear Kitty Grider; we had met the eloquent Colonel James D. Gould II, one of Mary's brothers, and thoughtful Potter Gould, another; we had met Colonel James's lovely wife, Clara, just before her untimely death, and their daughter, Clara Marie, and their son, Jimmy, and his wife, Mary Frances; and we already knew Ju-ju well from all the noontime dinners at the Everetts'. (We also knew by now that Berta, Mary, Fé, James, Potter, and Horace Bunch II—whom we hadn't yet met—were children of Anna Gould Dodge's brother James, who had been married to the Maimie of the cedah gahlans. And there had been Julia, who had died—Ju-ju's mother.)

So many Goulds had received us so warmly, gentle, fun-loving Dutch had long ago begun to call us "the Gould Girls"—the highest compliment we thought possible then. We hadn't felt like outsiders from the first day we'd walked up onto Mary and Dutch's front porch, but the day Mary announced that they wanted *us*—not *outsiders!*—buried beside them in Gould Row at Christ churchyard, we knew we were included forever.

"If you'd ever want to sell the lot, sugah, you'd have no trouble," Dutch offered, being the only practical person in the room at that moment. "The churchyard's almost full right now. Lots of folks would like to have a lot there. But"—his blue eyes danced—"Mama, here, she just had to come right on up to see if you wouldn't like to have first crack at it."

Dutch offered to close the deal for us, and I handed him the check that day.

Once he had it tucked safely into his jacket pocket, Mary sighed happily and said, "Now, some sweet day we'll all be right there together —side by side—where we can hold hands for all eternity!"

Unable not to kid her now and then, I asked, "But, Mary, aren't we going to heaven when we die?"

Her face fell. "Well, yes," she said hesitantly. "Of course we are, but don't you think the good Lord will let us come back to that beautiful churchyard once in a while?"

To all the old-timers on the Island, Christ churchyard is—of all things beautiful—at least *next* to heaven. To the rest of us too.

———————

In those days, before all the horror of the sixties finally erupted —before the divisiveness of the 1964 presidential campaign—a Confederate flag was a symbol of the Southerner's pride of place. To us Yankees and to Agnes Holt, it was merely part of a forgotten past— a quaint symbol at best. Since we had no telephone and since Agnes totally respected our need to work, she hit upon the bright idea of sticking a small Confederate flag in our front yard by the driveway when she wanted us to call her. The three of us had had a lot of fun over that flag, and when the day came for us to drive away from White Cap and head back to Chicago, I saw Agnes's little silk flag sticking forlornly in the front yard. We had planned to stop for a minute at the Tabby House anyway for a personal good-bye, after I'd made one quick thank-you visit to another woman. This other one had helped me enormously with sorting out the fundamental history of St. Simons Island, and she had no idea she'd done it. Her name was Burnette Vanstory, and her long-popular book, *Georgia's Land of the Golden Isles,* had come to be my second Bible.

I ran up to the Ship House while Joyce was making our travel lunch and called Mrs. Vanstory, who lived only a few blocks away on East Beach. She told me to come right on over, and in those final moments on the Island, a friendship and working relationship were begun that have buttressed all the other novels I've done, have comforted us both in sorrow and tragedy, and have been a part of our very lives through the years. Burney and I loved each other on sight—at least I loved her—and leaving became still harder when, at her door as we said good-bye, she told me that she and her husband, Van, were also rabid baseball fans. The first we'd found on St. Simons except for Dutch.

I returned to White Cap and pulled Agnes Holt's Confederate flag from the sandy soil of our front yard, but instead of returning it to her when we stopped by, we took it away with us. Purely for reasons of the heart, that flag steadied us.

Hundreds of driving miles came and went before either of us could shake the near nausea we felt at leaving, and by the time we reached Michigan Avenue on the north side of Chicago, I had made up my mind. I didn't say anything then to Joyce, but I picked up Agnes's little Confederate flag and waved it mightily out the open car window.

My trauma at having to leave the Island abated when we came in sight of our dear old town house on Wrightwood Avenue. Its castle-like turret and steep slate roof looked good—good and welcoming. With Lorrie's help, we unpacked the car and settled in for the summer. Back in April, Joyce and I had made a memorable journey by following, as nearly as we could, Anson Dodge's steps as he once rode on horseback or went by boat from St. Simons Island to Blackshear, to

Waycross, to St. Marys, to Valdosta, to Burnt Fort, and to Woodbine, Georgia. He had founded or preached at the Episcopal mission in each of these small villages in the 1880s and 1890s. Under the spell of the man, it had been a hallowed journey for us, and even settled back at my desk in the third floor of our Chicago home, the memory was still fresh. So fresh that my concentration at the desk might be broken at any time by the remembered sight of South Georgia wildflowers choking the roadside ditches—bandanna daisies, white and magenta thistles, stands of the lacy foliage of mock bishop's-weed, and wildly vining blue butterfly peas. The remembered sights kept me feeling close and still familiar with the young man, Anson Dodge. Once my mail was handled, I rolled in a fresh sheet of yellow paper and went right on writing his story where I'd left off in the sun room at White Cap.

I was no longer apprehensive. I was only three quarters of the way through the rough draft, but I was living my first novel—even back in Chicago. This, I suppose, could have been because I so desperately missed Anson's Island; because I so deeply wanted to be a part of it for as long as I might live. A gift from God, perhaps, was the new nearness I began to feel almost as soon as I was writing again. I was somehow closer to the Island, and closer to my story because the Island and its people—both living and dead—were now real enough to comfort me.

At night before our fire I let my mind go free. Joyce, with her usual programming instinct, would select a stack of records, and with Vivaldi, Bach, and Schubert swirling through our house, I thought about many things. About myself as a writer, for one. It had never been difficult to use personal experience and the experience of others in my nonfiction books. That seemed natural, easy. Using experience, my own or someone else's in fiction was another matter.

I have been asked repeatedly how much of me is in a certain character in one of my novels. A good question, but almost unanswerable, because so much of what a fiction writer employs in the rounding out of characters is unconscious. Even in that first novel I was beginning to see that imagination is the great catalyst in coordinating both conscious and unconscious experience. There was, I mused before our fire that late spring, a lot of me in Anson Dodge. He had trouble slowing his own driving pace to the more leisurely tempo at which his Southern parishioners moved. He seemed to see a thing completed before it was ever begun. As do I. And of course I gave him my own

Christian philosophy where God's eagerness to redeem tragedy is concerned—God's eagerness *not* to see anything wasted. I'm not sure I had gone far enough then to realize that when a writer gets into the habit of using unconscious experience, of actually depending upon it, the creative excitement of bringing events and characters together into a plot takes over. I know now that it does.

I thought also during those long evenings about how I might be received as a novelist, since I had no intention of writing graphic sex scenes or of using four-letter words—both of which, by then, critics and thousands of readers seemed to favor. Or at least to accept. I can honestly say that a good review pleases me as much as it pleases any other author, but a review is, after all, only one person's opinion, regardless of how much harm or good that one opinion may do the sale of a new book. I did know that, in *my* opinion, I was going to be daring by the standards of contemporary fiction: I was going to count on a reading audience who preferred readable writing and a strong story, with emotions strongly felt and expressed, *without* the use of obscenity or detailed bedroom scenes. I wasn't then and I'm still not on a crusade for "clean books" per se; I abhor any kind of censorship. But I'd traveled enough and had enjoyed a large enough reading audience for my other work to know that such readers—"my people"—were out there. The J. B. Lippincott Company and the other houses which had also asked for my first novel knew it too. My approach was not a problem, but I thought about it during those long evenings.

I also thought about what I might do in future novels, if the first one was even slightly successful. Any writer wants success. If you find one who insists that it is not so, don't believe it. Writers, of all people, are human. It was taking me a lot longer to write a novel than a nonfiction book, but deep inside me, I knew I'd try another one if even a mere handful of readers liked my first. I also knew that I would never —could never—write a novel without God in it. Knowing Him to the extent I knew Him then, I was certain that, if I permitted it, He would walk naturally onto the pages of any piece of fiction I'd ever write. As He walks naturally into my conversations with almost anyone. The kind of so-called Christian fiction which sledge-hammers religious dogma through both narrative passages and dialogue turned me off from the first weeks of my own Christian life back in 1949. I could never do anything so rigid to the God who thought up Creation in the first place. If God meant anything to me, He meant *naturalness*—the freedom to be myself in His presence. Whether my best or my worst self, I could still count on His love and His naturalness with me; never once being anything other than Himself. The first novel presented no problem where God was concerned, since Anson Dodge was a Christian minister. I decided all that time ago that seeing God as I did, enjoying His presence as I had from the first faith in it, would eliminate any chance that I'd either leave Him out or drag Him in artificially. We were friends.

I thought during those long Chicago evenings, too, of how inadequate I was yet in this form so beyond my tried talents. Tay had seen about half of the Rough (the first rough draft) and had assured me that there wasn't anything so wrong that we couldn't fix it in a later stage. That was something, at least. I trusted her totally, and above all, I longed to learn from her. But I knew that, in spite of giving the writing of this book all of my concentration and energy, it was, at least in parts, plainly a "first novel."

A very long time ago, when I was in my mid-twenties, I read and digested James Joyce's *Portrait of the Artist as a Young Man*, in which he said something like this: The true artist works, but as he works, he sits in the corner and pares his fingernails. I had worked for years at achieving that kind of objectivity about my writing. It still holds me in good stead. I also give Jesus Christ a lot of credit for making me more objective every day. The next book I plan to write as soon as this one is finished is a short, nonfiction piece to be titled "Leave Yourself Alone." Where work is concerned, leaving oneself alone is not an easy accomplishment for any creative person.

My back hurts often when I type, and I do type everything on a noisy old manual, needing the "fight back" its rough action gives me. Electric typewriters give me the jitters. Undoubtedly my manual Olympia is hard on my injured back, but I've been able to turn out book after book—*leaving my back alone!*

It is somewhat less easy to leave one's writing self alone. Here the ego fools you. You *want* to be read and appreciated. You *want* good news from the publisher and affirmative reviews. There is a sneaky tendency—for a young writer in particular—to think that just because you've put down a sentence that sounds pretty good to you, it must be immortal. Thank God, I've never written an immortal line, and thank God still more, I know I haven't. Tay's whacking and cutting didn't bother me at all. I can hear other more successful authors than I laughing me to scorn on that line, but it is true. Whatever I have to toss out should have been tossed out anyway, and there is beneath me always that certainty that I belong to the One who thought up Creation in the first place. It requires time often for me to realize it, but another way to handle that discarded scene or chapter will come. Another, more workable idea. And so I can be a little patient with myself most of the time. I was learning then from Tay the basics of how to construct a novel, although I couldn't explain those basics now. I am still learning from the doing. I hope I never reach the place where I'm deluded into thinking that I don't need to learn much, much more.

On some of those long, musing nights by the fire, knowing that I was a novice novelist frightened me, especially if that day's work had not seemed to go well. On other nights it comforted me to be able to see myself sanely—to see exactly where I was at that time.

Tay Hohoff never, never gave me a compliment throughout the long months of labor, but I respected her so deeply that the very fact of her continuing to be my editor, of her caring about my book and about me, kept me going. A woman of her intelligence wouldn't be giving me all that careful work if she didn't believe in me a little bit. I believed in her so much, it was sufficient.

It was not the history of St. Simons Island that hooked me on the story of Anson Dodge and his little church. It was the people, Anson and those who touched his life. My obsession with Southern coastal history came much later.

On the recent publication of *Maria,* the second in my St. Augustine trilogy, I was asked to do a newspaper piece under my own by-line, and this is part of what I wrote:

> In spite of my personal involvement in these long ago (historical) activities, I must confess that to write readable, accurate, historical novels for history's sake alone is not my principal goal. My first interest, my abiding interest, is in people themselves, and so my work (so far) is not about fictionized characters who move against accurate historical backgrounds. Rather, it concerns itself mainly with real persons who actually lived through the events of those times. More than that, I have no particular interest in writing about famous figures from the past. Others have done and are doing this. Few of my characters are widely known. I have, almost from my first book, been blessed with a constant readership, and this I believe is solely due to the fact that readers can identify events and emotions and experiences in their own lives with

those of my characters—people whose real names I use for the most part. The majority of us are neither famous nor powerful. We are just people who muddle through, feeling helpless at times, as do the people in my novels, carried along by the rush of historical events around us.

Surely something of what I thought back in 1964 went into that recently done article. We become what we think. The unconscious, as I understand it, stores our thoughts and impressions for us so that, especially when one writes, the magic of remembering takes place or is reshaped by what has dropped into the unconscious. We say we forget. I wonder. Because so much returns—so much of what I thought was lost—when I put myself into the concentrated activity of writing. Even though I seem to have forgotten much of what I thought then, in a way, I credit those long spring and summer evenings of music and musing with much of the content of all my later work. Perhaps of this book in particular.

———◆———

In September of 1964, as we were busy clearing our desks and beginning to pack for one more October departure to St. Simons Island for the winter, a morning newscast chilled our hearts. Hurricane Dora had struck St. Simons Island, Georgia, and was still raging there, leaving in its fury enormous wreckage and damage. We did no work that day at all, not even packing, but stayed glued to the radio for fresh reports of the devastation of our beloved Island. We mourned also for Brunswick, the little town across the salt marshes and creeks on the mainland. According to the wild and winging news flashes, 40 percent of its buildings had been demolished!

In our Chicago house we had several extension telephones. Neither of us, as I remember, passed a phone very often that day without still another try at reaching Mary Everett, Edith Young, or Elsie and Walter Goodwillie. Of course, we couldn't even try to get Lorah Plemmons. Never mind that if we got only the recorded voice saying the lines were down when we tried to call Edith Young, we'd promptly try again with the Everetts' number or Elsie's. It was two days before long-distance telephone service was restored to the Golden Isles, and during those two days, if we'd ever had a doubt that the little coastal Island was *our* place, the doubt vanished. Mary and Dutch lived so near the ocean—and Elsie and Walter's Ship House was practically in it!

Lorah and the Youngs were a bit more protected by their surrounding woods, but our dread of what such a vicious hurricane might do to Lorah's dear house—and her in it all alone—was nearly unbearable.

When finally we reached Mary Everett, our hearts relaxed—although a few old beach cottages had been upended on the lower end of East Beach, little actual damage had been done beyond a lot of big limbs blown down. Mary only laughed when we mourned to her on long distance about 40 percent of Brunswick being destroyed. "No such thing, darlin's. We nearly blew away, but we're all just fine. I saw Frances Burns in the post office today and her dear Mrs. Plemmons is fine too. She goes into a closet when the wind blows that hard!"

Later, we found out that Walter and Elsie, badly needing a vacation anyway, had just packed up their car with Brenda and a suitcase and headed for the north Georgia mountains. The beach we'd loved was shifted seaward by the great tides, and although it is slowly returning, it may never in our lifetimes be the wide, wide silvery wonder it was when we found it. But our friends were all right, and we were thankful to be going back soon.

The overblown newspaper accounts continued to report the devastation of Dora. Even President Johnson made a flying personal survey, ordering the Corps of Engineers into action. The sandy beach we had walked daily was gradually riprapped with huge chunks of granite foreign to our Island shores. The wall is still called Lyndon's Blessing, or Lyndon's Blunder—depending upon where the speaker's political loyalties are.

Oddly enough, we worked like Trojans in our Chicago garden during the remainder of September. Looking back now, I think our mood was a strange one. We were leaving our home again soon—and excited about going. Yet, after a spring and summer back there, we seemed to love it as much as ever. I have to laugh now, remembering the three long trips we made to the suburbs for large loads of already blooming chrysanthemums for the garden—knowing full well that we could enjoy them only briefly. Such extravagance probably salved our divided hearts.

The long, narrow strip of backyard no longer looked like a bowling alley the bright October day we drove away, headed once more for St. Simons. The garden was a picture and we were glad, because Lorrie Carlson, who would move in again, loved flowers. Perhaps, too, the Island warmth and friendliness were reaching all the way north to

Chicago. City neighbors seldom know one another well, but as we drove away, the folk who lived in the tall buildings on either side of our house were hanging out their windows waving.

Was it only the pretty garden which made them seem more friendly? Or could it have been that I had begun learning on St. Simons Island how much people need one another? Being what society thinks of as neighborly isn't natural with me, no matter how outgoing I am in public. I'm a private person all the way. I can stay inside my big Georgia farm gate in our St. Simons house, writing, reading—the days passing, especially if Joyce is away—and two weeks can rocket by without my once realizing that I haven't been farther from the house than my mailbox at the end of the lane. Only now and then do I indulge myself to this extent, but I do love being alone. Maybe the toppling of my ivory tower by a new sense of community is the greatest gift the Island and its people have given me.

After a happy visit with Joyce's parents in Indiana, where we left her Olds, we were back in White Cap by the last day of September. I was nearing the end of the novel. In one way, at least the *Beloved Invader* manuscript (titled at last) had more tender loving care than any I've done since. It wasn't that I loved it more; I love them all during the time they're being written (although I do have favorites), but *Invader* was the first, and being so unsure of myself made me more careful. Elsie had been patiently cutting her stacks of stencils almost from the beginning for both the Rough and the Smooth. They were everywhere. It grew to be funny, actually, when there no longer was an open space for a guest to sit down in our living room. The funniest part of all was sorting the stencils (hard to read at best) according to pages Tay had read and approved and pages Tay had not read. (I'm thankful for the way Xerox machines multiplied before the second novel was finished!) Fred Burk at Lippincott wanted ten copies. Easy to run off, once I'd okayed all the stencils, but far from easy to collate once they were run. What to do?

"Frances Stankiewicz." Elsie spoke the name like an announcement. "She's wonderful at collating and she'd love to help."

We knew Frances and her husband, Mitch, from the happy late afternoons and evenings at the Ship House with the Goodwillies. And so, armed with boxes to put the collated manuscript in, Elsie, Frances, and I drove to the vicinity of the Island airport, where Elsie, with her usual resourcefulness, had arranged for us to work in an abandoned little-theater building.

"The Island woman's club meets there," she said. "Our long tables are still up. They'll be just right for the job."

The *Beloved Invader* manuscript has long since been in the Mugar Library Special Collections at Boston University, where all my papers and junk are housed. I can't check its length, but although it's shorter than most of the others, it seemed long enough to me that day. Elsie and Frances enjoyed the collating—or pretended for my sake that they did—and finally, at about six o'clock, we carried a stack of ten boxes out to Bonnie and laid them in that big, commodious trunk. (These days, no car has a trunk to compare with Bonnie's.)

As I recall, Agnes Holt took care of sending the ten boxes to Fred Burk in Philadelphia via American Express—then still a flourishing business. The nice Express delivery man picked them up at the Tabby House and charged it to Agnes's account.

"We'll settle it later," she said airily. "He'll have to weigh them first."

It took quite a chunk of money to settle later, too, believe me.

But the copy that was to go to Tay in the New York office was held for Joyce and me to send airmail at our cozy St. Simons post office. It was quite a ceremony. Frances Burns, the attractive lady who worked at the post office and whom we'd met often at Lorah Plemmons's house, officiated. In fact, beginning with *The Beloved Invader*, because we were so fond of Frances, it became a tradition for *her* to weigh and stamp every manuscript I sent from the Island, until she retired from stamping not long ago and "went to fishing." I remember as though it were this morning that Frances pronounced some magical kind of incantation over the big package—she's an authority on folk legend and history—and stamped it elaborately with every conceivable variety of rubber stamp. After that anticlimax, I walked out of the post office beside Joyce in silence, already lonely for my book.

The waiting for word from Tay set in. Joyce put aside her work on the biography of Sir Wilfred Grenfell and spent the jittery days with me, driving up and down the Island the way we did at first, visiting Lorah Plemmons and the Youngs and the Everetts almost every day, moving a little out of the Golden Isles area to explore the old historic towns of Darien and Midway, bird watching, bird watching, bird watching, picnics on the beach, shelling, more bird watching, and more visits. There hasn't been such a nervous waiting time on any manuscript since that one, thank heaven. But in a bit over a week, another telegram came. My heart soared: REASONABLY FEW CHANGES. HURRAY! TAY.

She had read it rapidly first without editing it, so as to quiet the jitters she knew perfectly well I had. In two more weeks or so, her carefully—and in spots humorously—edited manuscript came. Joyce says I didn't say a word for the hours spent devouring Tay's scribbles in the margins. One thing I should make clear: she never, never told me *how* to fix anything. Of course, she marked nothing "good"—not one line—but she did mark with a vengeance what was wrong. I remember some of those notes—many of which continued to appear until she died. "Pew!" was a favorite; "Come on, Genie," another. "Oh, really?" appeared when I'd put Anson and Anna or someone else in a physically impossible position—legs where legs couldn't be if arms or heads were where I'd placed them. Her caustic comments scared me, but I laughed too, and that was her genius. I have never had more downright fun and agony in all my life than I had with this amazing, contradictory, and brilliant woman's editing. (I'll never forget, when I was writing *New Moon Rising*, her blasting me for having no sense of motherhood. "You haven't fed or changed this baby for three chapters!")

For days and days—no way now to remember how many—I labored over the changes, as Elsie cut needed new stencils without a word of complaint. About a hundred new stencils, as I recall, because I was so fussy about the way my manuscript looked. If it wasn't altogether professional, at least it could look that way. I have always been a stickler for *not* being the one to cause those printer's typos. The least a writer can do is submit a clean manuscript. Certainly the least this writer could do, since she had the expert help of dear, efficient Elsie. (I remember that was when I convinced her that she didn't begin to charge enough per manuscript page, and she raised her rate. I'm still proud of my victory.)

Finally, there was another only slightly less ceremonial pilgrimage to the post office, and Frances Burns got off the changes to Tay, who wired (my, how I miss delivered Western Union telegrams!) that it would be going at once to the Philadelphia office to be copy edited.

Charley Granade, now head of another department at Lippincott, meticulously supervised the copy editing of *Invader,* I okayed or over-ruled (only now and then) the copy editor's suggestions, and back it went to Philadelphia, on its way to be set in type. And then I received the letter from Tay for which I'd been waiting—her reactions to the finished manuscript. It struck her as a "good book. Not a great one, but definitely a good one."

She still thought I had been wrong to insist (the one time I'd dug in my author's heels with her) that the sermon which appears in Chapter 35 should be left in. Tay had wanted to delete it as repetitious of certain sections earlier in the book. I took almost every suggestion she made, but on that one I was adamant. To this day, I'm glad. The passage is Anson Dodge's resurrection sermon—the setting forth of his (my) firm belief in the Ongoing Life after physical death. I have now lost count of how many letters I've received from persons for whom this one short message has had special meaning in times of personal grief. The book was published in 1965. These letters continue to come.

Most meaningful of all to me was something Burney Vanstory's granddaughter told me recently in Christ churchyard as we all stood talking quietly around Ann Vanstory Teeple's still open grave. Ann Vanstory Teeple was the girl's mother, who had died before her time —and my beloved Burney Vanstory's only child. And she was my friend. "Miss Price," the girl said softly, "I just had to tell you that in Atlanta at Mother's service there, our pastor used the resurrection sermon from *The Beloved Invader.* It helped us all."

Ann's daughter's eyes brimmed with tears—as did mine. I'm sure Tay is glad now that we left it in.

I admit to having had a sweeping moment of deep embarrassment because all those mimeographed copies had to go off to Fred Burk without Tay's changes, but her letter had declared the novel good, and I would be content. Without her telling me, I already knew that it was not great. But it was finished, and as suddenly as the title, *The Beloved Invader,* had come while Joyce and I were waiting in the optometrist's office for our first reading glasses, peace came. A different kind of peace. I had done the best I could at that stage in my writing life.

The new peace lasted for several days, as I remember, and then —the book completed and out of my hands forever—I began to feel an almost depressing inner restlessness. It was late February 1965. We had at least two more months left on St. Simons before the high summer rentals would send us scurrying back to Chicago. Gradually, with Elsie Goodwillie's willing and skillful help, I was catching up on a huge stack of personal mail. I should have been lighthearted and carefree. I wasn't. And I knew why I wasn't.

"I can't wait a minute longer to say something—to ask you something," I said to Joyce one morning over coffee. "Why should we go on being sick every time we have to drive back across the marshes and head for Chicago? Writers can live anywhere typewriters can be set up. I'm not taking a packed speaking schedule again—not ever. I don't feel in the least compelled to go on with that. I'm a writer—for better or for worse. So are you. Why don't we sell the Chicago house and move here—to stay? *Inside,* I need to be a part of this place."

Joyce set down her coffee cup and leaned back in her big chair across from mine, her whole being relieved. "I wondered when you were going to bring it up again," she said. "I'm ready. I wouldn't even mind living for a few years right here in little White Cap, would you?"

That was it. We would go back to Chicago with our shining secret kept closely guarded except from our parents and Lorrie Carlson. Surely it was no secret to Mother that my entire life had taken on a new dimension since I'd found St. Simons. Just yesterday, as I write this, Mother said to me on long distance, "I've been rereading some of your letters from back then, darling, and I still get tears in my eyes at the new joy in you—more joy than I had ever seen in you before you found your Island."

Mother wanted to stay in Charleston but, as always, I was left free to do whatever might seem to complete me. As was Joyce by both her parents. Oh, we raced from the Goodwillies to the Everetts to Lorah Plemmons to the Youngs, to Agnes Holt at her Tabby House, to anyone on the Island who might be glad at our decision, but except for Lorrie we said nothing to our Chicago friends. Best to wait until we were back there again in April or May.

At the Christian Booksellers Association convention the summer before, 1964, Joyce had become instant friends with one of the most lovable people in the publishing world, Richard Baltzell, who was then Lippincott's promotion manager. I was in the Zondervan booth for the entire convention, signing copies of my newly published *God Speaks to Women Today* for the booksellers, who came from all over the United States and Canada. Joyce, who from the beginning of our friendship so many years ago had been a veritable extension of me, made friends for me that year with my new fiction publishers at the Lippincott booth. Excitedly, she brought Richard Baltzell around for an introduction. I loved him on sight. And in the spring of 1965, *Invader* finished, Richard made the first of many pilgrimages to St. Simons Island. Pilgrimages which, happily, continue to this day.

Plans were forming for a large reception for me to be held by Lippincott that year, 1965, at CBA in Philadelphia. A nice place to take Mother, I thought, and was generally pleased. Richard and I also discussed a tour on which he would accompany me, visiting all or most of the Zondervan Book Stores in Michigan and Indiana. That would be tiring, but I was gratified that my longtime friends at Zondervan would be supporting me in my new fiction venture with another house. They have been nothing but encouraging and proud of what success I've met so far, and of course I had no intention but to go on doing nonfiction books for them.

Richard's plans sounded exciting, but most important, his first visit to us (he loved his room at Goodwillies' Ship House overlooking the sea) began a cherished, lifetime, three-way friendship. To this day, whether there is business or not, we all seem able to go just so long without hearing one another's voices. He is a gift I might have missed had it not been for *The Beloved Invader.*

We enjoyed, enjoyed our Island friends; we missed few evenings chasing the sunset either at the pier in the village or at Frederica, where we parked by the old abandoned Yacht Club to watch and photograph the changing colors and the reflection in the calm waters of the Frederica River. It was during this time, as I recall, when our bond of love with Lorah Plemmons had grown strong and sure, that she first told us of the influence on her childhood of one Indian man in the Georgia mountains. He taught her how to select and preserve curative herbs, how to know one lichen from another, how to walk noiselessly through dry woods, how to kill a snake with one blow of a flexible stick.

She who always welcomed our visits as a time for "a good talk" actually talked so seldom of herself that we hung on every word. And to this day, I remember vividly the first time we actually saw her—at age eighty-nine!—give a rattler a deft whack behind the head and finish him off. I also hear that good, merry chuckle as she hobbled along beside us back to her porch "to talk some more."

It was during that nearly idle interim, too, that we arrived one day to find her chopping pine splinters in the backyard. More activist than I, Joyce just had to take the big ax and try it. Lorah let her make a few wobbly blows at the big chunk of fat pine and said, "Lordamercy, child, give me that ax! You'll chop your foot off!"

The next time we rolled into her yard under the big camphor tree, she had not one but two boxes of pine splinters chopped and ready for us to take back to White Cap. She had diminished the once huge chunk of fat pine to a mere shapely knot. We took that along, too, and still use it as a doorstop on our own back porch, at the kitchen door.

And then—the earth took a sudden extra turn for us both. One night at the Goodwillies', between piano numbers, Elsie swung around to us and said, "Oh, by the way, I know you said you might not buy anything down here for a few years, but Marian Stevens—I'm doing her manuscript right now—says she *thinks* her husband, Ben, might be willing to sell off a beautiful point of land they own in the Stevens family tract at Frederica. Four acres. Do you want me to have her call you?"

"Yes!" we both chorused. At once the fun and the frustration and the excitement began. We were definitely going to sell the Chicago house that summer—just as soon as we got back—and land was not yet expensive on St. Simons Island.

Elsie, who does everything yesterday, had Marian Stevens on the telephone in five minutes or less. There would have seemed little time during the remainder of that year for property buying or moving. *Invader* would be published in the fall, as would Joyce's biography of Sir Wilfred Grenfell. The first in her beloved series of children's books, *Suki and the Invisible Peacock*, was just out. It might be premature, but we wanted, oh, how we wanted to own more of St. Simons than the tiny lot in Christ churchyard! As I reached to take the telephone from Elsie, I had a shaky feeling in the pit of my stomach. What if Marian Stevens's husband, Ben, didn't want to sell his property?

A brief moment later, I hung up and said, "She'll ask him again.

When she broached the subject yesterday, he said no."

The next day we decided to call her in the late afternoon, hoping she'd had a chance to sound out the already mysterious Ben Stevens, who hadn't refused the first time Marian had approached him on the sale of the beautiful four-acre point of land, but who then did refuse.

I stood nervously in a village phone booth and dialed the Stevens residence at Frederica. Ben himself answered. A quiet-spoken Southerner of few words, he didn't say yes, but he didn't quite say no. Would we call again the next day? This went on for a torturous week. Finally, he agreed to have us come up and look at the land on an old plat he had. The four-acre point was inaccessible by car.

Were we ready to buy it without even having seen it? Yes!

And after a month of on-again, off-again conversation with this handsome, gentle man with the disarming shy smile, we had his word. That word was enough for us. Ben Stevens and his equally kind-mannered brother, Curtis, owned adjoining land—a rather vast tract of it. At that time no one in the Stevens family had ever sold a foot of land to strangers. Old Captain Stevens (an important character in my later novel, *New Moon Rising*) had once deeded a portion of his land to Christ Church, but since then, through good times and bad, the Stevenses had held onto their precious land. And precious those four acres had become to us—sight unseen. We were familiar enough with St. Simons' woods to picture it in its present state: standing with magnolia and gum and old oak trees, sprouting dense undergrowth of vines, scrub oak, myrtle, and cassina—and of course pines, always pines. Our coveted point was virgin land, Ben Stevens said, where not even a cotton field had ever been planted. Oh, his grandmother's cattle had crossed the point from one marsh to another, grazing, but it was otherwise untouched. A pie-shaped point of land, surrounded by Sidney Lanier's marshes of Glynn and a dense growth of "dear dark woods." A perfectly secluded spot for two hardworking writers who had fallen hopelessly in love with the north end of the Island, where we felt near the church—Anson's little church which had started it all in the first place.

News had spread already that I was the author of a new novel about St. Simons, and our once-blessed solitude at White Cap—until then broken only by the dear ones we welcomed—was already being invaded. Strangers appeared at the door wanting to illustrate the book, to do the jacket painting, and so forth. All, of course, completely in the hands of my publisher. Tourists found us on 11th Street in the accessible white cottage. The idyll had begun to dim a bit for us both—until Ben Stevens gave his word. We had the money for a down payment and we made it fast—only two days later—with the help of Mr. James Gilbert, the Brunswick attorney who handled the closing and who became a much-cherished friend.

On air, we glided back over the marshes that afternoon from James Gilbert's office, and of course we went straight to the Goodwillies, our good-luck people. This may sound too pat, but once more—in the midst of a rendition of "I'll See You Again"—Elsie swung around to us from the piano, remembering that Walter's sister, Joannie Goodwillie, and her friend in Chicago were looking for a house to buy on the north side of the city.

That very night, Elsie called Joannie long distance and set up an appointment for us to meet them and show them the Wrightwood Avenue house almost the minute we returned to Chicago.

All of this happened in about three weeks, and even though we owned the land, we still had not seen it except on Ben's map! So one night, John Golden, our fine firewood man, took us in his heavy truck through head-tall palmettos and undergrowth as far back toward our point as the truck would go. We dared not get out and walk the rest of the way; inspection of another piece of land at West Point had taught us about ticks in the light-filled St. Simons woods. And so we sat there, high in John's big old truck, and reveled in the beauty—without a worried thought toward what was to be a huge, expensive, chaotic development job. Coming from a part of the country where one simply dug a basement and built a house, we had no way of anticipating what lay ahead.

That afternoon, John asked if we knew the Harry Parkers. "That's their lane," he said as we left the property. Harry Parker, we knew, was Ben's brother-in-law, married to Ann Stevens Parker, Ben's sister. Both Parkers had written reams of research material for *The Beloved Invader* at Edith Young's request, and so I felt close to them. Still, we wouldn't have moved an inch past their Private Road sign for anything in the world. (It is still an amazement that tourists pass ours as though it read, "Welcome, we're waiting for you!")

Every evening after work, we drove as far as Bonnie would make it into our dear dark woods, fascinated, as always, by the special, ethereal light that lay, we knew, at the end of Parkers' lane, and the end of Ben Stevens's lane, too. And that lay over our own mysterious, still unseen four acres, even more remote to us. There was yet no way to get to our property.

I still remember Mother sitting at the end of the road with me in Bonnie, one late afternoon during her spring trip to the Island. "I don't know how you bear not being able to see it better!"

I didn't know either, except that there were those millions of ticks and redbugs.

Mother was as excited as I—well, almost—and we talked of nothing else on our flight in the Bluebird from St. Simons to Atlanta. I was accompanying her home to Charleston for a week, to take care of some family business. In Atlanta, with three or four hours to wait for the Charleston plane, I made Mother a proposition:

"Now, we have lots of time between planes, and if you'll make a firm promise *not* to insist upon going into the book department, *not* to say one word to anybody we meet in the store—clerks or anyone—that I've a novel about St. Simons coming out, I'll take you to Rich's and buy you a new summer outfit. Is it a promise?"

She laughed her musical laugh and said, "Why, you know I never mention your name!"

A complete and charming falsehood, since her favorite pastime (and my father's when he was with us) is boasting about my brother, Joe, and his sister, Genie, and her books. For years, this boasting had been a standing joke in our family—especially between Joe and me.

I reminded Mother again in the cab on the way to downtown Atlanta. I emphasized that Lippincott was setting up my first autographing party with Rich's famous and hard-to-convince book buyer, Faith Brunson, and that I wanted no boats rocked now. The party, if Faith Brunson agreed to have one, was to be on publication date in September, just a few months away. It is rewarding at times for an author to be recognized by strangers, but there are times when it isn't, and this was one of those. I really wasn't much worried that anyone in Atlanta, where I'd never appeared or spoken, would recognize me, but I'd learned from experience to watch Mother. One of her favorite things was to browse in bookstores and drop her daughter's name, but I felt that at least I had her promise, and so by the time I was making out the check for the items we'd selected in one of Rich's ready-to-wear departments, I had put the whole thing out of my mind. Then I handed the check to the courteous salesperson.

Examining it, she looked up suddenly. "You're not *the* Eugenia Price, are you?"

"Well," I replied, embarrassed as always, "Eugenia Price is my name."

Mother could stand the pressure no longer. "My daughter is the author, Eugenia Price," she said, beaming her best smile.

"Oh, I've read all your daughter's books," the salesperson declared, speaking directly to Mother, as though subconsciously sensing an ally. "I don't have another customer right now, and I'm taking you both right up to the sixth floor to meet our Miss Brunson!"

"No," I said quickly, my long-held aversion surfacing for authors who peer at bookstore shelves to see if their titles are in stock, or authors who sweep into a bookstore expecting its personnel to be impressed that a real live writer has honored them with his or her presence. "No, thank you." I tried to modulate my voice. "Mother and I have a plane to catch."

"Oh, but not for two more hours," Mother chimed.

Helplessly, not wanting a scene, with Mother and the ebullient salesperson on either side of me, I was herded toward the escalator and up to the sixth floor. Neither of them seemed to notice my nervous silence—nervous because I'd heard that Faith Brunson could be totally unapproachable. But unless I made a scene before the strange and well-intentioned salesperson and drew still more attention, which would have embarrassed Mother, I had no choice but to follow them up the escalator. Follow!—for five flights, they kept me in the middle between them!

We walked into the spacious, well-stocked book section, and a pleasant-looking lady in a green smock approached us.

"Oh, Mrs. Goldstein," our guide said. "I have Eugenia Price here —*Eugenia Price* and her mother. Will you get Miss Brunson right away?"

Dismay, confusion, and dread passed pronouncedly across Margaret Goldstein's intelligent face. "Well, I'll see if she's busy."

"Please don't bother her if she is," I said quickly, extending my hand when Margaret Goldstein offered hers, first to me and then to Mother. "We, uh, we just want to look around the book department. I insist that you don't bother her at all."

"It'll be no bother," our ready-to-wear clerk exclaimed. "You're one of Rich's best sellers, Miss Price!"

I frankly doubted that; in fact, I'd have sworn it wasn't true. Margaret Goldstein gave no sign that she knew the name as she excused herself and vanished into another room at the rear of the section.

Mother could contain herself no longer. "My daughter has a new novel about St. Simons Island, Georgia, coming out from Lippincott in the fall," she said in her best grande-dame manner.

"Oh, how exciting," the salesperson said. "I know Miss Brunson will be so eager to meet her."

After a few moments—not many, really—Margaret Goldstein reappeared, walking slowly, almost reluctantly, down the long aisle toward us—alone. "Uh, Miss Brunson is—on long distance," she said with a weak smile.

At this point, I must pick up the story as I've heard it a dozen times since from both Faith Brunson and Margaret Goldstein. On that first trip to Faith's office at the rear of the section, Margaret had been totally rebuffed by a very busy book buyer.

"I sell her books—of course I sell her books," Faith had shouted. "I'll sell her new novel. I'm having her for a party. But I don't want to meet another religious author until I have to, and I don't like *any* author who comes snooping in my bookstore! Say I'm busy with a salesman—on long distance—anything. Just get rid of her."

Margaret had chosen to say long distance.

"Then we'll go," I said quickly. "We have a plane to catch anyway." I took Mother's arm and started back toward the escalator.

"No, wait," Margaret said, not looking at any of us. "Just wait, please." She walked determinedly back down the long aisle and vanished once more into the room off the rear of the book department.

"Faith Brunson, you listen to me," Margaret vows she said, striding into Faith's office again. "Just because you're afraid of religious authors is no excuse for being rude. Anyway, Eugenia Price isn't like a lot of other authors. She doesn't even seem to want to be here in the first place. I think that lady from ready-to-wear dragged her up here!"

"I don't care who dragged her where! She's snooping, and I don't like snooping authors. Tell her I'm busy."

Poor Margaret reappeared and again urged us to wait. And according to her, after she'd made another trek down the long aisle, she accosted Faith with something like this: "Now, get up off your duff and go out there. I think you're making a big mistake. She's not the typical author at all!" With that, Margaret got Faith by the arm and brought her out bodily.

A smartly dressed, attractive woman in her late thirties, Faith managed to introduce herself. My embarrassment showed plainly—at least, she vows it showed plainly and I'm sure it did. I introduced Mother and apologized for disturbing Faith. Margaret Goldstein sneaked away.

Then I laughed. "I don't think you wanted to come out here and I didn't want you to," I said. "I hate authors who go peering around bookstores to see if their books are on the shelves. Will you forgive us? This was really a—kind of mixup."

Faith looked at me for a long moment; then she laughed too and extended her hand. "You're one of my best sellers. I'm delighted to meet you—and your mother. Would you like to go with me for a cup of coffee? We can talk about the autographing party I want to give you for your new Georgia novel."

By God's grace or some stroke of magic, and probably by both, I had struck exactly the right note with the woman who has been one of my most valued friends since that peculiar meeting. But I had simply told her the truth. I *did* dislike snooping authors; I thought them gauche. Anyway, it was the far-out beginning of what still goes on as a meaningful friendship as well as a profitable professional relationship. To this day, I call Faith when I'm stumped on a publishing question and usually talk over any new book ideas with her. She's a natural in the book world, highly respected and influential wherever her name is known in publishing, which is everywhere. Her humor remains delicious, and if my memory is correct, I haven't brought out a book since we met that the publication date was not set in order to hold the first party at Rich's with Faith Brunson, who gives Mother credit for starting it all.

I must add that I don't believe anyone less than Margaret Goldstein could have gotten her boss out to meet me that day back in 1965.

Early in the summer, back in Chicago, we were lyrical to find Joannie Goodwillie and her friend, Edith Steele, interested in buying our beloved Wrightwood Avenue house. In fact, the way was paved for our move to the Island far sooner than we dared hope it would be. By the end of July, the deed for the house was in their hands and, in ours, the deed to what Joyce was calling Price's Point. Now that our house is here on the blessed four acres, our home for as long as we're physically able to look after ourselves, we call it The Dodge. After Anson Dodge, of course, but also because it is the perfect place for two busy writers to dodge interruption.

In this book, I am using old letters of mine, kept and shared now by a few close friends—Amanda K. Borders especially, to whom I wrote at length in those days both about my writing and our passion for St. Simons Island. I am referring also to carefully kept letters to Mother, but all letters from me after mid-1965 are scarce. We were far too busy for personal correspondence. Just the job of sorting our books for shipment to Georgia required, I remember, incredibly long hours. It seems irrational to ship tons of books from place to place, but we think of them as friends and form attachments to them. The day the movers began to cart them out to the big van parked in Wrightwood Avenue, we wondered if we'd ever be able to build a house large enough to contain them!

Most of the very few items of furniture which we planned to keep for our house-to-be were going to storage in Brunswick—my desk, my old swivel chair, Joyce's bed, two handsome Chippendale chests and a mirror that Mother had given us, Joyce's dining console, one small Oriental rug which I cherished, *and* most of the books. These were labeled "Storage," while boxes stuffed with the contents of our files and desks, along with the books we couldn't do without and our kitchenware, were labeled "White Cap," so they could be separated by the movers, who would arrive in Georgia ahead of us.

Chicago, which we had both loved for so many years of our lives, did not give us a very fond farewell. Knowing how exhausted we'd be once the big van pulled away, I had made reservations in a motel on the South Shore where the room service was excellent. I had one more speaking engagement scheduled in Chicago—an advertising-club dinner and speech at the Art Institute, as I recall—for the following night. Our plan was to get a good night's sleep at the motel after the usual pain of packing and rest the next day; we'd keep the engagement, and then Joyce would take me to a Delta plane for Atlanta and that first, all-important autographing party for *The Beloved Invader* at Rich's. She would drive Bonnie to her parents in Indiana, where I would join her later.

The plan sounded perfect. The plan was, but plans don't always work out. Smudged and exhausted from the move, we made it to the motel, by now a symbol of salvation and comfort to us both. I dragged myself into the front office, a smile of anticipation on my haggard face, and asked for our rooms.

"We're sorry, madam," a cold-eyed young man said, "but we've had a convention holdover. There are no rooms available."

I stared at him, remembered that I was a Christian, and tried courteously to explain that I'd made a reservation a month before.

"That can't be helped," he said and turned away.

"Well, could you recommend another good place?" I pleaded. "We're both totally exhausted." When he didn't answer, I added, literally choking back tears, "We've *got* to have a room—and room service!"

He did finally make a call for me, but only after I had insisted again.

Wearily, following his directions, we headed back up South Shore Drive and turned into what appeared to be a rather has-been place. At that point, it would have to do. Our spirits sagging, shoulders and backs screaming, we had to carry our own luggage up a flight of stairs because the bellman hadn't shown up for work that afternoon. Of course we were starved, but unlike the motel which had turned us away, this one had no eating facilities whatever. Joyce got out the Yellow Pages and had delivered some warmed-over Chinese food, which we gladly ate. Grateful for clean beds, we fell into them and died until morning.

For breakfast and lunch the next day, we took turns walking blocks for carry-out food. I don't remember what we ate and I don't think I want to. When evening came, we dressed for my speaking date and went down to my car, parked in an underground garage.

We found old Bonnie where we'd left her, waiting, but hemmed in by two other locked automobiles! It took so long to find help, and so much expensive charm to convince the doorman to grant that help, that I arrived at the Art Institute after my dinner audience was half finished with the meal. Always prompt, I was embarrassed, harried, and tired all over again. I wondered if there was an ounce of charm left for the people who had paid their money to hear me speak.

The next afternoon, when Joyce went to unlock the car before I carried my Atlanta-bound bags down the motel stairs, she found poor Bonnie hemmed in again! After another wild hunt for help, we headed toward O'Hare airport. I just made the plane. When we waved good-bye as I climbed the steps to the cabin, we were both laughing. Why not? We had made it. Our furniture and books were en route to St. Simons Island and I was about to be en route to Atlanta, where Faith Brunson and Margaret Goldstein, at least, would greet me.

I generally dislike being met at a plane—or seen off, for that matter—so I'd arranged to take a taxi to the old, now vanished Dinkler Plaza Hotel. I walked toward the registration desk, still smarting from the final Chicago frustration and a little jittery about the success or failure of the appearance at Rich's. My thoughts on the plane as we sailed through high-piled white clouds had been happy thoughts; it was beginning . . . something new and unknown was now beginning for me. Still, relaxing during the flight, I was aware of how thoroughly tired I was. I longed for a polite clerk at the Dinkler Plaza desk. It was not at first a conscious longing, but I suddenly realized that I needed someone to be kind to me. In the lobby, smiling wistfully, I identified myself to a middle-aged gentleman who seemed almost to be expecting me. Of course, Faith Brunson had made the reservation, but what happened next seemed *personal.*

"Well, good afternoon, Miss Price!" He smiled broadly. "Welcome to Atlanta!"

For a moment, I could think of nothing to say except, "What a nice surprise to have you glad I'm here." After the icy big-city departure, I was warmed all through. In fact, I remember breaking down and telling that courteous Southern gentleman at the Dinkler desk all about my recent troubles.

In my room was a huge basket of fruit from Rich's, a sheaf of literature about this wonderful store and about Atlanta, lots of little flags, and a card welcoming me a second time to my new Southern home.

I had a long way to go before the Island. Two days at Rich's and the remainder of the *Invader* tour, including the long trip with Richard Baltzell to the Zondervan Book Stores, still lay ahead—but I was on my way at last. The day would come when I could fly to Indiana to pick up Joyce and her Olds; then, one in each car, we could begin our final trip South. Our first trip *home.*

PART FOUR

The Dodge

TAY Hohoff had long before gone on to other manuscripts for other authors. I had become, with the publication and promotion of *The Beloved Invader,* the "property" of sales and publicity for the novel on which she and I had worked together for such a long time. I missed her—and was overjoyed when, just before the move from Chicago, a call came from Richard Baltzell in which he told me that Tay had actually agreed to appear with me—even to stand in the receiving line—at the planned reception that year in Philadelphia.

"I hope you know that's an honor," Richard said. "She's mighty proud of you or she'd never agree. Tay hates functions. And besides that, she's wary of all religiosos."

Richard and all his helpers at the Philadelphia office of Lippincott slaved to be sure that everything went exactly right at my big "do," which was to be held in the ballroom of the hotel housing the Christian Booksellers Association convention. Mother and Joyce would, of course, go with me, and Mother, at least, would revel at the idea of standing in the receiving line. Richard explained further that at a certain point, after all the booksellers had been "received," Howard Bauernfeind, Chairman of the Board at Lippincott, was to lead me gallantly up an elaborate stairway overlooking the ballroom, deliver a brief speech welcoming me to the ranks of Lippincott authors, and then present me for a response.

Richard's description of it all sounded touching and tiresome— my feet always hurt in dress shoes, since I go barefoot most of the time —but of course if Tay was willing, so was I. There were to be elegant refreshments and a small musical combo playing show tunes and romantic music. Not only everyone at Lippincott but also Bill Moore, then Executive Director of CBA, worked to make the entire affair a rousing success.

It was just that. Mother still likes to talk about it, and she looked lovely in a brown metallic cloth suit almost the color of her red-brown hair. I was in black, I remember, as was long-suffering, noble Tay. Of course, I was flattered that a house like Lippincott wanted me to the extent of such an affair, but mostly I was pleased that Tay stood beside me in that receiving line.

There was no time at the reception for the two of us to talk, and I was relieved when she informed me hurriedly that she was staying over in Philadelphia—at *her* hotel, the Warwick, "away from all this crowd"—and would be expecting me to come there tomorrow morning at ten. Her parting words, when she finally made her escape that evening, were, "We've got to discuss the next novel!"

Later on, after we had grown close, I tried to tell Tay how excited I'd been that she actually wanted to do another book with me. Her response: "Pooh. That's ridiculous. All editors like to edit successful books!"

On the day when Joyce and I had checked in at the Everetts' to say good-bye the preceding spring, Mary had said to me in a most offhand manner, "By the way, darlin', I just thought of something that might interest you."

It must be remembered here that Mary had spent hour after hour with us during the more than two years of research for *The Beloved Invader*, had entertained those who might be able to add even a fragment of information, and time after time had insisted upon driving us in her own car to Berta's house and to verify certain Island locales related to the story. The blessed woman had done all any human being could have done to help, and yet—on that last day—she seemed almost unaware that she was about to drop a bombshell.

Casually, she left Dutch and Joyce and me and went to her bedroom. We heard a drawer open.

"I expect Mama's found a treasure of some kind." Dutch grinned. "At least she thinks it is. And did you notice? She almost forgot to tell you."

Proudly, her eyes shining, Mary rejoined us bearing a stapled sheaf of typewritten pages. "This, dear Gould Girls," she said in her best oratorical manner, "is the history of 'The Goulds of New St. Clair and Black Banks.'"

For a minute, Joyce and I could only stand and stare at her.

Finally, Joyce took the sheaf of papers and began to fill the silence against which I was still helpless. With all my heart, I wanted to do the story of the other Goulds, but saw little chance of ever finding sufficient material, since no one living then remembered Horace Bunch Gould, Mary's grandfather and Anna Gould Dodge's father. Everyone to whom we'd talked also appeared very vague about Horace's father, James, the lighthouse builder, who had been the first Gould to set foot on St. Simons Island. Oh, Horace's charming wife, Deborah, had died in this century—Mary and Berta, her granddaughters, remembered her —but that was far from enough. And even with the cooperation of our friend Dr. Junius Martin, rector of Christ Church, who gave us access to Anson's journal, it had been hard enough to piece together a more recent story. So, when Mary suddenly "materialized" the history of the Goulds of New St. Clair and Black Banks, I felt almost faint.

"Go on, take it, darlin'," Mary said. "It's my only copy, but I think my brother Potter might have one, and I'm sure my brother James's daughter, Clara Marie, has one. I think she typed this from Cousin Agnes Hartridge's handwriting. But even if mine is the only copy in existence, take it—take it right on back to Chicago with you."

The previous spring I had signed another contract with Zondervan, to do a book to be titled *The Wider Place* with a long-cherished friend, Floyd Thatcher, who had just succeeded my late Zondervan editor, Peter deVisser. *The Wider Place* would have to be written first, of course, but in Philadelphia at the big convention, the thought of spending a whole morning—"or as long as you like"—with Tay to talk out another novel about the Goulds had me whirling. *The Wider Place* would not be as hard to write as another novel. I could do it while we were settling in and enjoying our first months on St. Simons as permanent residents. So, an hour ahead of time, I was up and dressed and waiting for ten o'clock and my visit with Tay. Joyce and Mother went downstairs at our hotel to wave me off in a taxi to the Warwick.

Tay met me in a dark-red, floor-length dressing gown. I can still see her sweep toward me across the bottle-green velvet carpet which covered the floor of her spacious room.

"I don't blame you for preferring this hotel," I said, sitting down in a chair across from hers. There was an awkward moment, and then

I smiled at her. "I know the whole thing was hard on you last night. I appreciate it more than you guess. Thank you too for staying over to see me today. There was no way I could have gotten away from the convention last night after the exhibits opened. I'm kind of an exhibit, you know."

"Yes, I know." She gave her surprisingly childlike smile. "The best of the lot."

"I hope you mean that. It means . . . more to me than you seem willing to believe."

With an airy wave of her hand, she shushed me, settled gracefully back into a big wing chair, and looked me straight in the eye. "Now, what will our next novel be about? When you're ready with another good story and have the time, we're eager to sign another contract."

I had read and reread Mary Everett's Cousin Agnes Hartridge's history of the Goulds of New St. Clair and Black Banks. As far as the information on those pages went, I knew it by heart. Choosing my words carefully at first, I ended up rattling off the story as my enthusiasm mounted. I told her of James, the first Gould to set foot on the Island back in the 1790s. My dates were a little fuzzy, but I already knew that Tay brushed off all dates, leaving them entirely to the copy editor and to me. I covered a long period of time in a few minutes, and before I was finished, Tay was smiling and smug.

"My dear," she said, when I'd run down, "we have not just another novel—we have a trilogy! The antebellum and Civil War eras for Horace Bunch Gould and another, laid earlier in time, for his father, James Gould. Don't you see?"

I did see and could have hugged her, although we weren't that free with each other yet. "I've signed to do another nonfiction book, but that won't take but a few months to write. I'll be living on St. Simons Island. I see no reason why I can't write that book and enlarge my research for—for the trilogy at the same time."

Whenever I mentioned being able and willing to break off a large amount of work, I could see Tay's eyes light up. She was a worker, too. That may have been our first big bond. (I *am* a hard worker. As I remember, *Don Juan McQueen* is the only book of the twenty-four I've published which did not make the agreed-upon deadline. Research simply became too involved and difficult.)

In an hour or so, Tay and I said good-bye, and I went back to the convention hotel to tell Mother and Joyce all about the *St. Simons*

130

trilogy! I took a cab, of course, but I could have flown.

That all-important visit with my editor in the Warwick that day was the beginning of *New Moon Rising*, although, as usual at that point, there was no title.

Sometime that fall before Joyce and I moved from Chicago, I wrote to Mother:

> Tay Hohoff is God's special gift to me. She's not only thoroughly imaginative, she's going to keep my nose to the proverbial grindstone. I can do it too. Even with packing up ahead now, settling on the Island, the development of my land at the Point, I can write *The Wider Place* and I can handle new research on the second St. Simons novel. I don't feel capable on my own, but there is God and there is you and there is Joyce—and now, happily, there is Tay too. And there is that blessed Island. We have, as I think I told you, engaged Mr. John Golden, our firewood man, to supervise and build the road back to my house-site, and all the grading and filling of the land. The prospects seem to have lifted his spirits too. There is magic at the Point—true magic. Mr. Curtis Stevens, a descendant of old Captain Charles Stevens and Ben's brother, will dig our well. Curtis is one of those rare, open, totally honest gentlemen whom one can trust. Thank heaven! Because we certainly know nothing of digging wells! I will talk to John Golden long distance tonight about his laying out our road. My instructions are that the road must *wind* and that a minimum of trees must be cut down. I began this letter by talking about Tay, bless her. And there is no end to my regard for the woman, but as always, I've ended up with the new house-site and that beautiful place tucked up there on the north end of the Island in the light-filled woods. Oh, Mother, I've never known such joy as I know these days. Never, never, never. I've written a novel at last—I have another ahead—and after searching the country over for just the right place to put down roots after the hard speaking schedule could be ended, I've found—St. Simons Island—in of all places, Georgia!

Mother came to the Island for Christmas on December 18, that year of 1965, and after two happy days together, she and I drove Joyce to the airport to catch the Bluebird for her holiday flight home to her parents. After we waved her off, we headed straight for The Dodge—of course. By then, the beautiful four acres looked a bit ragged. Uprooted undergrowth was stacked high along the newly cleared road.

But John Golden's road *was* there, laid out perfectly. It would circle the house one day—but Mother and I could drive it even then, which we did, round and round in old Bonnie, imagining.

"Bonnie had better last a long time." I laughed. "All this fill dirt will guarantee that I don't buy a new car anytime soon. No one had better ever tell me again that anything is dirt cheap! Dirt ain't cheap."

At night, Mother and I continued what Joyce and I had begun —long hours before the White Cap fire poring over decorating magazines, discussing the preliminary sketch for our new house that Joyce had drawn on the back of a Lippincott envelope. One thing we all knew —there would be no white-columned, antebellum replica for us. Such palatial mansions were *not* old St. Simons. We knew this because Edith and Nix Young had permitted us to study their excellent collection of photographs and sketches of the old Island houses—now gone, all of them—in which the Kings and the Goulds and the Coupers and the Postells had lived in the prosperous days before the Civil War. John Couper's house at Cannon's Point appeared to have been the largest —three stories, big and square, overlooking the Hampton River—but there had been no white columns even there. The Kings at Retreat Plantation had lived in a truly modest cottage, planning to enlarge it or build another more suitable to the needs of their large family, but the war had prevented that. There was a small sketch of Black Banks, an inviting but rather modest coastal house, and although there is no picture of James Gould's house, Rosemount, at New St. Clair, Potter Gould and others of James Gould's descendants still living had been able to give me some idea of its size and style, since, as children, they'd roamed the burned-out tabby ruins. It too had simply been a large, roomy tabby structure.

We wanted our house at The Dodge to be truly harmonious with the Island landscape. One that would give the look of a solid, wind-resistant coastal home—two-storied, so we could see the marshes and the salt creeks for miles around—and with a traditional kind of simplicity. Of course, it must be a functional house, suited to our needs as writers, but in feeling and style, we wanted it to fit into its setting the way Black Banks had.

"Just be sure," Mother warned, "that you build your rooms—all of them—large enough. I don't think there's anything worse than feeling cramped in a house. You'll get it paid for. Think very carefully about the size of every room. A house doesn't need to be pompous-looking in order to be spacious."

I cringed a little, thinking of the cost, but I fully respected Mother's opinion where houses were concerned. She had not only designed and built three in my growing-up days, she'd restored a lovely old Victorian house right in the middle of World War II, when almost no one could find adequate help. Joyce and I both cared about the atmosphere of our home. And we gave our mothers credit for that. Colors were of supreme importance inside—color and space and no clutter.

Before Joyce had gone home, she and I had spent an excited hour with Lamar Webb and John Baldwin, two attractive young architects just getting started in business on the Island.

"We want it to follow this sketch," I said during our first visit with Lamar and John, "and most of all, we want it to look *old* when the last nail has been driven!"

They sparked to our idea, and although Lamar—who of the two became *our* architect officially—didn't finish the preliminary sketch in time for Mother to see it before she flew home on January 2, it was ready for Joyce by the following week. In fact, I took it to the airport when I went to meet her. The whole thing looked perfect to me—even to the sketch Lamar had done of the two of us on the upstairs porch, with two flashy pileated woodpeckers in the oak tree nearby.

In the car, still parked at the airport, Joyce studied the sketch for a long time in silence.

"What's wrong?" I asked. "Don't tell me you don't like it!"

"Oh, I do like it," she said in that quiet, reserved way she has of expressing forthcoming disapproval. "The overall effect is beautiful— I like the way he's angled the guest room and garage unit, and I love the pass-through between that and the main house. Looks just like an old plantation house with a kitchen pass-through. Exactly what we asked for."

"But what?"

"Well, look carefully—it's a matter of proportion—do you think the roof is steep enough?"

"Why—sure. I suppose. I hadn't noticed."

She covered the main portion of the sketch with her hand. "Doesn't that roof look rather contemporary to you?"

It did. I honestly hadn't noticed before, but of course, she was dead right. I tend to see things as I *want* them to be instead of as they are. She has the good eye in this family for line and form. This distinction between us may be the reason that I am a novelist and she is a biographer. But the instant she pointed out the pitch of the big roof line, I knew. It just wasn't steep enough.

"Let's run by right now and get Lamar," I said, "and take him down to see that old building behind the big Aiken house on the ocean. Isn't that the kind of steep roof line we want?"

"You're reading my mind." She laughed. "Let's go."

Lamar saw at once what we meant and redrew the sketches exactly right. With a tabby first story and the second board and batten, stained (as Joyce planned to do it) the color of live-oak bark, there was no way —once the cedar shingles had silvered—that The Dodge could look contemporary. Not with that roof line.

Joyce was due to leave again early in the new year, 1966, for a huge Nashville children's book fair, so we "scheduled" our daily trips to Frederica and the new house site as though they were speaking dates. She would be gone for only a few days, but she would be out of sight of our beautiful four acres and the light turning up and down in the woods and over the marsh. We got up earlier than usual for a while and worked hard in the forenoon—I on *The Wider Place* and Joyce on the second of her Suki series, *Suki and the Old Umbrella.* By two o'clock each day we were "up there"—just sitting in the car looking, if the rains were coming down, or if not, walking around and around our winding road, picturing the house as it would be one day.

We both worked unusually well, and the days and evenings flew by on wings of sheer joy. Of course, everything at the property went too slowly to suit us, but Curtis Stevens was about "halfway down" with our well, he figured, and we slowed the progress there inadvertently, I now know, because we liked so much to talk with Curtis and his charming brother, Ben, who was helping him. Finally one day they hit water, and we all celebrated by drinking several thermos cups of it, never once acting as though its high sulfur content nearly choked us.

"We all have sulfur water," Curtis said in his slow, philosophic way. "You just want to watch your silverware; it'll turn gunmetal-blue. But this is good water and not nearly as deep as we thought we might have to go with her."

In his office one day, Lamar said, "There's one man who would know what to do with every inch of this house! His name is George Barry, and he's never built a house off Sea Island. In fact, the man came down here to retire, but he's so young for his years and is now so in demand as a builder, I wonder if he ever will. One thing I know—he could really execute these plans."

"Then let's get him," I said.

"That might not be so easy. He isn't looking for work, and all his equipment and tools are on Sea Island. He lives there. I'm not at all sure he'll do it, but he would understand what you want. You both want it so authentic, it's got to be custom-built. George Barry would do the best possible job—*if* we can get him."

"Does he have a wife?" Joyce asked.

"Why, yes. Mrs. Barry handles the business accounts for him. She's a terrific lady! Why?"

"Does she read books?"

"Incessantly."

"Then Genie can try to influence her. We'll go to May Korb's new bookstore and get a copy of *The Beloved Invader*. Genie can sign it specially to Mrs. Barry and enclose a note begging her to persuade her husband to build our house!"

I can still hear Lamar's approving laugh. Mine too, although Lamar's praise of Mr. Barry's skill and the fact that up to then he'd built only those handsome places on Sea Island rather discouraged me.

We had just heard about May Korb's new bookshop called the Shorebird in Longview Shopping Center—newly built since our arrival on the Island. Ben West, at our favorite hamburger spot in the village, had raved about May, and we had found him totally right. She became almost at once and has remained through the years one of our favorite friends. St. Simons had no bookstore until May opened the Shorebird, and we had greeted her coming with great appreciation—not only because it meant a local outlet for our own books but because we'd finally have a place right on St. Simons where we could go on adding to our library.

Joyce shopped at the new Brooks grocery store nearby while I went in the Shorebird to initiate our Phyllis and George Barry conspiracy.

I greeted May warmly and said—too loudly—"Do you know a lady named Mrs. George Barry?"

May put a warning finger to her lips and said in her most proper, Southern-lady voice, "Eugenia Price, I'd like you to meet one of my best customers, a very interesting lady, Mrs. George Barry."

I tried not to whirl around but I probably did, and from the rear of the tiny shop came a lovely-looking, perfectly groomed, graying lady carrying not one but three copies of *The Beloved Invader* in her arms! I loved her on sight, not just because she had beaten me to the punch with three copies of my book, or because we had our eye on her husband's building prowess. I loved her for herself. She was so gracious in telling me how much she'd liked *Invader* and so easy to talk to, I just threw all caution to the breeze and told her about our conspiracy to get her husband's attention.

"I think that's a marvelous story," she said, laughing. "George will love it—and as a matter of fact, he's just about to finish a Sea Island house—I think in the next month or so. You'll have to talk to him, of course, but be hopeful." The nice smile came again. "Be hopeful. I am."

George Barry did build our house, but new houses have to be paid for. And here I must say that there is no way for me to express my indebtedness to the beautiful gentleman who then headed up the mortgage and loan department of the American National Bank in Brunswick—the bank to which Agnes Holt had sent us. In my use of the word "indebtedness," I intended no pun. I *am* still mightily indebted to the American National Bank for the house, but I write now of a deep kind of personal indebtedness to this soft-spoken gentleman. His name is Dan McCook, and he has, by his expertise and patience and Christian love and concern, delivered me from a lifelong dread—hatred, in fact—of anything resembling taxes, insurance, mortgages, and balancing checkbooks—business of any description. Through all the years in Chicago, I loathed it. Anita Woodman, the intelligent and witty lady who came periodically to the Chicago house to do my accounts, made the first chink in my defense against learning any more about the icky business end of things than I could possibly get by with. Dan McCook finished it off.

"Don't tell me any more than you have to tell me," I said grimly to Dan on about the second or third visit to his office. "I've decided I want you to handle everything for me—I'm not considering any other bank but American National—you've checked on my past income and think I'm worth the loan, so let's leave it there. Just tell me what I have to scrape up and where to sign, and don't say any more about anything. I'm too happy with the thought of living on St. Simons Island. If you give me a stream of details, I may be too scared to take the plunge."

We were already friends. Because of Dan's kindness and gentleness with me, especially on such a frightening transaction as actually building a house from the ground up, I had come to like him. I didn't dread visiting him in his office, but I wanted to keep it that way. And

I thought it only fair to let him know right off.

He looked at me with his deep-set brown eyes for a long time, unsmiling. Then he said, "I think you'd better listen to me for a minute or two now. I'm just as fond of you as I can be, and we're all as pleased as punch to have you and Joyce become a part of our Island. We're downright proud that you're here. But do you know you've almost insulted me?"

"*What?*"

"Your mind is so closed to *my* work, which is finance, that if I didn't know you better, I'd really be insulted after what you just said. You act as though you've got the only really creative work on earth! My work with money—helping people handle their business affairs— is just as creative as yours, and if you'll simmer down, I'll teach you not only how to stop hating the money you make, but how to understand your own financial affairs."

I was speechless. I sank back in my chair across the desk from him and began to smile. "You're right, of course, Dan. Forgive me?"

He reached across the desk and we shook hands. He forgave me, and now, more than a decade later, as I write this, I *am beginning,* thanks to Dan, Charlie McMillan at the bank, and my fine attorney, James Gilbert, to understand a little of what is involved with my business decisions. They're still comparatively simple, God knows, and I mean to keep them that way, but in all ways—by arranging the best possible terms for me on the house and by his patient teaching through the years—Dan delivered me from one of my more formidable blocks to reality.

Of course, the very next day after we met Mrs. George Barry at the Shorebird bookstore, I hied me again to Dan's office in Brunswick.

"You couldn't settle on a finer contractor," he said. "Why, do you know that man, George Barry, needs no bonding at the bank? He'll want to do it on a cost-plus basis—won't make you an estimate—but you're much better off doing it that way *with him.* He's a man of integrity and the best builder anywhere."

The day Lamar called the Ship House to leave the message that George Barry had agreed to build our house, we dropped everything and celebrated. We packed a picnic lunch (as we'd done many times before) and headed up Frederica Road to tell the property that Mr. Barry was going to build the most beautiful house in the world right smack on its cherished four acres. The land seemed as glad as we, and so did Lorah Plemmons, who didn't know George Barry from "who shot John." We were seeing Lorah every day then, since we were soon going to be neighbors. The old darling, always ready for a celebration, went over to the property with us for a Frederica picnic and a long walk around our woods.

When the Glorious Day arrived, the day set for the actual staking out of the house according to Lamar's gorgeous drawings, Joyce was away signing books. We had talked for hours about positioning the house, but I felt nervous giving the orders without her. She simply had more common sense about things. Still, the time had come, and she reassured me long distance that I'd do it just right. I met Lamar and Mr. Barry and his foreman, Mr. Bob Forbes, at The Dodge, and down went the stakes, and back and forth and across went the cord that would outline the shape of our dream.

I had signed the second fiction contract with Tay at Lippincott for a still untitled novel about Horace Bunch Gould, the second in the planned St. Simons trilogy. Work on *The Wider Place* was going well; I was rather far into Chapter 9, as I recall, the day the house was staked out. The dear ones at the St. Simons Library had given a beautiful tea in my honor to which the people who lived on my Island came and stood in line for autographs, and my cup was brimming over.

The day Joyce returned, we raced up to The Dodge so that she could see how I had positioned the house. We wouldn't have to chase the sunset anymore once we lived there. I had decided that the living-room bay window should face it. That evening, we stood on the spot and watched the big red ball of sun go down over the marshes to the west.

Back at White Cap, I read aloud a letter I'd begun that day to Mother:

> Yesterday, after a hard rain, as I sat in Bonnie right on the house site, I was suddenly overcome with a kind of homesickness to live there! Each time I have to drive out the sandy road we've built and come back to East Beach for the night, it seems harder. Isn't it something that I love those wilds this way after all my years of city life? Even the Island storms and bugs and dampness and snakes and deer flies—charm me. I want to learn the Island as Anna Gould Dodge knew it. I am so captivated by the dear dark woods that I now find the ocean almost dull.

When I finished reading, I asked, "Do you find the ocean dull?"

Joyce laughed. "No, not dull. I'll always love the sea, but the magic is up there for me too."

"It's late," I said. "You should go to bed. You've got to proof all those galleys on Sir Wilfred Grenfell tomorrow."

"I know, but I'd much rather sit here and talk about the Island than sleep."

"Me too. Do you sometimes feel things are going just too smoothly to last?"

"Sometimes, yes."

After watching the dying fire for a few minutes, I said, "Did you notice how different everything was at my St. Simons Library tea?"

"Different? I know it was beautiful."

"Yes, but I've been given dozens of beautiful affairs in the past years. I meant—the people. The people here are just—different. Even those who haven't been here much longer than we have. Am I imagining that? They don't seem to—smother me. I—don't have to be anything or anybody but me. Is that because they—at least, our old friends like Lorah and Mary and Dutch and Berta and now Captain Doug Taylor—and the Youngs—is it because they all knew me and loved me before they knew I'd published a single book? They don't seem to do or say anything exaggerated that leaves me wondering how to answer. Do I make sense? They just seem appreciative and glad I've written about their Island—and that's that. That—and the ongoing warmth toward us."

"I know. And we don't need to understand it. I guess we just need to make the most of all this joy God's giving us now. Might help us accept some future time when things might not be so good." She yawned.

"We'd better turn in," I said. "You've got a long day's work tomorrow on Grenfell, and I've got to meet the bulldozer man at the property at eight thirty."

———◆———

Our longtime friend, Frances Pitts of Duluth, Minnesota, was to make her first trip to St. Simons soon. She would stay at the Goodwillies' Ship House and spend her days while we worked as only she could spend them, walking the Island lanes, tree and bird watching. Frances was, as we knew she'd be, wild about our wooded four acres. At every chance, we took her up with us on our regular inspection tours, and I can see her now—as I've seen her often through the years—standing in our lane, looking up into the heavy branches of a big tree, wondering as a child wonders.

Frances had been on the Island for about a week when, in the midst of a hard day's work, there came a knock at our front cottage door.

I opened it to my attorney, James Gilbert, and his associate, Joe Whittle.

"We have bad news," James announced in his slow coastal speech. "There's been an injunction filed against you. Work will have to stop on your house."

Stunned, we both asked all the wrong questions because we didn't know the right ones to ask. Neither of us could imagine why anyone would do that, and so the first moments of that traumatic conversation, softened only by the gentle manners of the two attorneys, are still a blur. But it seemed that another longtime Islander had felt that he owned the back acre of our four. He contended that Ben Stevens had had no right to sell that acre to us. Every tap of work—Curtis's final stages of the well, John Golden's clearing—everything would have to stop. Joyce, I think, understood a little better than I what an injunction was, and even if she hadn't, the long legal battle had begun. And it would last for what we remember now as several months.

Two things in particular during that frightening, suspense-filled time are vivid. First, we spent every free hour with our friends, who consoled us. Every evening with the Goodwillies, afternoons with Lorah or the Youngs or the Everetts. It all seemed so horrible to me, I honestly can't remember now whether or not I told Mother. The second thing I remember is that, by God's grace, I kept on working on *The Wider Place* and it strengthened me.

Enough here to say that in the late spring, thanks to the indisputable memory of aging Captain Douglas Taylor, who went out in a boat to point out an old surveyor's mark in the marsh, and to the expertise of my attorneys, we were at last free to finish the well and the clearing and begin building. (Every time I make a mortgage payment now, I'm reminded that during that horrid period of stalemate, interest rates skyrocketed!)

Then, when Lamar found that Mr. Barry was still free to do the building, our hearts only sang for joy. That picturesque back acre with the cedar tree bent over the marsh did belong to us after all! For days, when I visited The Dodge, I literally touched the palmettos and the cassina berry trees (which Frances Pitts calls fairy trees), and my gratitude for the miracle of the whole four acres grew. Of course, so did our regard for the original owners, the Stevenses, who had stood firmly with us through it all.

A few of the stakes had blown down during the long, windy winter, but under Mr. Barry's expert supervision they were quickly replaced and the sagging cords tightened, and one evening in early May we drove up after work to look for the very first time at one side of the actual foundation of our house. My bulldozer man was re-engaged, and for at least three weeks two huge machines ground away all day every day, one scooping up the solid bed of palmettos, the other digging holes in which to bury them as part of the necessary fill for the site, which turned out to be much nearer sea level than any of us had believed. (I say again—anything that's "dirt cheap" is made of pure gold!) But, in spite of our general revulsion for the bulldozer, we grew fond of quiet, expert Mr. Mauldin, who operated one of the giants, and watching him came to be my favorite thing to do.

On June 22, I had my fiftieth birthday, and neither of us will ever forget the philosophical lecture gentle, handsome George Barry gave me as we stood together on the subflooring of what would be our comfortable, light-filled living room.

"You've got it made now," he began, his blue eyes twinkling. "I always believed—and when I reached fifty myself all those years ago, I found it to be true—that the age of fifty is the beginning of a new kind of freedom." He made a sweeping gesture around the unfinished house and out over the marshes and the woods. "You've reached a measure of success in your work, you've made most of your big mistakes —the kind that bring you trouble which *you* could have avoided by the mere use of better judgment. You know a little something about yourself—what you're really like, what you want from life, what you mean to give back to life." He patted my shoulder. "Oh, Genie, this time of life is it—from now on, this is it. I'm up in my seventies. I should know!"

He did. I have found it so.

———— ✦ ————

Because of the house, I hadn't visited Mother on my birthday that year, 1966, so Joyce and I went up to spend a week with her in July. Although I certainly didn't know it then, on that trip I met two people —Nancy and Mary Jane Goshorn—Mother's neighbors, who would become more important in my life and Mother's than any of us could possibly have guessed. Mary Jane was a couple of years younger than Mother, tall, slender, silver-haired, and seemingly good all the way through. Nancy, her niece, eight years my junior, also enviably thin as a rail, with curly auburn hair and direct blue eyes, was attractive, extremely courteous, but so quiet I found myself talking too much when I was with her. Which wasn't but once or twice that trip, as I recall, when we talked over the fence that separated their properties.

Mother had written of how much she valued her neighbors, and I was glad. But I confess that I had no inkling of how deeply I would come to value them myself as the years went by.

Joyce, who had gone through the tiny gate in the fence to take pictures of Nancy and Mary Jane in Mary Jane's spectacular flower garden, got to know them both first and discovered to her delight and mine that Nancy is a baseball fan too. For those readers who are not fans, the next pages may be skipped, but the American pastime played an important role in establishing the permanent bond between Nancy Goshorn and me. Baseball has always played and still plays a dominent role in my non-working hours and so cannot be left out.

By then, we all knew that the Braves were coming to Atlanta. Joyce and I knew too, as I've told, that we would, in our newfound love of the South, switch overnight to become Atlanta Braves fans. Nancy got an enormous charge out of this seemingly fickle behavior. She entered still more into our new enthusiasm when Mother remembered to show her a copy of a column of mine, requested by Ward Oury, sports editor of a suburban paper, and promptly reprinted in the *Chicago Daily News* just before we left the city.

Here, for the rootin' tootin' fans and for anyone who wonders if I'm always researching and writing in a serious vein, is the piece I wrote:

WHY IS A CUB FAN?

"Why is a Cub fan?" Why is a wild morning glory! If one is a Cub fan and has always been a Cub fan, one can no more become a Sox fan than a wild morning glory can become a radish.

The analogy holds. At least to Cub fans: radishes are White Sox and morning glories are Cubs. Granted, the Cubbies may be considered short on glory, but they are not of this earth as radishes are. They grow on fences—exceeding their reach by merely winding back again—like the glorious ivy on the glorious brick walls of beautiful Wrigley Field.

True, one can gather some sustenance from a radish, and there are almost no calories in it. Still, there is the passing wonder of a morning glory . . . not dependent upon artificial lights at night, transient, collapsible, delicate, gone with the sun . . . like Cubs. There is also the trouble of having to pull and clean and pare a radish . . . there is the trouble of having to chew it. No one troubles to plant a wild morning glory, just as no one thinks of trouble at all at beautiful Wrigley Field. This is simply a place where the Cub fan goes on a sunny afternoon about twice a year to be glad about morning glories.

I am a Cub fan because I care for peace of mind. With a new book coming out this fall, I thank my Cubbies that I do not have the added strain of a pennant race to harass me. I not only love peace of mind, I love solitude . . . one can always find it at beautiful Wrigley Field with the Cubbies and the ivy and the space around one in the boxes. Cub fans always live longer and less troubled lives in their comfortable, familiar, peaceful homes in the second division. Home, with morning glories, peace . . . no strain, no stress . . . quiet, predictable living. The Cubbies will stay where they are, we need not despair because we need not hope. Where can this be found anywhere in the 20th century but at beautiful Wrigley Field?

I will miss my Cubbies next year, though . . . will miss the peace and the quiet and the rest of no contention. The delicate dependable Cubbies will go on as they have gone on for the thirty years I have adored them, but alas for me, I am moving to Georgia and must do battle with the "hard driving men" of the NEW Atlanta Braves!

I can almost hear knowledgeable baseball fans exclaim in total incredulity, "The *hard-driving* Atlanta Braves?" I know. I know. As of now, more than a decade later, they flounder in last place, fully as wispy and fragile as the Cubbies had ever been. No matter. We *are* Braves fans and that means that we believe and have believed since 1966 that one day—one sweet spring and summer—they will drive hard again.

The year 1966 not only began the love affair with the Braves for us and the new friendship with Nancy; it also began a love relationship with Burney Vanstory and her husband, Van. Until we came to know the Vanstorys, neither Joyce nor I had ever expected to find anyone else anywhere as mad about baseball as we. Wrong. The Vanstorys not only scheduled their lives so as not to miss a single radio broadcast of a Braves game; they understood every nuance of baseball. As the months wore on, Joyce and I not only began to despair of the Braves, we longed to appoint F. P. Vanstory manager in place of Bobby Bragan. Naturally, we didn't even know Bragan. But if it is kept in mind that we are true fans, there will be no perplexity over the fact that, by then, *nothing* could be wrong with our club—it had to be the manager's fault. (That a true baseball fan really knows better than this is beside the point, of course.) There is even a picture in this book of Joyce and me carrying a large sign reading BRAGAN MUST GO. Joyce and I lettered the sign and carried it while we picketed back and forth in front of the Vanstorys' house.

Nancy Goshorn was, naturally, since she lived in Charleston, West Virginia, a Cincinnati Reds fan, as my father had been all his life and as Mother is yet. We didn't sway Nancy then, but as the years passed and she and I became so close I didn't like to go on a promotion tour anymore without her, and since novel tours for me always begin at Rich's in Atlanta, she switched too.

"Which city do you visit more often?" I asked. "Which city do you really love? Atlanta or Cincinnati?"

Nancy has a logical mind. She realized the place of her true loyalty at once. She is, foolishly now, also a Braves fan. I doubt that we'll ever win Mother away from the Reds, but once the Braves' eccentric, lovable current owner, Ted Turner, took over, Nancy committed herself wholly.

I don't remember exactly what the Braves did in the standings during the year of 1966, but it doesn't matter. They were *our* new team, in the state which was our new state, and a radio station right here in the Golden Isles carried every game!

————

The summer weeks passed and The Dodge began to take shape in its muddy, sandy, cleared space in the woods at Frederica. There aren't pages enough in this book to write out our near delirium as we drove the wheels nearly off Bonnie going up and down the Island from East Beach to that blessed four acres. I do remember the moment of exhilaration when, with the subflooring laid for the second story, Joyce and I climbed, single file with Lamar and George Barry, up a ladder propped against the front of the house and stood seeing for the first time the serpentine salt creeks and the vast marshes from the elevation of the second story. It was breathtaking. Joyce still has the same view from her office and bedroom windows on the west side of our house. In fact, it seems pertinent to say here that no two people could possess a more tested friendship than ours. We are both decidedly individualistic, opinionated women, but, unbelievable as it may seem, we built and decorated the entire house without one single disagreement! This probably shows less maturity on both our parts than it may imply, since the truth is we simply have phenomenally compatible tastes. But without either of us even asking the other, we ended up with the views from our office windows which we each actually preferred—she the wide marshes, I the wooded front of our property, with the road winding out to our old-fashioned Georgia farm gate which holds its huge copper mailbox for depositing the many cartons of books which come to us.

The day in December when The Dodge was at last roofed over, we bought a staggering amount of refreshments of all kinds and gave a rooftree party for the workmen—a tradition in New England, according to George Barry and his lovely wife, Phyllis. The carpenters, led by foreman Bob Forbes (who now, in retirement, still takes care of The Dodge's carpentry needs), set up long plywood and sawhorse tables in our living room, and it was dark, as I recall, when the party ended. George Barry's crew was composed not of "pickup" workmen but of craftsmen. Men who not only cared about the quality of their work, who not only revered their boss, but who enjoyed talking about building. Of course, everything bored us at that point except talk of our house, so no one had a better time than we on that gala afternoon.

There were two such parties at The Dodge. The second one had its own air of excitement, but there was one regrettable difference: our master brick mason, Mr. Wallace Ledbetter, was not present at the second party. Wallace, a soft-spoken gentleman with a sensitive face and ready humor, had managed to impress us both greatly with his unique skills. Lamar had informed us that Wallace was the most skilled craftsman in his line on the entire East Coast. We believed Lamar because our respect for his genius and knowledge of building had us in awe, but we believed him also because we could see with our own eyes what Wallace Ledbetter could do with bricks. And we loved every single brick that would pave our first floor and form our backyard wall, the back patio, the front walk, and the porch floor. We didn't love each brick only because they were ours and would be a part of The Dodge. We loved them for their old beauty and patina. We had been fortunate. Mr. Barry had somehow managed to have sent down from Savannah exactly enough bricks to handle our needs—and they were each one precious, since they were the last remaining from the demolition of Savannah's revered old DeSoto Hotel. It was pure joy to watch Wallace and another warm friend, Wallace's partner, Mr. G. L. Buchanan (whom we called Mr. Buck), work with the lovely old bricks, handling each like the treasure it was.

Joyce and Wallace, with the blessing of Wallace's wife, Fraser, our equally beloved St. Simons librarian, became special friends. Joyce has the faculty for analyzing crafts as well as their results. She would stand for an hour at a time, watching Wallace's strong, deft fingers fit the bricks and place them as though they'd grown there.

Together, Wallace and Mr. Buck laid the interior floor, the porch, and part of the front walk. But, for the same reason that Wallace could not attend our second Dodge party, Mr. Buck had to finish the job without him. Wallace was fatally ill. Ours were the last bricks he laid.

I think of him almost every time I think about the beauty of our floors. And I can still see him, after he knew of his illness, standing in the doorway, his ever-present hat at a jaunty angle, and hear his warning: "You can just be careful in the kitchen because of the bricks. They're art pieces. And don't you ever let *anyone* talk you into waxing or shellacking them! Do you hear me? Leave that natural old pink glow." And then he laughed and pointed his finger at me. "If you let anyone wax those bricks, I'll be right over there in the churchyard and I'll come back and haunt you!"

From Wallace Ledbetter, that was a command which we have obeyed. And the bricks, of course, are still beautiful.

Mother came down again for our now traditional Christmas with Lorah and Sarah and Mary Plemmons, and there was the added fun of a brief visit early in January of 1967 by Joyce's parents, the Reverend and Mrs. Leroy Blackburn, en route to Florida for the winter. Joyce's father, Leroy, is gone now too, but I can still see him walking round and round the lane, clapping his hands in boyish pleasure over our new place. A couple with enormous capacity for joy, the Blackburns' happiness with our new property was as satisfying to me as my own mother's joy in it. They would be back in the spring, and surely, by then, they could sleep in our guest room at The Dodge.

———•———

Mother hopped another plane in February, this time to Washington, D.C., where I was to speak at the First Lady's Prayer Breakfast. *The Wider Place* was published, and I had signed a contract to do my first nonfiction book for Lippincott. Tay agreed for me to do the nonfiction book along with our novel research because I had told her that it was one I'd always wanted to do—*Just As I Am*, based on the old song. Another reason I was persuaded to do it was that Richard Baltzell had become religious book editor.

The rough draft was finished by February, and I agreed that Richard could meet me in Washington for a look at the rough manuscript the day before I was to speak on the vicissitudes of building a new house with God in the picture. (One of my points, as I remember, was a fresh one, out of my own experience at The Dodge: the necessity for God's grace to be operative *in the homeowner* when painters finish an entire room in the wrong color and when the outside tabby is mixed a shocking raspberry red instead of the ancient lichen pink it was meant to be!)

I will never forget my quick windup of that talk. I was the main speaker and had been allotted exactly eighteen minutes. The Secret Service had to be pacified when Muriel Humphrey, Ladybird Johnson, and I had met them behind a big screen before the breakfast began, because I couldn't hand them a printed copy of my talk. I have never been able to oblige in that way, since I don't even use notes. But Senator Len Jordan's wife, along with another lady or two who were in charge, assured them that I wouldn't be saying anything derogatory about the government, and so I was allowed to wing it. From my years of producing radio, I have a kind of built-in clock in my brain so that somehow I know when a period of time is nearing its end. That day, in view of my impressive surroundings and knowing that President Lyndon Johnson, who had spoken to the Men's Prayer Breakfast at the same hour, was due to drop by our ballroom for a greeting to the ladies, I even looked at my watch to be sure that I still had three minutes left. I paced myself and what I had to say accordingly.

About halfway through relating a humorous incident—and before I had made my point—a commotion started at the rear of the huge room, and from the speaker's rostrum, I could see the quickly recognizable Secret Service agent, Youngblood (who had saved Johnson's life in Dallas), enter the room in the company of about half a dozen other watchful agents; and towering above them all in the middle was the President of the United States, in full stride down the open aisle toward the platform where I stood.

I will never again have to wonder if the Lord puts words into our mouths as He promised St. Paul He would do. He does. I could hear and see annoyance sweep over the sea of feminine faces before me, and down the speaker's table about two places I heard Ladybird Johnson say "For goodness' sake!" But the President had a schedule and on he came, as I, ready or not, wound up quickly and sat down—amidst a roar of applause which could have been for either the President or for me because I'd made it. I will never know, of course, and if it was for both of us, that's fine. All that mattered at that moment was that I *had* made it.

The highlight of that trip was an afternoon spent with Muriel Humphrey, one of the warmest, sanest, most enjoyable persons I've ever met. She was interested at that time—during her husband's tenure in office—in writing a book and wanted to talk publishing with me.

After Richard and I took Mother to the airport for her flight back home, he dropped me in a cab at the Watergate, where the Humphreys lived then. Mrs. Humphrey and I talked book publishing, but mostly we talked as two human beings, and although, having seen the quantities of her mail that day, I wouldn't presume to continue our first flurry of correspondence, I treasure the hours spent with her and admire her deeply.

Richard and I spent another long evening on my rough manuscript, which he liked as much as I did, and then he took me to my train. Yes, I had taken a train up. I love trains, and Joyce had discovered that the Silver Meteor left nearby Thalmann, Georgia, for Washington at an hour that would get me there reasonably on time. Looking back now, the train ride, in spite of the jolting roadbed and the dated sleeping accommodations, was another highlight for me.

Still another was my hat. In those days, women still wore them (may the ghastly habit never fully return!), and of course I had none, since I'd been roaming in blue jeans for a long time. Joyce had gone shopping for me while I finished the Rough of *Just As I Am* and returned to White Cap with two hats—one that cost $30.00 and one that cost $3.00. Knowing me, she, of course, didn't mention their prices until I'd tried them on. I chose the $3.00 creation, and even Agnes Holt, who worried a lot about my ultracasual dress, thought it went well with my designer's suit when she accompanied us to the Silver Meteor that morning. The First Lady didn't notice, I'm sure.

·

PART FIVE

New Moon Rising

BURNEY Vanstory, whose knowledge of local history is respected by everyone, had agreed to begin some research for me, which I would need immediately when I finished *Just As I Am* and was ready to start the second St. Simons novel. Joyce's notebook had, of course, begun to fill up during conversations with the living Goulds and her own research in my behalf. Burney was working on basics: what they wore, their houses, and the background of St. Simons' involvement in the Civil War.

She filled two folders with material which I cherish and use to this day. The still-untitled novel about Horace Bunch Gould was under way even before I was free to write. And Tay kept track too. Not one period longer than three weeks to a month passed during any work in progress that she didn't call or write—just to check. Just to say, "I hope it's going well. I'm thinking of you."

That practice is as important a practice as any editor can have—it is such a morale booster to hardworking authors, who, no matter how experienced they are, never get over hoping for some small contact from their publisher. I should think it equally valuable to the publisher. All sorts of mental aberrations and depressions can attack a working author, and do—even one blessed with a rather even temperament. I know. I have been told that I'm not a particularly moody person, but I've had my share of black periods during stretches of hard writing—especially novels.

I began experimenting with the opening pages of the Horace Bunch Gould story shortly after my trip to Washington, but the new house took precedence as well as time. Lamar Webb and George Barry stood staunchly by when a finishing touch that might have been completed in hours began to take days—as always happens. Because they stood watch, the house is truly *finished*. Neither man would accept slipshod work from any subcontractor. And so, finally, with a few very rough chapters of the novel packed away carefully in a box from my desk marked Vital Stuff, I joined Joyce in squaring my shoulders for the move. The Day had come.

"You can move in," Lamar announced triumphantly, "on March sixteenth!"

We did move in on that one day—March 16, 1967—but we couldn't have made it in one day or maybe ever without our friend Marie Richardson, who came all the way from Chicago to help, as she'd promised before we left there. Marie had worked for me for years, and our good-bye, difficult as it was for us all, was possible only because we promised to bring her down to St. Simons Island to help with the big move into our new home. No one knew as Marie knew about the contents of all those boxes and crates which had been stored at Whittle's in Brunswick for all those months while the house was being built. Neither would the move have "moved" as it did without the help and good cheer of our longtime Island friend, Holland Sheppard, or our late, beloved Mable Hillery, both of whom we'd met and come to love when they worked at the Ship House for the Goodwillies. Beautiful Mable of the unforgettable singing voice and the laughing brown eyes is gone now—at age forty-one—but if she were here, she'd help us again in the same way, in spite of the fact that she'd long since stopped being a domestic when the Ford Foundation retained her in New York to teach Sea Island slave songs to city schoolchildren.

When all the furniture was in place—some old, some new—the final touch arrived in a delivery truck bringing Joyce's house gift to me —the mellow, handsome antique hutch which Agnes Holt had *not* tried to sell at the Tabby House for all those years. I look at it every night from my favorite chair in the living room and am still pleasured by it.

While I had worked during the days preceding the move on the first chapters of the novel, Joyce finished her lucid biography of Theodore Roosevelt. But once in The Dodge, we decided just to enjoy for a while—to enjoy the glorious fact that, at long last, our new address wasn't even on a street! We were now the proud possessors of a rural box number on Route 4, Frederica.

When Joyce's parents returned for a few days en route back home from Florida, the house received their blessing. By then, after their several trips to the Island, our friends were theirs too, but the day Joyce took them to see the Everetts, she was shocked and saddened to see that our beloved Mary did not recognize them at all! Between the severe headaches she'd been having for some weeks, Mary seemed herself. She was sweet and gracious to the Blackburns, but our fears for her began—fears that perhaps those splitting headaches had been caused by one or more small strokes. We prayed not.

I have just been surprised to note that the year of publication of my book *Make Love Your Aim* is 1967. Somehow, somewhere in this busy time I had written that too. Perhaps turning fifty had accomplished some of what dear George Barry had promised. I was surely working better, and perhaps—now that I'd reached the golden age— I was wasting less time dramatizing myself, less time on mistakes. Writing has always been my first love, and since those days were happiness days, and since I'm not really happy unless I am writing, the output shouldn't surprise me.

———————

Our second houseguest at The Dodge was Richard Baltzell, who had contracted with Joyce for a biography of Georgia's inimitable educator, Martha Berry, founder of Berry Schools near Rome. Richard had then met Joyce in Atlanta, and together they had explored the vast Berry College campus and had fallen under the spell of the warm hospitality of the president and faculty. When I met them at the St. Simons airport, where they returned their rented car, and asked why they'd driven back to the Island when they could have taken the Delta Bluebird, Richard said, "Wait till you see the trunk of this car." It required two trips each by all three of us to transfer from that trunk to Bonnie's the cartons of priceless materials which President John Bertrand had entrusted to Joyce.

So the first books written at The Dodge—Joyce in her quarters overlooking the marshes and the Frederica River and I in mine, where I see the winding lane and the tall trees overarching it—were *Martha Berry: Little Woman with a Big Dream* and my second novel, eventually to be titled *New Moon Rising.*

Early that summer, I wrote to Amanda Borders:

> I have begun the new novel and as usual I'm struggling, although I feel I have selected the right place to start. Horace Gould is on his way home from Yale, where (like a lot of young men in the 1960's) he has just taken part in a campus rebellion. I plan to have the novel ready for publication in the spring of 1969, but some days I wonder. I'm taking no engagements of any kind, though, and for once, have no other contracts signed for any book aside from this one. Oh, I did take a week or so early in June to catch up on the mail by dictation to my good Elsie, and another time with Mother. Joyce and I flew to Charleston, then drove with Mother in her car into the mountains to a picturesque school called Alderson-Broaddus. They had kindly asked to be able to decorate me with what I call my "horse collar," and they did. In case you're wondering, the elegant blue and gold academic hood means that I am now a Doctor of Letters. Honorary, of course, since at the age of fifty-one, I have never graduated from anything but high school. Enough university credits to graduate about a time and a half, but they go together, those credits, only in that, as a writer, I know something about a variety of subjects.

Our exodus from East Beach to Frederica on St. Simons somehow seemed complete when Elsie and Walter Goodwillie sold the old Ship House and moved into their own home, with a charming backyard for Brenda and Elsie to putter in and with no one's towels and sheets and complaints but their own to see to. In spite of the fact that Walter had suffered a stroke two years before they moved, it had not altered his charming, dry humor; it only made it difficult for him to climb stairs. But with help, he could make it fine up our low back-porch steps, and with Elsie driving, the two of them visited us several times a week. Usually, if they didn't come up Frederica Road to The Dodge, we went down Frederica Road to their house. They loved their new place as much as we loved ours, and Elsie, with the indomitable spirit which had seen her through not only Walter's stroke and the sale of the Ship House, but a broken kneecap and a kidney-stone operation, stood ready at all times to dive into more manuscript for me. That woman can't bear to miss a beat!

I had studied a large, impressive book, *Early Years in Coastal Georgia* by Margaret Davis Cate, in which she had preserved invaluable material on the Island's distinguished, well-born black society. There, I had looked long at a handsome photograph of a sturdily built, older Negro man named Rufus McDonald, sitting on the step of his cottage beside a bright-eyed boy who appeared to be looking at something in sheer wonder. Mrs. Cate, in her continuity on the opposite page, wrote: "While playing around in the yard, this child, like all people who live much in the open, was quick to notice the new moon which had appeared in the western sky. Turning to look at it, he clasped his hands . . . and said, 'God bless the new moon!' "

I was so struck by the photograph, by what she had written, and by the child's exclamation, "God bless the new moon!" that for months —in fact, until the final manuscript had gone to Lippincott—my novel about Horace Bunch Gould was called "God Bless the New Moon." I used the phrase within the body of the book. It was appropriate and most people liked it. But someone at the house suggested *New Moon Rising,* the novel's last three words. The latter title won, but I have sat looking again today, as I write this, at Rufus McDonald and the boy —and I find I am still moved by "God bless the new moon."

According to a letter written to a friend at the end of 1967, I had completed the rough draft of Part I of the novel. Much of that summer and fall had been spent in research and in settling into The Dodge. In the letter I wrote, "Now that November has brought the inevitable change in the very color of Island air—from summer white, it has changed to autumn yellow—I still find it almost impossible at times to believe I'm actually living here. I am, I know, but part of the time I simply accept it by faith."

Another special guest early on at The Dodge was our wise and humor-filled and much-loved friend, Dr. Anna Mow—the merry saint who at this writing is eighty-four and still energetically speaking and turning out books that everyone should read. Anna has been my spiritual rock for almost all the years of my Christian life—but she is more than that. She is my friend, to whom I can tell anything—with whom I can *be* any way I feel. Enough said. Joyce and I had begun our life together in 1961 with the particular blessing of Anna Mow, and what she blesses, I have learned with the years, comes from the Father —straight from the Father. She reveled in our new place and, in her usual perceptive way, missed nothing—saw more, even, than we knew was here.

I doubt if Anna guesses just how much her encouragement in the writing of my historical novels means to me. When she reads a new manuscript (and I usually manage to get a copy to her before it goes to my editor), her wholehearted "Bless you, it's good!" frees me entirely. That means more than reviewers' praise of my characterizations or my style. Anna's strong *"Bless* you!" means that what the novel says is true. True, according to her uncommon insights about God and people. Her visits are too infrequent and always too brief, but The Dodge had pleased her, she had sensed the peace in its rooms, the beauty outside in the light-filled woods, and she had blessed it. We were content and invigorated, as we are each time we're with her.

———

One of the best things about being at work on another novel was being in touch with Tay again. During the promotion and opening sales efforts, an author feels almost estranged from the editor. Fred Burk and Richard Baltzell had managed to make the promotion of *The Beloved Invader* fun, but life took on another dimension when Tay re-entered it on an almost daily basis. Oh, we didn't talk that often, or write that many letters, but she was always "with me" when I worked on any book for her.

Invader had done extremely well, she told me—especially for a first novel—something around 50,000 copies just between its September publication date and Christmas of 1965, its first year in print. Tay seemed proud, and I worked day by day into 1968 with a new sense of confidence. I didn't begin to have enough confidence to try a novel without Tay, but I did seem to feel a bit more secure, as though I knew a little of what I was about. I work almost entirely by instinct, but I had never kidded myself concerning my own ignorance of how to construct a readable novel. When I call a book "readable" I mean that it is one which I want to finish once I've started reading it. If, out of a sense of justice to the author or because I need to know the content of a book, I have to force myself to keep on to the end, that is not a readable book. The most encouraging letters I get are the ones that declare, "I couldn't put it down!"

After my hectic 1967, I remember 1968 as a peaceful, pleasant, almost predictable year. Joyce and I worked long hours during the day, and in the evening we read aloud from what we'd written. Or we listened, during the season, to the baseball games. Being Lorah's neighbors now, we visited her often, and I don't remember popping in a single afternoon that she didn't have something ready—a complete dinner or a freshly baked loaf of her banana bread. (Lorah's cooking was always hard on the diet!) Of course, we continued to see our other friends too, and almost every night after an Atlanta Braves game there was a telephone conversation between our house and the Vanstorys' analyzing who should have done what for a better Braves showing. Burney and Van came to our place often, as did Clara Maria Gould —especially after our first party at The Dodge. That had been a Gould party, to which we invited the Gould clan as a small thank-you for all their help and encouragement. We had met Clara Marie before that afternoon, but somehow, in spite of the fact that I spent most of my time on our back porch talking to her father, Colonel James, she and Joyce and I hit it off in a special way from that time on.

The year 1968 seemed too good to last, and indeed, as our beloved Mary Gould Everett grew more and more anxious and changed, we should have been forewarned. Our sadness over Mary was eased somewhat by the strengthening bonds of friendship with her "little sister," Fé Gould Powell, from "Al-benny," Georgia. Fé came more and more often now to the Island to support Dutch, especially when, not long after the Gould party—where Mary had been the belle of the ball— Dutch had been forced to move her into the Brunswick Nursing Home. In spite of his deep love for her, his own age made the move necessary. We went on checking in with Dutch, but the familiar living room was starkly empty.

As before, we talked to Elsie every day, but we saw less and less of her and Walter. His health had worsened; it was more and more difficult for Elsie to help him into the car for their ride up Frederica Road to our house . . . more change. But rather than allow the new sadnesses to depress us, we tried to be philosophical—to remember something Joyce's mother had warned us about years before. We were both getting older—were reaching the time of life when one's friends begin to sicken, even to die. Once accepted, sorrows can become more creative. We had no guarantee that life would go merrily along as it had been, even on St. Simons. The impending change frightened me especially, I realized, because living on the Island had taught me, in a way I'd never known, how to love. Sincerely, from my heart, I *loved* people with whom I had little in common—except that we belonged here together. Life on the Island, especially in those days, tended to level one's prejudices and pretensions.

Spirit-lifting events took place too. Early in the year 1968 I was greatly pleased when our newly formed Coastal Georgia Historical Society presented me with an attractively framed recognition "for the outstanding contribution made to our knowledge of the customs, habits and life of those who lived in former days in the Golden Isles of Georgia." I, so recently an outsider, knew better than anyone else (other than Joyce) that the "knowledge of the customs, habits and life" had been made freely available through the long talks with the Gould family and our other Island friends and through Burnette Vanstory and our helpful local librarians. And most notably by Mary Everett the day she handed me the family history, written by her Cousin Agnes Hartridge, of the Goulds of New St. Clair and Black Banks.

For a long time I had acted only as a sponge, soaking up all these other people's knowledge, but the award stimulated me to still more careful research for the second novel. This was based on the life of Horace Bunch Gould, the father of Anna Gould Dodge, and took place before and during the Civil War.

Another strong stimulus to my work was the friendship which had begun at the CBA reception in Philadelphia between us and the president of the company, Joe Lippincott, Jr., and his delightful wife, Fifi. They had stood beside Tay, Mother, and me in the receiving line and had met Joyce later. In October of 1968, Joe and Fifi came to neighboring Sea Island for a short holiday, and one evening when the sun had just begun to drop toward the marsh, the four of us—Joe in an old jacket brought for the occasion and armed with shovel and bucket of fertilizer—ceremoniously planted our Lippincott Tree in the big front yard.

He and Fifi had given us instructions to order from a local greenhouse just the kind of tree we wanted. Our longtime friends, the Esteses, delivered a five-foot live oak, which stood in its burlap blanket awaiting Joe's expert planting. Fifi and Joyce and I stood by while the dear man labored, each meticulous square of sod stacked neatly beside the hole he dug. Finally, he set the tree triumphantly into the ground

Mary Gould Everett with her beloved Dutch and Ginger

Captain Douglas and Berta Taylor

Brothers Potter Gould and Horace Bunch Gould II

The other Gould brother, courtly James D. Gould II

Fé Gould Powell and Ann Stevens Parker with me at New Moon Rising *party, St. Simons Island*

*Captain Nix Young's "lady,"
Edith, in "her" chair at home*

*Beautiful Lorah Plemmons in
her favorite chair on her back
porch*

*Elsie and Walter Goodwillie at
the Ship House with the
people-dog, Brenda, about
1964*

Sarah, Mary, Lorah Plemmons, and I clown it up at my house.

Two Atlanta Brave baseball fans with picket sign urging the ouster of still one more manager! Left to right, Joyce Blackburn and Eugenia Price in front of White Cap, spring 1964

My mother (left) with me in the receiving line at the Invader reception, Philadelphia, 1965

My "editor, dear," Tay Hohoff, with Shadrach

I revel in seeing the actual octagonal foundation of James Gould's original St. Simons light tower during archaeological digs

Our wonderful friend Johnnie Wilson when our ileagnus bush was young and Johnnie was well and in full charge

I perch on back wall at The Dodge with Joyce

Inside the keeper's house (now our Coastal Museum) signing the last copy of Lighthouse *that Big Day with Kitty Grider and Joyce*

Joyce (left) and Jean Alexander before the present St. Simons light and keeper's house at the end of Eugenia Price Day, October 2, 1971

and gently and lovingly sifted in the fertilizer—by hand—layer after layer, alternating with rich topsoil we'd had hauled in.

Since the J. B. Lippincott Company still uses the beautiful old tree colophon on its catalogues, letterheads, and so forth, we always get a special lift out of seeing our real live Lippincott Tree still standing—flourishing—in the front lawn of The Dodge, between a clump of palmetto and a little woodsy cluster of pine and sweet gum. The tree stands; and Joe's early confidence in what I try to do with my novels still supports me. He and Fifi have come to be dear to us, and I hope he realizes how much his faith and encouragement mean to me.

Looking back now, it appears that I had my head screwed on a bit straighter in the research for *New Moon Rising*. At least, we weren't rummaging only in the old trunks and dresser drawers of our Island friends. For the opening sequence, in which young Horace Bunch Gould had just been kicked out of Yale, I had access via the mails and long distance to archivist Dorothy Bridgewater and to the excellent archives at Yale University. Besides that, Potter Gould had let me borrow for an indefinite period the actual yearbook from Yale which had belonged to his grandfather; and when Ms. Bridgewater's Xeroxed accounts of the Yale Rebellion arrived from New Haven, everything fitted together. She had sent not only the account and the reasons behind the rebellion, pro and con, but copies of photographs of the Yale College campus exactly as it looked when Horace had walked its tree-lined paths and sat on the famous old Fence.

Of course, Burney Vanstory's fine materials stayed beside my typewriter for constant reference when I needed to depict an aspect of living in the nineteenth century or to tell what Horace or his sister, Mary Gould, might be wearing in a certain scene.

I remember, too, a full day's attention from Lilla Hawes, who was then director of the Georgia Historical Society in Savannah and who became and still is one of our favorite people. Lilla took an entire morning to work with me in the Society's fine archives so that I could learn what I needed about the old city of Savannah; she then spent the afternoon driving us around the town to acquaint me with its streets and squares as they were in Horace's time. It was Lilla, too, who "decided" that young Horace, during his stay in Savannah, could well have roomed at Miss Platt's boardinghouse on the corner of Bull and Congress streets. There actually was such a house. I had no proof that he did stay there, but with the standing of his St. Simons family and under the auspices of his father's factor, Frank Lively (a fictitious name), Miss Platt's seemed the likely spot. If I've done a book since without some help from Lilla Hawes, even in the St. Augustine trilogy, I don't remember it.

From the Brunswick Library, where our close friend Theo Hotch was still director in those days, I was able to find excellent material on old New Orleans for the wayward period in Horace's life before he returned to settle into respectability on St. Simons Island. Librarians (once a somewhat remote breed to me because I've always been a believer in buying my own books) have become indispensable. Our frequent, happy contacts with the state's librarians have been another gift from Georgia. So many books needed for research are not available on the market, I have become a library nut. For instance, Ellen Dodge's death from fever in *The Beloved Invader* would not have been nearly so graphic without the good research of Fraser Ledbetter at St. Simons Library, and that is only an isolated example.

It is true that I do have to master the material, once found, so that I can write freely, with little or no reference to the stacks of copied material and reference books which clutter my office during the writing of one of these novels. But without librarians I couldn't even get started.

Sometime during the writing of Horace's life when he was in his thirties and falling in love with his charming Deborah, Richard Baltzell came down again to sign me to two more nonfiction books for Lippincott—*Learning to Live from the Gospels* and *Learning to Live from the Acts*. Richard came also to work with Joyce on the nearly completed manuscript about Georgia's Martha Berry. No one is more welcome at The Dodge than Richard, but during this visit—to illustrate how involved my own heart becomes with these people about whom I write —Horace Bunch Gould was the man in my life. I was living with Horace day in and day out. One afternoon, with Joyce and Richard hard at work downstairs, I suddenly found need of some information from a tombstone in the cemetery at Christ Church. I left my typewriter and invited them to take a break and go with me. While I hunted for the date I needed from the old Gould plot—in those days a tangle of briars and ivy—Joyce and Richard wandered off to another part of the cemetery. In my search, I came suddenly upon the simple, elegant obelisk which marks the burial place of Horace Bunch Gould—and tears sprang to my eyes! Horace was so young and so alive to me that day in the pages of my manuscript, it seemed impossible that I'd seen that tombstone a hundred times and not felt sorrow before that afternoon. We all laughed at me, but my sorrow was real.

This memoir is dedicated to the Goulds of St. Simons Island—a dedication which of course includes those members of the family who no longer live here. But a mere dedication in no way demonstrates the depth of my gratitude to them all. The Goulds have shown me only graciousness and love and faith, from that first day when Mary Gould Everett opened her arms and her heart to the two Yankees climbing her front steps. There were the hours spent with Berta Gould Taylor and her handsome Captain Doug—who actually remembered Anson Dodge—and the happy, helpful visits of Fé Gould Powell, who gave me so much encouragement as well as understanding of her Aunt Anna; and now that I was working on the second novel, there was the excellent and colorful help from the Gould men: dashing Colonel James; quiet, scholarly, genial Potter; and sensitive, tender Horace Bunch Gould II, who lived in Jacksonville and to whom I was to dedicate *New Moon Rising*. Joyce and I made a memorable journey to Jacksonville one day that year to visit Horace and his Emmy in their home and were not only received royally, but were given, along with Horace's valuable reminiscences, a copy of the only picture extant of the first Horace Bunch Gould, as an old man. It was beautiful.

And there was one more gift. "Now, Genie," Horace said in his musical voice, "there's something else I want you to have—to keep nearby for as long as you're working on this novel. It's my treasure, but I trust you with it totally. It will bring you the success we all wish for you from our hearts." Then he handed me a small box containing an old medal "given for valor in the battles of Atlanta and Savannah to Captain Horace Bunch Gould by the United Daughters of the Confederacy."

I took the treasure and just looked at Horace—just hugged him, unable to say anything. The medal stayed by me until the novel about his grandfather was finished. I returned it with reluctance.

Colonel James Gould's children, Clara Marie Gould and her brother, Jimmy, told me at dinner the other night that, unlike their Uncle Horace, their father and their Uncle Potter, although gallant and courteous on our every meeting, had really not taken me too seriously at first. Neither gentleman had heard my name before our meeting at Berta and Doug's Oatlands Plantation, the first time we had been included in the annual Thanksgiving barbecue out under the Taylors' great oaks. Both were courtly gentlemen, justly proud of their family heritage, educated men of the world. Joyce and I had been thoroughly charmed by both of them, and any doubts about me they may have harbored when we first found St. Simons had evidently vanished by the time I began work on the second novel, which was to be solely about their antecedents. They could not have been more cooperative, more patient with my many questions, more astute with their answers.

I remember well the sunny afternoon when I drove across the marshes and salt creeks to Brunswick to keep an appointment with Mr. Potter Gould at his office in the First National Bank Building. He was a busy CPA, but he gave me all the time I needed and seemed to enjoy himself as much as I did. Potter had not only lent me the Yale yearbook I mentioned earlier; he was going to be my main source, I learned that afternoon, for discovering everything knowable about Rosemount and New St. Clair, the house and plantation owned by his great-grandfather, the original James Gould of Massachusetts.

I had not plotted or even thought much about *Lighthouse*, the third in the planned trilogy, but, painstakingly, Potter drew a clear map showing the lay of the land owned by the Goulds, the land included in both plantations, New St. Clair and Black Banks. He described as best he could—better than anyone else had been able to do—the imagined look of Rosemount, remembered clearly by him in his younger days as it lay in its crumbling tabby ruins, hidden from Frederica Road by dense woods for the hundred years since the Yankees had burned it. I made use of Potter's map in the writing of both *New Moon Rising* and *Lighthouse.*

Gentle, attractive Fé Gould Powell, although a worrywart like her sister Mary, also had an irresistible, childlike gaiety and guilelessness that only made her astute observations more impressive. I shall never forget her concept of her three brothers, Potter, Horace, and James: "Potter is my spiritual brother, Horace is my sweet brother, and James is my cavalier brother." She was right. Potter Gould, always a leader in his church, is a man of deep spiritual sensitivity; Horace is by anyone's standards a thoroughly sweet man; and James? Well, handsome Colonel James has been gone now for three years, but anyone who knew him must think of him as I do, as a man in action—in gallant, suave, premeditated action. He wasted no word and no gesture. All were designed beforehand to impress, to convince, to entertain, at times to shock. At carefully calculated times, of course.

"I've spent hours with Potter and Horace," I said one day when Colonel James's only daughter, Clara Marie, was visiting us, "and they both helped enormously. But my sixth sense tells me that your father can throw an entirely different kind of light on his ancestors. Would he see me?"

"He'd be pleased as anything." She laughed. "In fact, I think he'll be insulted if you don't ask to see him. How about coming to our house for lunch one day next week? Daddy'll take the afternoon off from work to talk to you. There's nothing he likes better, so be prepared."

Colonel James's lovely wife, Clara, had died shortly after we found the Island, and he lived with Clara Marie in the large, comfortable family home in Brunswick, where the Gould Motor Company had thrived for more than fifty years. Jimmy, Colonel James's only son, was running the business by then, though not without the constant counsel and guidance of Daddy.

Dinner, the Colonel's term, was the name for the copious noon meal prepared by the Goulds' longtime cook and family friend, Beatrice, though Clara Marie's invitation had been for "lunch." It was, of course, delicious. Jimmy came too, and the talk was as good as the meal. But each time I attempted to get in one of my many questions, the colonel would quickly change the subject or say plainly, "Now, we save all that for later, young lady."

"Later" came at last. Jimmy returned to work, Clara Marie and Joyce went to another part of the house, and I was escorted by the man himself into his den and seated with more gallantry than I would have dared to write into a nineteenth-century scene.

"There now," he said, "I've seated you with forethought beside *the* famous family heirloom." He gestured toward a handsome, dark wooden chest no thicker than a small trunk and strapped at each corner with beautiful brass ornamental hinges. "That, my dear, is my great-grandfather's writing desk—his travel desk. James Gould, the light-house builder, took that with him on every journey he made! It's rosewood."

As I have said, I hadn't reached the first James Gould in the family history yet; he wouldn't enter my life until the third novel, but a tingle of identification went through me as I examined the magnificent travel desk. Then, once the tingle had passed, I tried to rid myself of the sinking feeling that Colonel James, who had seemed so astute, so "with it," was going to ramble into talk about other members of his family with whom I was not then directly concerned. I was wrong, of course. He simply had to show off that desk—and who could blame him?

But after he'd carefully and mysteriously demonstrated the desk's secret drawer, where James Gould had kept his money when he traveled, he said, "Now—I know this novel is about my grandfather, Horace Bunch. What would the charming lady like to know about that gentleman?"

"Almost anything that comes to your mind." I laughed. "I have a photograph of him as an older man. He did look a lot like Robert E. Lee."

"Yes, so you wrote in *The Beloved Invader*," he said. "Tell me, how did you know about that fact?"

"Before I saw the photo? From the Gould family history which your sister Mary gave me."

"Oh? Well, it's been a long time since I've read it. Fine thing Cousin Agnes Hartridge did for the family, to write all that down as she did."

"Fine thing for me, I know. What stories do you remember hearing about life at Black Banks and New St. Clair? Funny, tragic, superstitious—stories about the servants"—I had learned not to call them slaves—"about your grandparents, especially. Of course, anything about my hero, Horace Bunch."

Colonel James leaned his handsome head back against the chair where he sat, the haughty Gould nose and neat mustache giving him an added air of authority—of being in charge, which indeed he was.

"Well, let me see," he mused. "Ah! I can give you a story that will make your hair curl! One I feel you might get from no other member of the family."

It was my turn to sit up. I flipped open Joyce's notebook as he began a colorful, somewhat gruesome narrative about the murder of a young black girl by a runaway slave from Hampton Plantation at the north end of the Island. The man wove such a spell that I didn't write down a single word. I couldn't. I knew I didn't need to. No one could forget one facet of that story. Colonel James was a master storyteller. That incident, which of course I used—embellished still more from my own imagination—drew more critical acclaim in *New Moon Rising* than any other section of the book.

Perhaps the most interesting part of this entire episode, though, is that Colonel James was dead right when he said no one else was likely to give me the same story. Did it happen? I've asked Potter, Horace Bunch II, Jimmy, Clara Marie, Mary, Dutch, Berta, Berta's daughter, Kitty, Mary's daughter, Mary Jane—anyone and everyone who might have heard a glimmer of such a fascinating event. Not one person had ever heard an inkling! Clara Marie did say that as a boy her father had spent time among the older folk asking questions, and so easily could have heard the tale then, but that's as much of an explanation as I ever got.

Of course, even if Colonel James made it up that day out of whole cloth, I was scott free as a novelist to tell it. There are no rules governing such things. As for my usual insistence upon historical accuracy, didn't I hear it straight from the eloquent lips of a genuine Gould descendant?

From Potter I received the needed facts about the land owned by his family; from Horace, the picture and the medal and the usable tidbit that in the early days the edges of a marsh were called "marsh margins"; from Colonel James, a look at the lighthouse builder's travel desk, a good grisly murder story—true or not—and an unforgettable afternoon with a vanishing breed of Southern gentleman.

After *Invader* came out, letters began coming from other relatives whom I'd neither met nor heard of, and two of these come easily and happily to my mind. Another of Horace Bunch's granddaughters, Mrs. Deborah Diggs, who lives at Patrick Henry Airport in Newport News, Virginia, wrote soon after the publication of *The Beloved Invader.* She and I have continued to exchange letters, and with her daughter, Angela, Mrs. Diggs even stopped for a visit one sunny afternoon while our house was being built. We had to entertain our guests in a half-finished kitchen with no place to sit down and only a subflooring on which to stand, but our time together was of a piece with the Gould tradition of love and charm to which Joyce and I had become accustomed.

Much later—in fact when my valued historian friend Dena Snodgrass and I were en route to Charleston, South Carolina, to begin research for my novel *Maria*—I stopped at Hilton Head to do a speaking date and experienced a typically warmhearted "Gould moment" while I was still standing on the platform. I had spoken on learning to love the South, and of course the Goulds were prominent in all I had to say. I had been asked to conduct a question session at the close of my talk, and about halfway through the session, a refined, pretty lady stood almost shyly and said, "You don't know me, Miss Price, but I'm Horace Bunch Gould's granddaughter Ruby Owens, from Augusta."

The auditorium, filled with five or six hundred people, buzzed with sudden excitement. Dear Ruby Owens was baptized that day into the strange phenomenon of Gould fame through my novels. The Island Goulds and I have many laughs over the fact that my readers look upon the Goulds as near celebrities. "How I would love just to look at a real live Gould," said one of my letters only last week.

Well, a busload of women from New England got to do just that once in the churchyard, at the end of a little tour I'd just given them. Jimmy Gould's beautiful and obliging wife, Mary Frances, had agreed to meet me in the churchyard that day to help out, and unknown to me, she had arranged with Jimmy to leave his office and appear also. Jimmy is unmistakably a Gould—tall, broad-shouldered, handsome, and with a genuine sweetness in his face and manner. The group and I were deep in conversation at the church door when up the old brick walk strode Jimmy. When I announced that a real live Gould was approaching, *oh*'s and *ah*'s circled the churchyard. I lost their attention at once, as half a dozen women hurried down the walk to shake Jimmy's hand and exclaim over him.

The Goulds and I share a similar humor, but no one—not a single Gould and certainly not I—experiences anything but a kind of wonder and a measure of awe that this family which has so enjoyed itself on the once obscure little coastal Island is now known across the world—including wherever my novels have been translated into foreign languages. My English readers are especially loyal. Hodder and Stoughton, my British publisher, brings out beautiful books, and only last week an English lady wrote, "How fitting that dear James Gould, with the book of his story, *Lighthouse*, in my hands, has in a sense returned to England where his family began so long ago."

Horace's granddaughter Mrs. Ruby Owens has come to be very dear to me. In fact, it was through her that one of my cherished prayers was finally answered. Ever since the first days on St. Simons when Ruth Backus let me see a copy of the rare, privately published volume of Ellen Dodge's writings, I had longed for a copy of my own. There were precious few copies in existence, I knew. Actually, I'd seen only one other, during a visit with our neighbors the Harry Parkers. But on that memorable day at Hilton Head, Ruby Owens told me after the meeting that she wanted to send me her copy of Ellen's poems, essays, and stories! When it came after I returned to the Island, I could hardly believe it was mine.

Starting, perhaps, with just the thought of my everlasting gratitude to Ruby, I confess here to having sat for a while—not writing; dreaming, my eyes half seeing the sharp black summer shadows of the tall pine trees across my front lawn. Dreaming? Yes. Because there is a dream quality to every St. Simons contact related to the writing of the three Island novels. The loving acceptance shown me by the entire Gould family is beyond the wildest novelist's dream. To say it is a gamble to undertake even one book based on the antecedents of living people—to attempt to portray their ancestors as they might have been, risking the disapproval and criticism of the living members of that family—is to understate. Truthfully, I've declined to write a dozen or more stories for this very reason. You see, the Goulds have spoiled me. From the first time we walked onto Mary Everett's front porch, we not only were made welcome as Island newcomers, but were literally taken by one member after another into the family circle. I didn't understand it then, nor did Joyce. But we did know it. We still don't understand it, but a happy Gould reunion dinner party just the other night proved beyond the shadow of any doubt that even after I had published two novels laid elsewhere—even after the passing of the years and of almost all the early Goulds who welcomed us—the bond is still authentic. Perhaps stronger than ever from the years of being neighbors, Islanders together, and from the shared grief at the loss of the older members of "our family."

Without realizing it, I'm sure, the Goulds have made me a more trustworthy person. How? By trusting me. At dinner the other night, we laughed a lot, remembering how, once the novels were published, we all got confused trying to figure out (especially with the older Goulds dying one after another) what was actually true—what had really happened and what had "happened" in my writer's imagination and found its way into the books.

Joyce told one of her favorite stories at dinner that night about Watson Glissom, the sexton at the churchyard, who relished the pastime of putting tourists on. Needing a villain or two in *Invader*, I fictionalized (from some fact) the P. D. Bass couple—strange provincial folk who caused Anson and then Anna a lot of "needed" trouble. Needed in that I, as the author, needed some trouble or conflict; no minister ever had a church filled only with saints, I knew, and so the Basses came into being. Then, as *Invader* began to be widely read and folk began to come into the churchyard hunting the graves of my characters, Mr. Glissom's fun began.

"He knew, of course," Joyce said, "that Genie had fictionized the Basses, but when an unsuspecting tourist inquired after the location of the Bass tombstones, Watson cocked his head, rubbed his calloused old hands, and said, "Well, now, of course it's hard to know about these old-timey graveyards. Stones get moved and all. But it seems to me like this very morning when I was cuttin' brush over there—way over there by that back fence—I seen a Bass grave.' "

He would then—naturally—stand chuckling after the unwary tourists, books in hand, as they plodded away "over there by that back fence" in vain. (Watson Glissom has gone to Baptist heaven now, so any information you might be given at Christ Church these days will be factual, though perhaps not nearly as colorful as before he went away.)

And speaking of confusing what really happened with what I made up, I still remember how Mary Gould Everett, one day after publication of *The Beloved Invader,* told me quite seriously that she was sure she could point out the exact live-oak tree which Anson Dodge had hugged on his first trip up Frederica Road. Actually, Anson's hugging the tree had been merely wish fulfillment for me—it was what I had so much wanted to do on my own first trip up Frederica Road, then so picturesque. I don't know whether I ever did set dear Mary right on the tree hugging—it wouldn't have mattered to Mary. Enough that my Island books expressed Island truth.

———•———

Although I was able to research portions of *New Moon Rising* in the more orthodox ways—from the archives at Yale University, from books and old published letters from Confederate soldiers who had fought with Horace in the battles of Atlanta and Savannah—I went on depending upon my living friends for more than they realized. When the time came for material I needed on the Kings of Retreat Plantation, Dutch Everett introduced me on his front porch one day to the best possible source—his nephew, Mr. Richard Everett, of the Cloister Hotel on Sea Island, an area historian of note. In fact, Richard Everett had inherited the cloak of his mentor, Margaret Davis Cate, who for years had lectured to Cloister guests on coastal history. At her death Richard continued the erudite lectures, and so, although Dutch only meant me to meet a relative of whom he was proud, in reality he introduced me indirectly to the Kings.

No one had done more research on the family and descendants of the famous Thomas Butler King of Retreat than Richard Everett. Fortunately, by the time I met him I had practically memorized Burnette Vanstory's *Georgia's Land of the Golden Isles.* The book was a lifesaver; it had me ready for an interview with a historian who, I gathered from that first meeting on the Everetts' front porch, would not be inclined to brook stupid questions or bother to answer them. I must have asked the right ones, for Richard visited our house the next Sunday—and often thereafter. His charming wife, Liesle, was abroad at the time of his first visit, which Joyce and I remember with great pleasure. Richard was vastly informative about the King family, and ultimately there was much good laughter all around.

The time came when I felt comfortable enough with him to ask bluntly, "Now, don't feel any obligation to answer this, but Joyce and I want very much to know *why,* in all her fabulous material about other Island families, Mrs. Cate saw fit to give such short shrift to the Goulds. Their two plantations combined made them among the largest landholders. The family is still prominent by name in our community today. Do you know why she practically ignored the Goulds?"

Richard Everett gave me one of his highly probing, almost patronizing looks, then glanced out the windows toward the big marsh. "Yes. Yes, Eugenia, I do know why. There were perhaps two reasons. One, Mrs. Cate and Colonel James Gould never, but *never* hit it off. They liked each other, but they were always at loggerheads. Temperaments, I would think. However, the second reason is, I'm certain, more germane. You see, Mrs. Cate was active in the United Daughters of the Confederacy and had direct access to military records of all Georgians." He took a beat. "She knew for a fact that *no Gould ever served the Confederacy!*"

Joyce and I exchanged looks. We both liked Richard Everett so much and respected his reverence for the Island historian who had coached him since his youth from her vast store of knowledge—and yet, we *were* the Gould Girls. *We* knew better. Just a room away from where we sat that afternoon—in its tiny box in a drawer—lay the proof that Captain Horace Bunch Gould had indeed served the Confederacy with "valor in the battles of Atlanta and Savannah."

Neither of us said a word. I simply got up, walked through the kitchen and into the dining room, opened the drawer, took out the medal my dear Horace Gould II had let me have for inspiration as I wrote, brought it back, and handed it silently to Richard. He opened the box and read the inscription. He frowned, his quick mind taking in the unlikely truth—Mrs. Cate had made an error which had held all those years!

"Well," he said. "Well!"

And then the three of us had another of our many laughs together. Richard is gone too, now—gone too young, far too young. We still miss him. I miss him always at the end of a novel. His detailed criticisms of each one gave me a comfortable, safe feeling that I'd at least made no unconscious errors in the history.

In the year 1968 the death of someone else who was "too young" affected us both deeply because it shattered the life of our friend and helper, John Golden, who had not only laid out and supervised the filling of our acres, but had cared for them on a regular basis since the day we moved to The Dodge. For weeks, we had been praying for John's beautiful, critically ill wife, Lucille. We had visited her often in the Brunswick Hospital. One day on our way home from the village, we stopped outside John's home in Harrington to inquire after her.

John saw us from the window of his house, and the minute the screen door opened, so slowly, and he started toward our car, I knew Lucille was gone.

"She just left me," he said simply. "I don't know what to do."

All his adult life, Lucille had been his rock. During the desolate weeks following her death, we watched John begin to suffer physically as well as emotionally from the weight of his loneliness. I talked to him hour after hour, but the once energetic, ambitious man seemed unable to shake his cloud of grief. From my office window, I could see him laboring to move his big power mower across the wide expanse of our front yard. His steps dragged, and twice I ran down to comfort him when I saw him stop walking behind the mower and crumple above it, his thin shoulders wracked with sobs. The least exertion tired him. He owned a good truck, a tractor—all implements needed for his work— and we could tell that even the upkeep of those prized possessions was becoming too much. He needed relief desperately.

Then one morning, as he and I stood out in the middle of the front yard, he said, "I don't think I can go on with all this hard work. I . . . just feel like I can't haul another load of fill dirt or fire up that tractor one more time. Even startin' the lawn mower's too hard. What would you say if I sold all my equipment—and much as I like you ladies and have liked working here—get me just a plain job where I didn't have any overhead and not so much responsibility? I won't ever get used to that empty bed, but . . . maybe if I didn't have anything much to worry me when I get home at night, I'd do better."

In a special way, John Golden would always be our friend. He had been with us from the beginning—from that first load of live oak and fat pine dumped at the back door of Go Native. His ingenuity and responsibility had made possible the landscaping of our home. Still, I knew we were losing him, and his nerves wouldn't stand a long delay —in fact, it seemed to me he wanted me to free him that very day. So—we shook hands, I gave him the most generous bonus I could afford (nothing would ever show our appreciation), and we said good-bye.

Even as I had asked myself, during those days of sensing John Golden's impending departure, what we would do without him, I had thought longingly of another John we knew—Mr. John Wilson, a broad-shouldered, handsome man in his middle sixties (who looked forty!) who had already worked for us on occasion, making our many-paned windows shine and doing a far better job of cleaning the house in a few hours than Joyce and I had managed by giving our entire Saturdays to the job. Holland Sheppard, bless her, had sent him, knowing well our needs from her own association with us. Whenever he'd worked for us, Joyce and I—who usually dreaded the confusion of someone cleaning while we wrote—had begun to look forward to the days when John Wilson came.

And not only for his work; the times we had talked with Johnnie —as we were eventually persuaded to call him—we had warmed to his quiet, easy manner—spiced here and there with unexpected and delectable humor.

Now—if he could only give us more time! For years, he and his intelligent, rich-voiced wife, Ruby, had lived in New York, where he had been a butler and then supervisor of a section of a large plant. As far as I knew, he had no tractor and only a small pickup truck, but John

Golden had done all the heaviest yard work at The Dodge. Thank heaven, we needed no more dirt hauled.

When John Golden had gone, I ran into the house to call Johnnie Wilson.

"Good morning!" Ruby Wilson's vibrant voice greeted me. (I have since come to depend on that elevating "Good morning!")

I'm sure I sounded excited. After all, if there was any chance that Johnnie could come to us on a regular basis, I'd get out of all that Saturday cleaning—and I already envisioned him as being in full charge of both the house and the big yard.

"Well, I'll just have to have him call you when he comes in," Ruby said, and then came her low, throaty laugh. "I never make a commitment for that man, you know."

I tried to concentrate on my work. But every time the telephone rang all day, I grabbed it, hoping. About four in the afternoon, the ring was finally Mr. John Wilson, sounding—not quite but almost—as interested as I know I sounded. Yes, he was looking for a place, a place he could "operate." On Social Security, he couldn't work more than three days a week, and that, for us, would be perfect.

"I do want to work for just one family," he said. "I don't want to keep spreadin' myself around like I been doin'."

The next morning he came rolling up the lane in his pale-blue truck, and after that day and for as long as he lived on this earth—until late 1976—John Wilson was our man, our protector, our sensitive, understanding friend. He was in all ways a high-caliber gentleman (he had, in fact, to put considerable pressure on me before I could bring myself to call him Johnnie instead of Mr. Wilson); and still, with all his innate dignity, there was a sweetness about him, a near guilelessness toward us, which made me think of my own father. His views on politics, on black militancy, on almost any issue were so sane and balanced that he often kept me in check when I was stirred up.

He was never simply an employee, and there is no use pretending that we've learned how to live without him even now; we haven't. But when the missing grows too sharp—and it does at times—we give thanks for the years in which we had him and for the years in which he had us. Our regard was mutual; he loved us as deeply as we loved him. Now and every day since Johnnie went away, Ruby and I talk each morning before I begin work. It helps us both. She came to dinner when Joyce's mother was here a few days ago and will come again soon.

She and Joyce and I have two common bonds, strong, unbreakable bonds. One is the missing, the daily—sometimes hourly—missing. The other, a sure faith that we will all be with Johnnie again one day. That doesn't help Joyce and me to remember when to send the laundry or pick up the cleaning or buy more birdseed, but it sustains us.

As I did with Tay's death, I have written first of Johnnie's so that now I can go on writing more freely about the unforgettable days when he was still here. Again I wanted the task behind me.

The winter weeks of 1968 moved busily for us through bright sunny days and heavy-skied rainy ones—both of us working, working. And *no* speaking engagements. Exactly the kind of winter I love. I would have to think a long time to find a day more to my liking than one reasonably uninterrupted, with a coastal rain falling outside, a ream of yellow paper beside me, and a book to write. That is my idea of heaven on earth, and there were many of those days that winter. As usual, we read aloud at night some of what we'd both written that day. I know of no better way to find out if a manuscript is readable than to hear it read aloud. Joyce was working on two books at once, fining down the third in her popular Suki series—*Suki and the Magic Sand Dollar*, the only one laid on St. Simons Island, and the rough draft of a juvenile biography of John Adams. I was nearing the end of the rough draft of *New Moon Rising* and feeling some pressure, since I'd promised the finished manuscript to Tay in the early fall.

My usual way with a novel is to write it all out—just get it down in a rough draft. Most often, these drafts will run from a hundred to three hundred pages too long. But I dare not stop the writing to cut and polish. Some authors do. With me, polishing breaks some mysterious flow that I cannot explain. Joyce tends far more toward careful writing on the first draft. But I'm in high gear most of the time and can't wait to put the story down. Tay said often that she felt this method accounted, at least in part, for the fact that my novels keep a reader reading. Maybe. True or not, it is the way I work best. I like the enormous feeling of freedom when that rough draft is finished—having the agony of putting it all together over with. (Rewrites are another kind of challenge.) At the end of the Rough, the main portion of the research is done, and most of the details concerning dates and places are straight. I can sit and pat that huge, fat stack of yellow pages and know that my story is there—however uneven. Pages and pages of the Rough are marked with large "Ick"s in the margin, meaning "terrible." And there are many, many "Fix"es scrawled here and there. At every chapter opening, I depend upon Joyce's notes to me at the top of the page. Faithfully, she reads my rough drafts, marks corrections, suggests better words, improves awkward phrases. I try to do the same for her. (Every writer needs a loving but objective critic in the family!)

In February, Joyce's mother called to say her father would have surgery, but he was in good health then and neither parent felt that she should leave her heavy writing schedule to come home. He did well. (The Reverend Leroy Blackburn was the kind of man who loved living on this earth as much as I'm sure he's loving life where he is now, right in the Presence of the Lord he followed.)

On February 18, Joyce finished the final draft of *Sand Dollar* and I was rolling along so well on *New Moon* that a feeling of celebration took us over, so that we were ready for a party when March 16 came —the first anniversary of our move into The Dodge. And although we planned nothing, it worked out to perfection. Lamar Webb and some of his associates from the office came, loaded with jonquils.

They seemed as gratified by the success of the house they'd helped to create as we were. It looked old already! We told them about a young fan of Joyce's who, with her mother, had asked directions to our place. When a neighbor said we lived at the end of the road, the mother said, "Oh, we've been down there. Miss Blackburn lives in a new place. There's nothing out that way but an old restored plantation house!"

That was one of our two favorite compliments. The other happened even earlier, before we moved in. One evening after a hard day's work at White Cap, during one of Joyce's visits to her parents, I had driven up to the nearly finished Frederica house alone. I was sitting on the front steps, just watching the sun go down, when I saw Burney Vanstory walking slowly toward me up my lane with her beautiful cat, Sandy, in her arms. At that time, the workmen still had a locked chain stretched across the road a little way from the house site, so Burney had parked her car and walked in. We waved, and then she called in her lilting drawl, so soft and Southern, "Genie, it loo-oks like it grew from a seed!"

Judging from my date book, we evidently celebrated The Dodge's first birthday and the finish of my Rough several times. With Lamar and the fellows from his office, with the Youngs for vegetable soup, and with Lorah Plemmons for chicken and dumplings. I remember the two or three days off from both work and diet with only happiness. My favorite time in the entire process of doing a big novel had come—the final rewrite. Rewriting means long, backbreaking hours at the typewriter, but the book is there. I can watch the thick stack of Rough diminish and the thin sheaf of Smooth begin to grow. Long evening readings begin, and within a week or so I can start to feed it to Elsie Goodwillie for the final typescript. Of course, even the Smooth is covered with my chicken-scratching and Joyce's more legible notes, but not only is Elsie a superb manuscript typist, she edits me, watches my spelling, *and* can read my scribbles.

I remember working almost night and day during the month of March and the beginning of April. When we learned that our super friend and one of our favorite writers, Eileen Guder, could spend a week with us, we were lyrical. I would work only part of each day while she was here, and then, for the first time in the years of our friendship, Joyce and Eileen and I could talk—and talk and talk—with no holds barred. We did.

By the end of May the completed manuscript—completed, that is, until Tay discovered the rough places—went off to New York. I'm sure I just answered long overdue letters for the few days Tay required to read it and report to me. Bless her, she never kept me waiting beyond endurance. She would never bother to say that she was going to try to read it as fast as possible to protect my nervous system. She didn't have to bother to say it. She did it. On June 10, the date book tells us, she called, and was—for Tay—most enthusiastic. "A far better book than *Invader*."

That's all I needed to know. If I can improve any novel even slightly over the last one, I am content to keep on trying. Tay's editing came back promptly, and I made the changes she wanted—she was right on all counts. By June 20 Elsie was cleaning up the pages I'd redone, and the whole manuscript went off to Philadelphia for copy editing.

I must say here that, with *New Moon Rising*, there began a rare new relationship with a superb copy editor at Lippincott, Peggy Cronlund, who has been with me ever since. And who grows more essential with the preparation of each manuscript for publication, especially now that Tay is gone.

Joyce brought her parents to the Island for a week's visit while I spent my usual June time with Mother. My birthday, Mother's wedding anniversary, and my father's birthday all fall in June, and when at all possible, I am there with her for those dates. I was back on the Island for the Fourth of July, and since I had two other books coming out that year, *Just As I Am* and *Learning to Live from the Gospels*, plans began to form for a tour that fall.

And then as I walked one morning—July 15 to be exact—across my office toward my desk to begin work for the day, the telephone rang. It was a friend of the Blackburn family to tell Joyce that her much-loved father had had a severe stroke. Joyce caught the first plane out and was away for something over a month, but Leroy improved and went home from the hospital, able both to walk and to talk again, and so improved that Joyce could meet me in St. Louis for another convening of the Christian Booksellers Association in August. Joyce's beautiful biography of Martha Berry was out, and she was being acclaimed not only by reviewers, but as a guest of honor at Berry College for Mountain Day.

Her description of the unique Berry College campus had made me eager to go there with her sometime to see for myself, and that wish was soon granted. In late November, we were due at Rich's for autographing parties for both *Martha Berry* and my two new 1968 titles. By then, we had already met and come to love dearly a select group (select for more reasons than their expertise!) of Atlanta and north Georgia librarians, and so when Faith Brunson asked us to appear with Celestine Sibley, Wylly Folk St. John, and other prominent Georgia authors at a special "do" for the librarians at Rich's during a Georgia Library Association meeting there, we were delighted. Librarians Sarah Hightower, Grace Hightower, Virginia McJenkins, Sarah Jones, and their inimitable friend, Annie Taylor, were all on hand, bless them, their praise unbounded and their purses open to buy every new title we produced. Their appearance at our Rich's parties has since become a tradition. Joyce and I both did a lot of radio and TV in Atlanta, and when it was all over, she drove me north and west through the magnificent Appalachian foothills to Berry College.

It was Thanksgiving vacation, and although I wanted some day to meet her new friends at Berry who had been so helpful with the research for her book on the school's founder, I confess to being glad to see the highly scenic campus for the first time almost deserted, with little moving except the gold and red leaves on the myriad trees, which, following Martha Berry's dream, have been left standing.

Joyce drove me first along the roads crisscrossing the 33,000 acres of beauty and showed me the flourishing prize cattle farm, the two old campuses, the older school at Possum Trot, and Martha Berry's home, Oak Hill. Then, as though she had saved the best till last, we parked the car and walked under some bright yellow bowers toward Martha's grave on a slope beside the chapel, which was reconstructed exactly after the chapel where George Washington worshiped at Alexandria. In all that time we had seen perhaps half a dozen persons walking along the roads or across the silent campus—silent except for birdsong. We stood under the golden trees, beside the burial place of the woman Joyce had written about, saying nothing for a long, long time. A breeze sent a yellow leaf fluttering down to land softly on Martha's stone, and then, as though celestially programmed, there came from the open chapel windows the strains of Bach's Toccata in F, clear, pure, exhilarating, each honed phrase gliding down the sunlit slope to bless us.

We looked at each other and smiled. Not until we had returned much later to our car and had driven all the way back to the road that would take us south toward the Island did we speak.

We stopped in Milledgeville for Thanksgiving dinner at the Holiday Inn, one of our favorite spots in those days, and it tasted so good, and we were so happy, we simply stopped and had an identical dinner in Brunswick that night before we crossed the salt creeks and marshes to our home in the woods.

Mother came again for Christmas, and this was the most memorable time yet because she brought her young neighbor, Nancy Goshorn. No one could have fitted more aptly into our traditional Island Christmas at the Plemmonses'. I had liked Nancy so much from our first meeting—as had Joyce—but this Christmas stands out, at least to me, as the time when she became truly the sister I never had.

Early in the new year of 1969—the year of *New Moon Rising*—on January 13, Joyce and I lost our first beloved Island friend. Captain

Nix Young got up as usual that morning to prepare breakfast for himself and "his lady." He was quiet for such a long time that Edith went to look for him. She found him lifeless in his chair—unable to respond to her for the first time in all the years of their married life. We buried him in the churchyard, and back at the familiar house afterward, Edith sat in her chair as regal and composed as Captain Nix would have expected his lady to be.

We visited Edith often. The big empty chair where Nix always sat hurt our hearts, but the courage of this woman, well into her eighties, was still giving us courage long after she flew away on the Delta Bluebird—looking like a brave queen in an all-green outfit and her usual large hat. A sizable coterie of Island friends, Joyce and I among them, waved her off at the airport for her daughter Lucy's home in Sparks, Nevada. We didn't see Edith again, but her letters continued to come, her still keen mind moving ahead of her pen, until she joined Nix in the fall of 1972.

Then on March 1 dear Berta Taylor, who had suffered incapacitating strokes, took her place in Gould Row along the back fence in the churchyard. She did live long enough to receive an award from the vestry of Christ Church for her years as treasurer and for her dedication to the work of the Altar Guild. The day we buried Berta, the small church was filled with her friends as Dr. Junius Martin read the ancient, beauty-filled Episcopal service for the dead. Everyone in the church had loved and respected this woman, for many reasons. I shall never forget how weary and how beautiful her daughter, Kitty, looked that day—among her family but looking almost as though she were alone. In one very real way she was; it had been Kitty who had given herself for years to the minute-by-minute care of her mother. And now Berta lay under the simple purple-velvet pall with its white cross, used at Christ Church only for longtime communicants—old Islanders. A special honor.

And by then Berta's sister Mary Everett was no longer herself; she was ill for many weeks at the Brunswick Nursing Home. Faithful Dutch drove daily to spend hours beside her bed. Joyce and I went as often as we could, and each time we left with torn hearts. She always seemed to know us—at least, she clung to our hands and tried to smile. So far as I know, no one told her that Berta had gone to heaven first.

Another blow fell in April, the month before I was to leave on what would end up being the longest, most exhausting promotion tour of my entire life. On April 14, Joyce had painful surgery, and for ten days I spent my waking hours beside her at the Brunswick Hospital. Severe complications kept her there a week longer than we'd hoped, and after some rough oral surgery of my own, I pushed myself to shopping and packing for the long tour. We were both elated that *New Moon* was about to be published. My best sale to date of paperback rights had already been made with Bantam, the very house I wanted. Advance orders were excellent, especially in California and the Midwest, my old haunts.

Then another Island friend, Rabbi Greenwald, died. We both faltered a little—but only a little. I had too much up ahead, and I was too concerned about leaving Joyce so soon after surgery, to give myself much attention. If anyone could manage, she could, and anyway, the tour was set. I had no choice. Authors get hit with the same emergencies any mortal does, but the day is long past when an author merely writes a book and lets the publisher sell it. The author too must hit the road. I am always ambivalent about my tours. This one was not only set, but the schedule had been made by two persons, one on the West Coast and one in New York, who apparently—by some oversight, I suppose—had not consulted each other. Even a glance at it exhausted me before the packing was finished!

As usual, Snoopy, our mockingbird, knew all about everything going on with us. At breakfast one morning when I was about to falter again, he started to sing so courageously that I began to believe I'd probably make it after all. Anyway, the first days of the planned tour were exactly to my liking. That would help. I was to leave the Island on May 14 for New York, where I'd spend three or four days with Tay and Arthur in their apartment on 34th Street. Tay would give a party in my honor, and about that I was lyrical. There would be luncheon dates and visits to the New York editorial offices and long, constructive, stimulating talks with Tay about writing in general—about my hopes for my own books—about our tastes in music and reading, and best of all, about our next novel, *Lighthouse*. I left with a reasonably happy heart—and the best haircut my friend Dot Madden had ever given me.

The first copy off the press of *New Moon Rising* had reached me just before I took the plane to New York, and I gave it to Tay, signed with my love and more appreciation than I could put into a few words inscribed on a flyleaf. *New Moon* was a beautiful piece of publishing. As with all my titles, Don Bender, the talented art director in the

Philadelphia office who is responsible for Lippincott's generally superior jackets, had done his magic again on *New Moon*. I loved the binding, the feel of the paper, the type, and—as always when I open any new book—the singular smell of printer's ink. On *New Moon*, I even liked the jacket copy!

I had one more nonfiction book to do for Lippincott before I could begin *Lighthouse*, but not a long one, and Tay would edit that one too. Only the endless, tightly packed tour stood between me and the stimulus of tackling more work with Tay, and about that I felt a real sense of urgency. Her eyes were failing rapidly, and even though she had seen me through two novels, I still quaked at the thought of trying one without her.

From New York I flew to Los Angeles, where our dear Eileen Guder met me. My spirits lifted during the few days spent with her in her hillside home in Hollywood. The same things interest us both; we're nonstop when it comes to exchanging ideas, to laughing, to seeing things the same—to being totally ourselves together. I'm still grateful when I think of the rest I found with her before the horrific tour began.

As for the tour, I have no intention of belaboring the awful details. The good part was that two of the most cherished relationships I've known in the publishing world happened—spontaneously and joyfully —in the midst of the endless miles of driving California freeways from one speaking date to another autographing party to another TV interview to still another meeting with the press. The two dear ones responsible for the tour *and* for my ever making it in one piece (even if they had inadvertently scheduled me half to death) were my West Coast Lippincott sales representative, Ken Lockaby, and Lippincott's publicity director, Alice Allen. Alice and I each had a birthday en route, and neither of us, I know, will ever forget Ken's party for us—our own private dining room and two waiters, the room festooned with Ken's handiwork (paper streamers and balloons), and beautiful gifts for us both. I hope Ken remains my West Coast rep forever, but I wish he were nearer Georgia. I miss him. And although Alice is now Alice Donald and in her own business, we also remain close.

Over Memorial Day, I had a semi-rest stop in Denver at the elegant Brown Palace Hotel, where the special experience of enjoying six or seven hours of book talk with one of America's foremost bookmen, Stanton Peckham, lessened much of my tiredness. Alice had set it up for Stan to come to my suite for dinner at eight. At eleven o'clock we still hadn't stopped talking long enough to study the room-service menu. We did finally eat about midnight, but our talk was so stimulating that the maid, who came every night at eleven to turn down my bed, automatically turned one down for Stan that night, too. This has come to be one of his—and my—favorite stories.

I worked my way across the country, a new sales representative meeting me in each city, and finally, on June 7, for just two days, I was back on St. Simons for a unique and meaningful autographing party at Left Bank Gallery. Mildred and Bob Wilcox had done the most effective thing anyone could have done for my exhausted spirits—they had engaged my beloved Georgia Sea Island Singers to renew me all afternoon. From the start of my deep friendship with Mable Hillery, she and her fellow members of the famed Georgia Sea Island Singers have been a fascination to both Joyce and me. That day Bessie Jones, Emma Ramsey, John and Peter Davis, Henry Morrison, and Mable sang me right into a burst of energy which kept me on my feet for the remainder of the tour.

Island residents don't appreciate what we had in that group. Joyce and I once saw them—our beautiful black friends from St. Simons— fill every seat in the Ayrie Crown Theater in Chicago on a night when the Beatles were doing their thing right down the street! On the Island, though, where they were all best known as servants, I fear they were not revered as we revered them for keeping alive the primitive beauty of the old coastal songs.

The first long segment of the tour had been arranged around an early publication date for the West Coast. Actual national pub date, at Rich's as always, was June 9, on what would have been my father's seventy-seventh birthday. Again, Faith Brunson and her people at Rich's did a superb job. I signed books until my hand ached—one of the most pleasant experiences I ever had. And a very good thing, too, since for most of the tour Joyce and my attorneys had been handling a peculiar IRS examination for me. I still don't understand much of what all the fuss was about, but if you are ever examined by the boys at IRS, it's a lovely idea to be away. Lovely and nerve-racking! Long before the lengthiest segment of the tour was half ended,

I had lost count of how many times I'd spoken—with variations, depending on my audience—on my subject: "My Two Conversions." One to Jesus Christ and the other to the American South on St. Simons Island. Of course, Mary Gould Everett figured prominently in every talk I made from the West Coast to the East. About ten minutes before I left my hotel room in some city on the last leg of the tour, my telephone rang. It was Joyce. Our beloved Mary was dead.

That afternoon as I spoke, there were tears in my eyes and in the eyes of my listeners as I told them about Mary.

———————

I honestly don't remember now where in Texas the last stop was, but I could have stayed over and had a good night's sleep before flying back to Atlanta, where I would catch the Bluebird home at last. "No," I said to Alice Allen long distance. "Get me back to Georgia! Even if it means losing a little more sleep. At least, get me across the Georgia border!"

About ten at night on July 3 I got as far as Atlanta. I showered and tumbled gratefully into bed at the Marriott. I didn't drift—I dove into sleep. My last conscious thought was, Tomorrow, two more hours in one more airplane and—home.

No.

At midnight, the fire bell clanged, and I spent the night with other tenants in my section of the hotel standing around in our nightclothes in the parking lot. At 6 A.M. we were told that it would now be safe to return to our rooms. I returned, ordered breakfast, and took a cab to the airport just in time to see the dear Island Bluebird taxi in at my gate.

I hardly remember, but Joyce tells me that I sat on the back porch for days and stared into space. No one meant that tour to be so brutally packed—it was not all that long—and certainly no one meant for me to have almost no rest time. It was one of those things that ballooned out of all proportion (like the national debt) and left me a zombie.

I mean never to do another one like that although, now that the years have brought them into focus, I treasure the memory of every stop. Especially the one where the people wept with me because Mary Gould Everett was gone.

The happy, busy, exhausting, fruitful year of 1969 had included for Joyce and me another tragedy—in one sense a distant one; and yet, not. Ralph McGill, publisher of the *Atlanta Constitution*, died. In Joyce's date book she wrote, "Ralph McGill is gone. We are bereft and poor."

McGill's original mind and compassionate, discerning heart had captured us way back in the very first days on St. Simons Island, when reading his column became a ritual. We had, of course, heard of Ralph McGill, but Yankeelike, I at least had not connected a man of his caliber with Atlanta, Georgia. We spent more than one evening before our fire that winter of 1969, talking of Ralph McGill as though we'd lost a dear friend. We had. I hope he knows now that he, along with Jack Spalding, Eugene Patterson, Celestine Sibley, and Harold Martin, played a part in moving us inexorably toward life in the South. The new South which we could *feel* emerging.

As the year 1969 closed, I thought a lot about McGill, Spalding, Patterson, Sibley, Martin—and that great lady, the late Lillian Smith. Consciences of the South. Consciences of humankind, really. When Jack Spalding wrote a favorable, penetrating review of *New Moon Rising*, I felt a kind of elation and humility that exceeded anything else that had come to me from all the work I'd done. His review made me feel that I was at last a part of this Southland which I had so unexpectedly come to love—and that it was now a part of me.

PART SIX

Lighthouse

CHRISTMAS 1969 was as merry and carefree as all Christmases ought to be. Mother and Nancy flew down again—a few days early so as to have some time with Joyce before she left for Indiana. Of course, we spent the Holy Day with our beloved Plemmonses, and at home I regaled Mother and Nancy with my own excitement at having met historian Walter C. Hartridge of Savannah at a meeting of the Coastal Georgia Historical Society, at the Cloister.

We spent our evenings in my living room, lighted only by the fire and the tiny white bulbs on the huge Christmas tree that stood proudly in the big bay, and I can still see Mother's smile, as always so responsive to my enthusiasm, as I launched into my report.

"This year," I began, "as program chairman for the Society, I'd called Mr. Hartridge to ask him to speak to us in November. He's so prominent and so much in demand, I wasn't very hopeful. He surprised me then by sounding eager to come, and the man's been surprising me ever since!" I laughed. "Honestly, he's unlike anyone I've ever met. He *lives* history. And the best thing of all for me is that he's not only done a lot of research on James Gould's wife's family, the Harrises of Savannah, he paid me all kinds of compliments on what I'm trying to do with coastal history in my novels. I never thought he would actually *dig* what I'm doing—he's such a scholar, I half expected him to be disdainful of mere historical novels. He isn't a bit disdainful! He's excited—and he *wants* to help me. Won't take a research fee of any kind, either. Just shook his head and told me not to mention it again."

Joyce and I were to visit him and his attractive wife in February, and of course I promised to keep Mother and Nancy posted on all developments.

I drove my dear guests to their plane in Jacksonville on December 29, and with Joyce home again early in January, I went back to work on *Learning to Live from the Acts,* a manuscript which I felt correctly would almost write itself. Few readers seem to have found this book —at least in comparison with my others—but finishing *Acts* started me out in high gear on the first year of a new decade, 1970. Two highlights of January were, first, the uniquely beautiful and sensitive adaptation of *New Moon Rising* that was performed by talented monologuist Marion Conner of Jacksonville; and second, my discovery and engrossed reading (the first of many) of John Steinbeck's *Journal of a Novel.* Both stimulated me to get going on my own third work of fiction.

My date book normally contains only cursory notes to remind me of speaking engagements, unanswered letters, bills to pay, calls to make, tax materials to hunt out and sort for my accountant, and scribbled notations concerning my daily progress on whatever manuscript I happen to be writing. But life seemed so good to me after the move to The Dodge, I find that I began to make personal notes as well. Jottings about particularly happy events, such as having Johnnie and Ruby visit us on a Sunday afternoon. One note—a small paean of praise—asks, "How could life be better than it is right now?"

With Johnnie to look after us, with our families well, with good work to do, and with a mockingbird who entertained us no end, it seemed that there could be no way to improve on anything.

Then a frightening problem arose. For some time we had both been involved in a community attempt to try to save our Island and its surrounding marshland from the industrial developers' bulldozers. Few seemed to know or to care that the marshes, far from being worthless stretches of tall spartina grass, were rich in food value—not there to be filled and developed. Discounting their beauty, they were veritable factories manufacturing a huge energy and food supply for our valuable marine life. We hadn't known this at first, either, but we learned. Our efforts to date had involved the struggle for some kind of protection from individual developers, some of whom had filled sections of marsh in the darkness of night—knowing that once that fill dirt was in, they would not be forced to remove it.

Suddenly Joyce learned that there was a far worse danger from a huge conglomerate, already purchasing marshland around Savannah. Armed with maps of our marshes of Glynn, they were planning to move in to strip-mine the marshes for phosphate! Joyce Blackburn has told the entire story of our battle to save the marshes in her excellent book *The Earth Is the Lord's.?* Nothing short of such a crisis could have slowed me at my desk, but this did. Joyce had worked in various ways already, but late in January I jumped into the fray too. Reid Harris, then our state representative, and his wife, Doris, were working night and day to get Reid's Wetlands Protection Act through the Assembly in Atlanta. The Harrises asked our help.

I had no business taking the time from my current manuscript or the ongoing research on *Lighthouse,* but I couldn't help myself. I agreed to go twice to Atlanta to speak first to the Assembly and then to a senate committee on behalf of *the people*—the people, in this case, who loved the Golden Isles of Georgia. On one return trip, via the Bluebird, I well recall that as I stood in line at the airport with some of the local businessmen who were fighting this legislation—all of whom knew me—I was given a unanimous cold shoulder. If you read Joyce's book, you will learn that ultimately the marshes were saved and our sense of place more valued than ever. I quieted my writer's conscience on one of my trips to Atlanta by doing some valuable research in the mornings at our magnificent Georgia Archives, which were within walking distance of the Capitol Building, where I was to speak in the afternoon.

In the Archives, Pat Bryant and Marion Hemperley were more than cooperative. In fact, working back from a fragment of information I had in the Gould family history, we reached the conclusion—a most important one for me then—that James Gould's Florida timberland must have been located at a place then called King's Ferry, now Mills Ferry. This doesn't appear to be earthshaking, but for me it was. The living Goulds and evidently Agnes Hartridge, who had written the family history, knew little about the East Florida period in James Gould's life. Only that he had been there. On the way back that night in the little airplane, I decided that, unless my instincts were wrong, Walter Hartridge, with his enormous knowledge of the East Florida period, could help me find a way in which James Gould might have come upon that tract of land as a young man. Walter had already sent me a rare copy of his early book *The Letters of Don Juan McQueen to His Family.* I would study it again before Joyce and I left for Savannah to visit the Hartridges, and surely the puzzle could be solved.

I had everything to do yet on the Massachusetts period in James

Gould's early life, but I had learned by then not to panic. To take one day at a time and one research problem at a time.

As I said, we did win eventually in our battle to save the marshes from desecration, but for a while I had trouble concentrating at all on the novel. Local opposition to our efforts to pass the Wetlands Protection Act mounted, and Joyce and I spent almost two weeks collecting signatures on a petition, writing letters, sending wires, and making local and long-distance calls.

My *Acts* manuscript was back from New York, corrected, and on its way north again within a week, and I dove into correspondence in behalf of James Gould—letters containing further questions to archivists at Bangor, Maine (Massachusetts in James's day), to the Georgia Archives, and to Walter Hartridge. I also answered a small mountain of personal mail. But I knew perfectly well that I would finish the correspondence any day and bang up against my most dreaded duty: cleaning my office before I began the actual writing of *Lighthouse*. The corners of my desk and every available shelf and tabletop were still stacked with Xeroxed research material and other clutter from two novels!

I looked around me in near despair, but someone came again to my rescue. Now, perhaps there's a question as to whether or not a bird can be referred to as "someone." A mockingbird can be. At least, our eccentric Snoopy can and must be. Through the more than three years at The Dodge, our weary and our happy days had been celebrated in song by that sleek and entirely unique bird. At least, according to any mockingbird "research" we'd ever done at White Cap, in Florida, or anywhere in the South, Snoopy is unique. He sings when no other mockers are singing, and he sits in judicial silence when other mockingbirds are cracking the sky with song. He sang me off on the long *New Moon Rising* tour and he welcomed me home. More times than I can remember, he has lifted my sagging spirits over a paragraph that won't jell or an important historical sequence that I've forgotten to develop in a story. His name is Snoopy because he is a dead ringer both in personality and activity for Charlie Schultz's irrepressible character in Peanuts—especially when he transforms himself before our eyes into the World War I flying ace and goes after his "Red Barons"—flocks of cedar waxwings, robins, and jays about to gobble up his bountiful supply of berries or wild cherries. Now Snoopy, completely out of season, sang me through the cleaning of my office, which took a week.

At any rate, my notations for the year 1970 tell me that by the end of February we were cheerfully on our way up old Route 17 to Savannah to keep the much-anticipated date with the Walter Hartridges. And we were going in my brand new Ford LTD!

Before I record that all-important visit, I must lovingly dispose of Bonnie, my incomparable 1959 Pontiac Bonneville. Faithful Bonnie, in which we had found St. Simons—into whose ample trunk we had packed our belongings for two winters on the Island and in which Joyce and I had traveled every Island lane and winding road not marked Private—had finally resigned from duty.

I should have had my warning that Bonnie's days were numbered when Mother and Nancy were here for Christmas—just a couple of months earlier. But to me, the car was immortal. Even at age eleven, she didn't look a bit old to me. Johnnie kept her shining, and I confess to having been surprised by two things that happened on the Sunday I took Mother and Nancy to the Cloister for dinner. But I was so blindly pro-Bonnie that I ended up laughing about them both.

The first happening took place as we were rocking along over my rough, sandy road away from the house. My mother doesn't have a phony bone in her body, but she does like elegance. I had bought Bonnie right after my father's death, and for the next few years Mother and I had taken many trips. Always, she had remarked on how handsome and comfortable our car was. I glowed and agreed. Okay, so Bonnie wasn't old then, but she *was* old that Christmas holiday as we drove out my winding lane to the hard road that would take us to the Cloister, one of Mother's favorite places to go. Still, I wasn't prepared for Mother's casual comment, spoken in such an extraordinarily kind voice that it wasn't casual at all.

"You know, dear," she said, picking a little at a rip in the red plastic that covered Bonnie's dashboard, "I think Bonnie at least deserves a strip of red tape over that tear, don't you?"

"No," I snapped. "No, indeed. Bonnie would far rather be in honest tatters than in cheap patches." I wanted her the way she was, no matter how she looked to anyone else!

Our dinner in the Cloister dining room was fine enough even for Mother. The maître d' hovered over us to see to our every wish and need, the details of the service could not have been more to Mother's liking, and we were assured repeatedly that it had been an honor for the Cloister to entertain us.

We finished our leisurely dinner, wandered out of the dining room to look at some of the expensive shop display windows, and finally, feeling quite elegant ourselves by now, walked out to where I had parked Bonnie. In front of the hotel, of course.

Unlocking Bonnie's front door, I noticed a small yellow card under the windshield wiper. "I wonder what this is," I said absently, slipping out the card to read it.

"What is it?" Nancy asked.

In answer, I burst out laughing! I handed the card to Nancy, who in turn handed it to Mother. They began to laugh too. I have saved the notice, and this is what it says:

> THIS AREA IS RESERVED FOR GUESTS ONLY!
> Employees must park in lot across from Laundry
> or next to Post Office.

Okay, so Bonnie *was* a dated model, her miles showing. Okay. So what? I was writing a column for a local paper in those days, and one entire column was devoted to the story of Bonnie's visit to the Cloister. Somewhere I have the gracious note of apology from my cherished friend, Mr. Alfred W. Jones, Sr., of the Sea Island Company. I hope he didn't doubt me when I assured him that it was merely a matter of my seeing one certain car differently from the way his conscientious security guard saw it.

It was not many weeks later that Bonnie's faithful engine suddenly began to pound more loudly than our pileated woodpecker, the Lord God bird, which pounds so loudly Joyce and I had once thought there was a man in our woods chopping down trees! I took Bonnie to Chancy's Standard Station, where Bud and Polly Chancy, trusted pals of ours, gave me the bad news.

"I'm not a General Motors mechanic," Bud said, shaking his head, "but they'd say the same thing. The engine block's cracked. And —I hate to tell you, I really do—but the car's not worth fixing!"

In dismay and not understanding their values at all, I found out that no one—not any car dealer anywhere—would give me anything for the beautiful white buggy which had been such a part of my life for eleven years. Finally, a junk dealer made me the insulting offer of fifty dollars. Tears stood in my eyes when I told Johnnie Wilson about it.

He thought a minute, looking down at his shoes, and then he said gently, his voice deep with comfort, "Don't worry about old Bonnie. I'll take her. I've got a friend who might switch the engine from my smaller Pontiac to Bonnie. I'll just drive her out like she and I were going somewhere together, and you won't feel so bad about seeing her go. That way, we'll keep her in the family."

I knew Johnnie would try to keep the old car running for love's sake, but even I doubted that it would work for long. I'm telling the whole truth when I say that I honestly don't know what finally happened to Bonnie. Johnnie did get the motors switched, and for a few months I would see him and Ruby riding around the Island in my big old white love. Then one day when we dropped by their house, Bonnie was nowhere to be seen. By some means Johnnie had spirited her off the Island without telling me, so that my grief would never be freshened by the sight of her steamboat dimensions bearing a stranger. If she ever again bore anyone anywhere. He didn't tell me where she went and I didn't ask, and now Johnnie is in heaven. And I don't intend to ask Ruby.

The only way I knew of getting over my grief at Bonnie's demise was to buy my first Ford. If I bought a Ford, I could have a decal on its bumper which read "Gould Motors." In those days, the big Ford dealership in Brunswick belonged to Colonel James Gould and his son, Jimmy, and I knew Jimmy would see to it that I got a good car.

The pale-blue Ford LTD I bought was promptly named Horace, after Horace Bunch Gould of *New Moon Rising*. (I now own a 1972 Ford LTD named James.) Having a Gould car helped enormously, but on the bright, crisp February morning when Joyce and I set out in Horace for Savannah, it wasn't the car—much as I liked it—which made me so peculiarly expectant. It was our destination. I also knew that Walter Hartridge, in anticipation of our visit, had already been digging out his Harris family notes.

A big factor in my high expectations for a fresh, productive working relationship with Walter was, as I'd told Mother and Nancy, his real enthusiasm for what I was doing. The man was obviously as much of an enthusiast as I—and if I'm not enthusiastic about a project, I simply don't tackle it. In fact, since one of the ways I check my guidance on whether or not to undertake a thing in the first place is by the level of my own enthusiasm, I drop few endeavors before they're completed. Of course, even my enthusiasm can flag as a work goes on, whether a writing job or an effort to preserve an old ruin or to save a marsh—I'm human—but I'm also blessed in that sooner or later I grow eager all over again.

I rang the bell at the Hartridge house, which had been in the family for generations, and as he would do repeatedly during the next few years, Walter himself flung it open, shouting, "Welcome to Savannah!"

Susan Hartridge greeted us too, and Walter and I went right to it. Sitting together in their parlor—that was the only time in the formal parlor; after that, every visit was spent in the family room—Walter and I could have told no one anything about either Joyce or Susan—what they did, what they said, even where they were. As it turned out, they liked each other—and a good thing, too!

Anyone reading this who knew Walter Hartridge—and many will because he was so widely known and respected—will recall how that tall, imposing man could go completely "out" on historical research. In fact, when he spoke, he held his listeners spellbound because he was spellbound with his facts. History, aside from his Susan and young Walter, was his life. He and I were to work together through two entire novels over a joy-filled period of five years, and I'm still dumbfounded at his vast knowledge. So far as I know, he was the only person who could, without glancing at a page of anything anywhere, give you in superbly chosen, fluent language the complete history of Georgia, Florida, and South Carolina. It should be no mystery to anyone why he was indispensable to me.

On this occasion, he had at his fingertips the complete history of James Gould's in-laws, the Harrises of Savannah. My need for such material was critical; Agnes Hartridge had not touched on the Harrises in the Gould family history which Mary Everett had given me.

And that was not all. Until that day I had hardly noticed the coincidence of Agnes and Walter's surnames; it was so long ago—a whole book ago!—that Mary, in giving me the history, had casually credited it to "Cousin Agnes Hartridge." Actually, I knew very little else about her except that she was a granddaughter of Horace Bunch Gould. I hadn't even known whether she was Miss or Mrs. Hartridge.

Now, as though Walter did not already have my rapt attention, I was suddenly galvanized to hear him mention "Aunt Agnes." That was when I learned that *Mrs.* Hartridge had been married to Walter's uncle, that she had nurtured Walter's interest in history from his boyhood, and that he adored her and had visited her often during the time she had lived alone in the Goulds' old Black Banks cottage. Then came the stunning coincidence that, on a visit to St. Simons when he was about sixteen, he had come up with the idea that she should write the history of the Gould family.

Although she had seemed to like his idea very much, he had never known for a fact that she had gone ahead with the history. *Much less had he ever seen it until I produced my copy of it that day!* And yet, if he hadn't suggested it in the first place, it might never have been written—and *I* wouldn't have had my primary source for *New Moon Rising.* So, although I came to know Walter only while working on *Lighthouse,* in this almost incredible way I owe the entire trilogy—not the first novel, but the trilogy—to him.

Sitting in the Hartridge parlor that day, I may have been more wonderstruck than Walter—but not much. Dimly, I recall poor Joyce and Susan, bundled in sweaters, bringing us occasional refreshments and stoking the fire every so often in the beautiful but drafty old house. Neither Walter nor I knew it was cold. I also remember that they made a joke now and then about our being in space, which we both understood and brushed off good-naturedly, from the distance of that blissful other world of history.

I had studied his early book, *The Letters of Don Juan McQueen to His Family,* and so had at least one intelligent question for him: "Don Juan McQueen seems to have owned land all over the southeast. Could James Gould have met McQueen at Pierce Butler's plantation on St. Simons Island? One of your footnotes tells me that McQueen was visiting there at the same time James Gould was on the Island. Could this persuasive McQueen have convinced the young Gould to take a lease in East Florida owned by McQueen—for the King's Ferry land?"

"Ah-ha!" Walter exclaimed, jumping up to his full six feet three or four. "Indeed he could have gotten the land in exactly that fashion! Splendid deduction. And no one can challenge you!"

I beamed under his praise. Historical research was new to me still. I was feeling my way, but catching on, I hoped, and loving every minute of it. Walter seemed to accept easily the fact that, provided a novelist holds to all the known history possible, his or her imagination must supply what cannot be verified.

Another jewel he handed me that day was his suggestion that I approach Dena Snodgrass of Jacksonville, who would, he felt, be happy to do some timbering research for me in the Jacksonville libraries. He both respected and loved Dena; and now that she has come to be one of my most supportive friends and researchers, so do I. One big bonus in having access to Walter Hartridge was that when he did not know something historical, he could direct me to someone who did—or who could at least give me a still further lead. (So goes following the trail of research—often a kind of treasure hunt.)

As the years went by, I came to depend upon Walter as deeply as I had always depended upon Tay Hohoff. In fact, it was an unfulfilled dream of mine that the two should meet in person. Unfulfilled? Perhaps not. Walter is gone now, too. He died suddenly in 1974, just the week before he and Joyce and Susan and I were to go to Charleston, South Carolina, to begin research on my novel *Maria*. His going was as much a blow to me as Tay's had been the year before. I did so want to be on hand when they met each other, but I like to think that my dream *has* been fulfilled—that they do meet and talk by the eternal hour. As with Tay, I miss Walter to this hour.

But during that extremely happy and productive winter of 1970, I still had them both, I had a new novel to write, and my spirit soared. Along with the good stimulation of writing came a new, enormous relief: my accounts and all my tax business had been put into the hands of a kind, astute CPA named Powell Schell. I was doubly in good hands when Powell gave me beautiful Beth Edwards as my account executive, and somehow I knew once and for all that I'd never have to agonize over tax business again. The problems would come, of course, but between Beth and Powell, I could rest.

When my manuscript for *Learning to Live from the Acts* had been edited by Tay, my heart lightened still more. There was, happily, very little additional work to do. My time and energies could now be lavished on the third novel, *Lighthouse*.

———

During the dark, trouble-filled periods in our lives, it is hard even to remember the weeks and months when everything went right. Still, outside of God, nothing is permanent but change. The dark times pass and merge into light times. The light times then change, sometimes suddenly, sometimes gradually, into darkness again. But change goes on. The darkness does lift. I have found both patience and peace from having learned this. Now that I am no longer young, I am never, never deluded about my good periods. I simply enjoy them, give thanks for them, and make every effort to make the most of them while they are at hand.

The early part of the year 1970 was a light time for me, when everything seemed to go right beyond even my inherent optimism. Every day something new seemed to come my way, something new and good. Mother and Nancy and her aunt, Mary Jane, had come to be a surprisingly close and happy threesome. They ate together, took trips together, and were utterly devoted to one another. I had no worries about Mother whatever. That period, of course, was at the very start of *Lighthouse*. The publisher wanted to bring it out in 1971—a tight squeeze for me for such a big book, but I had said that I'd try. If everything had kept on as it began early in the year, the goal would have been reasonable.

I was flying along writing at a rapid clip, even for me, because I had hit one of my windfalls. Quite by accident (God's kind of Accident!), one Sunday afternoon the windfall came when I meant to be doing no more than making a reservation at the King and Prince Hotel for a friend from the North. At the time we visited the Hartridges, I still had no information at all about what James Gould's early life in Granville, Massachusetts, might have been like. Agnes Hartridge's account had mentioned the town and that his father's name was also James, but had said no more. I didn't even know his mother's first name. During my telephone conversation with cordial Mr. Charles Morton at the front desk of the King and Prince Hotel, I had, of course, identified myself. He then told me how much he and Mrs. Morton had enjoyed my first two novels, and because I was so full of it all, I told him that right then I was drawing a complete blank at the point of Granville, Massachusetts, in the writing of another. I felt a little silly even mentioning Granville, Massachusetts, to a perfect stranger who lived on St. Simons Island.

Silly!—it was providential; the Mortons had come recently from a town near Granville, and he gave me at once the name of Mr. Paul C. Nobbs of Granville, who would surely be able to help! Within half an hour, I had Mr. Nobbs on long distance, and I also had his gracious promise to send me his only copy of a rare old history of Granville. From that I was to get every scrap of the information I needed.

The same extraordinary kindness was shown me by my friend Kathy Roach of Bangor, Maine, and by Mrs. Dorothea Q. Flagg of the

Bangor Public Library, who sent me not one but seven rare books on early Bangor, to keep as long as I needed them.

Buds were popping out on the sweet gums and fiddler oaks when, late in February, Clara Marie Gould came one night for dinner, bringing a Xerox copy of James Gould's actual will. Her cousin Barbara Whitlock had found it in the Glynn County Courthouse.

The days were too short to contain either my work impetus or my enthusiasm. Tay called often to encourage me in the always difficult task of beginning a novel, and by March 3 I had written two full chapters. Joyce's parents visited us and were, as always, understanding of the fact that I had to keep on working. And as I recall, it was about this time that dear Lorah Plemmons, whom we saw two or three times a week, began to give me her straight-faced lecture on working too hard. Lorah was ninety-five then, and without a hint of her merry smile (she could look right through you!) she would say crossly, "Genie, you listen to me. If you don't stop working so hard, you'll be in the same fix I'm in when you're my age!"

That, of course, sent Joyce and me into gales of laughter, but so help me, the old darling was still lecturing me in the same way just a week before she died, early this year. June 1977 would have marked her hundred and second birthday!

Joe, my wonderful, kooky brother, and his wife and daughter, Millie and Cindy, paid one of their rare visits to us late in March, and as always, after a few days of laughing with Joe, I felt happy and full of energy to go back to work after they drove off to their home in Nashville. Being with them did me so much good that, in spite of a bout with flu, the chapters grew as I worked daily on the rough draft of *Lighthouse*.

Spring on the Island, when the air changes from autumn and winter gold to clear, green-white, is distracting. Anyone who thinks we miss the change of seasons down here should try it through one year. Aside from Snoopy, the mocker, our other favorite bird is the rare painted bunting male which we have named Richard. (He is also understandably called a nonpareil.) On the coldest day in early March, with gray skies still low and a chill wind whipping around our point of land, there can come the long-awaited sound of his unmistakable call —silver bars pushed out at ten-second intervals into the bitter air.

"Richard is back!" I shout to Joyce. "Richard is back!"

According to our bird books, the tiny red and blue and chartreuse birds fly all the way from our feeders to Central America for the winter. And until that singular song reaches us again in March, we wait. We wait a whole month longer to *see* him, while he sings out of sight, in the tops of the tall pines, and then one day, one glorious day, there he is at the feeder, as much at home and in charge as though he'd never been away.

In a particular way, the tiny bird will always be connected in my mind with late summer and *New Moon Rising*. He was still here when Joyce read the entire manuscript aloud to me in our living room. For much of this long, time-consuming effort, Richard sat singing—every day as the reading went on—in the holly tree outside our living-room bay. At the end, Joyce was crying so that she could scarcely read my tag line. And while we sat there, with me realizing gradually that I had no more story to write and feeling lost and lonely—the painted bunting broke again into one of his louder paeans, as though he knew I needed cheering.

We can also chart the progress of spring in coastal Georgia by the thinning of the flock of white-throated sparrows which have lived all winter in the dense shelter of the yaupon hedge surrounding our house. When they begin to fly north for the summer, our year-round, faithful towhees are calling again in the woods and under the backyard azaleas. Cardinals, of course, have been around all winter too, gorging sunflower seeds and perching impatiently up and down the huge wisteria vine (like hopping red blossoms), ticking irritably when we're late bringing dinner. In the spring they begin to ignore our offerings and get so busy with nest building—out of sight—that invariably, we worry about the cat from the riding stable which adjoins our land. When the goldfinches stop by for thistle seed and the red-bellied woodpecker returns to the feeders, we know spring is coming. But it's here for certain the first day we find fifty to a hundred migrating robins in the front yard driving Snoopy out of his mind.

Beyond the birds, the fresh, green-white air, and the usual riot of jasmine, azaleas, and wisteria, the spring of 1970 is memorable to me because of one special visit to The Dodge. On a bright, soft April afternoon, Jimmy and Mary Frances and Clara Marie Gould arrived, their faces shining and a treasure for me in Jimmy's hand: the little tin lantern which his great-great-grandfather James Gould had carried for much of his life! Surely it was the one with which James lighted himself up and down the steep stairs at his St. Simons lighthouse. I would not only have the quaint, charming lantern beside me when I needed to describe it—beveled glass, four-sided, a sturdy bale for carrying—they *wanted* me to have it, as Horace had wanted me to have his grandfather's medal, for inspiration as I worked!

I was then still allowing myself to be talked into an occasional speaking engagement, and it was difficult to get back into the novel after three in a row in May. Speaking dates stimulate me, but for some reason they stimulate me away from writing. In my date book on May 14, I wrote, "Suddenly, *Lighthouse* going in all directions! I've lost my concentration. Was there such confusion during *New Moon Rising?*" Of course there was; there had been many such times. One tends to forget them from book to book. I also wrote in obvious exasperation, "I'm *so inexperienced* with novels!"

Whatever I am *not*, I am a pro, and I plugged ahead, aided in the work and in my spirit by the generous help of many interested people —our neighbors, the Harry Parkers, the librarians in Brunswick and on the Island, Dena Snodgrass, and B. I. Pennington, who not only planted day lilies for us, but shared with me, from his life spent timbering, technical detail that I needed.

As confused and frustrated as I felt with the writing, research help continued to come, often from unexpected sources. One day at lunch with Potter's son Joe and his wife, Katy, who were visiting the Island from their home in California, I happened to be complaining that I had to find a reason for James Gould's coming down from Massachusetts to St. Simons in the first place. The Hartridge history gave no reason. Joe's face brightened. "Why, I've always heard he came down to survey the timber used in the building of the frigate *Constitution.*" A mention of this to another member of the family triggered the same memory!

The pieces were falling together, and I was free to pursue my next mystery—some sort of detail about the old frigate itself. Joyce thought of that rare gentleman, Captain Alfred Brockinton, St. Simons expert bar pilot, and another valuable clue fell into place: Captain Brockinton owned the actual plans of the frigate *Constitution!*

My frustration eased, and I felt once more as though I were constructing a novel. June was coming, the month I always try to spend mostly with Mother, and we were already making plans for a trip. After

I stayed a few days in Charleston, the Goshorns would join us in a leisurely drive to Williamsburg. Then on to the Island, where we could all visit together for as long as I dared stay away from the manuscript.

Before I began the drive to Charleston, I mailed some 300 pages to Tay. It was far from a finished version, but I felt reasonably good about it. Clara Marie Gould and Theo Hotch, then our Regional Library Director, had read it. Joyce had read it. We all liked it. And so I bundled it off to New York and left for Mother's with a light heart the same day Joyce set out in her car for Indiana.

The trip with Mother and the Goshorns could not have been better. After a final stop in Savannah, so I could show them the lovely old city, we pulled into The Dodge on June 25, laughing, carefree, and not even tired. The only cloud on Mother's horizon was the fact that Joyce was still away.

I put off facing the enormous stack of mail which our good Johnnie had as usual sorted by dates for me. Then suddenly, about eight o'clock that night, as we all sat talking in the living room, I remembered the manuscript I had sent to Tay and, knowing her promptness, guessed that the familiar brown envelope from Lippincott might well be in that mountain of mail.

For some unexplainable reason, I did not say this when I got up to look. I simply went to the dining room and flipped through the letters and magazines stacked in Johnnie's neat labeled piles. It was there! I tore open the envelope and began to scan Tay's unusually long letter. "Dearest Genie," it began. "This is the most difficult letter I've had to write to you to date."

My eyes sped down the page. I had sent her over 300 pages of manuscript—a winter and a spring of hard work—and she didn't like it! My head whirled, and for a minute I thought I might faint. "You have begun in the *wrong place.* James Gould is too young to hold a reader's interest. It labors along." Those are not her exact words. I have sent that letter and the accompanying rejected manuscript long ago to Boston University, where my collection is housed. But that was the verdict—stamped in my memory forever. None of my 300 pages would do.

Publication date had been set for autumn of the next year, 1971. The year 1970 was almost half gone. Mysteriously, a publisher needs six to eight months to get a book out after the author is finished. Financially, I needed the book to be out on time. I could feel my confidence slide away before I was half through with the letter. And then Tay, bless her, brought it back—a little. *She* believed with all her heart that I could do it!

Back in the living room I kept the conversation casual, but when Mother and Mary Jane went to bed, I knew I had to tell Nancy. Someone had to help me accept the blow, and she had become such a close, dependable friend, able to weather all kinds of storms in her own life and in mine, I trusted her completely. Briefly I told her, then handed her the letter.

"We won't tell Mother and Mary Jane," I said, when she'd finished scanning Tay's honest but shattering evaluation. "No point in spoiling what's been a perfect trip for them. But I had to tell *you.*"

Charleston, West Virginia, where we'd both grown up, is just Southern enough so that members of a family frequently call the girls Sister. Joe had called me that since he was a little boy. Mother and Dad had called me Sister on occasion. And a while back, Nancy and I had begun calling each other Sister too.

She looked at me for a long moment, then her eyes smiled confidently. "I know this has almost knocked you out, Sister. But I also know you can do it. I'll see that everything stays on an even keel with your mother at home, so you'll feel free. And—well, I just *know* you can do it."

My mother not only works her ESP on me regularly but is one of the world's most perceptive women. But Nancy and I fooled her, she vows to this day. Neither she nor Mary Jane caught on that my world had crumbled.

After seeing them off on their plane, I spent the afternoon alone in my office going over galley proofs for *Learning to Live from the Acts.* Joyce was due home the next day, but by then I had experienced one more demonstration that God's timing is never wrong. Never early, never late. For a day and night alone I was confronted with the Book of Acts and my already earnest efforts to identify with the Christians who lived their hectic lives in the story of that Book. All over again in the proofs it was shown me that they were able to live victoriously because they *knew* that the Spirit of the living God dwelt *within* them, empowering them to act beyond their human capabilities. Joyce says now that I had so completely latched onto the knowledge that I, too, would be enabled to do that heavy, impossible piece of work on time, I almost gave her no chance to be shocked at what Tay had written!

204

"If the Book of Acts is true, I can do it!" she says I repeated again and again. "I believe it *is* true, so I intend to prove it."

For three days, between answering letters, doing my stint for the local United Fund drive, writing a promised article or two, and taking care of my usual round of desk work, Joyce and I talked about *where* to begin the novel. Tay had been able to offer no suggestions, since she didn't know the entire story as we knew it. Finally Joyce, as she had done in so many times of crisis in my life, came through again.

"Why not begin it during Shays's Rebellion when James was about eighteen or so? We know every young man in Granville went with Shays."

I began it there and the entire manuscript rolled off my typewriter without a hitch beyond the usual: time out now and then to exercise my aching back and to have the septic tank pumped out, and—not so usual—for emergency gall-bladder surgery for Joyce, about three quarters of the way through my rewrite.

Of course I stopped work again when the surgery took place. Joyce was more worried that I had to stop than about her own surgery, but I spent every waking hour at Brunswick Hospital with her. Considering the seriousness of her condition, she did well, and I managed to appear in Minneapolis at CBA, to catch up on mail and desk work piled high while she was in the hospital, and to be back with James Gould by mid-August. In October we drove to Atlanta, where we both received awards for our writing, and I did my traditional autographing party with Faith Brunson at Rich's. This time the book was *Learning to Live from the Acts.* And I had learned!

The entire period is rather a blur to me now, but I do remember that all through her long convalescence, Joyce would have worked two or three hours marking manuscript and making suggestions on the Rough of *Lighthouse* before I woke up in the mornings. As much as we do that for each other, her work on *Lighthouse* was beyond the call of duty or friendship. The Book of Acts was operative in her, too!

Darkness seemed to be giving way to another light period. Joyce's *James Edward Oglethorpe* came out to rave reviews—even from the Kirkus Reviewing Service, which has never, to this day, liked a book of mine.

And behind our brick wall in the backyard, the ethereal moon-flower vine was outdoing itself.

In October, our beloved Hartridges—Walter, Susan, and young

Walter—came to the Island for as long as I needed Walter's expert guidance on winding up the huge manuscript. When they left after several days, Walter had a copy of a nearly finished draft under his arm for further checking at home.

On October 28 he called—to say he liked it all enormously! The first two hurdles had been crossed. I now had both Joyce's and Walter's approval.

On November 12, nearing the end, an odd thing happened. I felt that there was one more chapter to be written the next day. Late that afternoon, the twelfth, after Joyce had laid our fire in the living room, I came downstairs with my day's work in my hand. She began at once to read it to herself. When she finished, there were tears in her eyes and she said, "It's complete. You've done it! Did you know this is the end?"

I looked at her, frowning, not daring to hope. "It is?"

"Listen," she said. And then she read the entire chapter aloud. It *was* the end. The right one. I was so certain that even Tay could not have talked me out of it this time!

Our friend Frances Pitts was visiting again from Duluth, and she agreed one hundred percent. Frances is another of my divining rods where manuscript is concerned. By the time we spent—as was now traditional with us—Thanksgiving Day with Lorah Plemmons and our beloved Goulds at Oatlands Plantation, I was far along into the final rewrite of the story of their great-great-grandfather, James Gould. Their love and encouragement surrounded me that day in a special way which I still remember with wonder.

Joyce was busy with autographing parties for her own new book, *James Edward Oglethorpe,* but she stuck with me—reading and combing through every page I turned out on the rewrite. By the time Mother and Nancy arrived on December 17, I had rewritten twenty-six of the thirty-nine chapters.

Joyce left for her own home in a few days, and in spite of the fun Mother and Nancy and I were having, they both knew that I was fidgeting inside over the work still undone. In fact, I had been writing too steadily even to reread what I'd finished. So, after we'd gone to Lorah's for an afternoon to trim her tree in time for her daughters' arrival, I began to read *Lighthouse* aloud to Mother and Nancy. All day and all evening they would listen, encourage, and criticize like troopers —one night until 2 A.M. I was, as I suppose most authors are at that stage, obsessed. I really wanted to do nothing else but keep pushing. Even our happy Christmas Day at the Plemmonses' was an interruption. Of course, I have long ago learned that life—daily life—does not stand still because one happens to be writing a book. Practically, I accept that fact and act on it. I try to remember to do the things that love demands, but my vagueness is by now legendary.

Tay called on Christmas Day, and we decided that I'd send her Chapters 1 through 26. She had already approved my new beginning with real enthusiasm. I sensed a fresh urgency in her that day when she called. Her eyes were failing rapidly. Their condition was beyond medical help. For two years, she had worked at editing with a high-powered magnifying contraption "which turns paragraphs into little hills," she said, but how she'd worked! On long distance that day, I knew deep inside for the first time that I had come to mean as much to Tay as an author as she had always meant to me as an editor.

"Send it on," she'd said, with that airy, young quality in her voice again—a quality I loved but hadn't heard often since the death of her beloved Arthur. "Having manuscript from you will brighten my New Year no end, Genie."

Mother and Nancy and I read manuscript until an hour before I had to drive them to Jacksonville to catch their plane home. I drove back to the Island in a downpour and, according to my notes, worked until 3 A.M. Elsie would have to clean up my working copy, since Tay now couldn't see anything typed on yellow paper. (One of my eccentricities is that I can't seem to write on white paper with any freedom.) But I felt okay about everything and thought almost every night before I dropped off to sleep about the truth in the Book of Acts.

———⊷⊶———

On Friday, January 1, 1971, with Joyce still away, I finished correcting twenty-six retyped chapters for mailing before noon the next day to Tay—and on New Year's Day I also rewrote Chapters 27 and 28. I was alone, as I usually am on New Year's Day, and I worked, as I usually do. When Joyce returned, for four days steadily we worked through the remaining manuscript word by word, and late in the afternoon of January 13 I had finished still more rewrites. Before February arrived, the entire thing was typed and in the mail to Tay.

Our dear Anna Mow had been here for a good visit and had gone on her merry way when, still at work on the small changes Tay wanted in the early chapters, a telephone call turned my world upside down.

It was Nancy, hating so to tell me that Mother had fallen in her kitchen and had shattered her left leg! She had fallen at dinnertime. Nancy and Mary Jane had taken her in an ambulance to the hospital, and by the time Nancy called me, the surgeons were waiting for more tests because of an old scar on her heart which showed up in the electrocardiogram.

Tay had been—for her—lavish in her praise of *Lighthouse* as a whole, but as always there were final changes to make—about seven or eight days of hard work for me. If someone has ever picked up the heavy end of a burden for you and carried it with cheerful abandon, then you may know how I feel about what Nancy and Mary Jane did for Mother in her suffering—and for me in mine. It was decided that surgery would have to wait a week, until another EKG could be done. And Nancy decided *for* me that I should stay right here and finish the all-important rewrites.

"Your mother wants you to," she insisted. "Joe will come for the surgery, and I'm with her every minute. The Duchess"—Nancy's name for Mother—"wants you to finish that novel! After all, she refused to come to our house for dinner the night she fell because she was afraid she'd slip on the ice outside and disturb *you*. How's that for irony? She fell in her own kitchen, but she was trying as always to protect you from worry at this tough stage in your work. So, Sister, stay put, do you hear me?"

I stayed, and somehow I managed to concentrate enough to handle the rewrites. Except for eight chapters I had not yet corrected, the rewrites were all in the mail to Tay by the time I took a plane to be with Mother three days after her surgery. I made those final corrections in the bathroom of her hospital room, sitting on the john and using the top of the step-on waste can for a desk.

Nancy and I had just gotten Mother home in an ambulance and ensconced in a hospital bed—set up in her dining room, which we had stripped of furniture—when Tay called, half laughing and half apologetic. "I hate like the devil to tell you this, Genie, but it's as much my fault as yours—more, in fact. I *know* about small boats and skiffs. You don't. You've got James Gould and his family escaping down the St. Mary's River, the Indians in hot pursuit, and James's boat doesn't have a tiller or a helmsman!"

"What's a tiller? The thing you steer with? Maybe they didn't have one!"

"Silly girl, of course they had one. Otherwise they'd have gone in circles. I know things could not be worse for you there, but you'll have to redo that scene and put a tiller on the boat! Let James do the steering."

Things could have been far worse than they were. I could have been trying to care for Mother without Nancy and Mary Jane. But I had them, as I've had them every day since. The scene was rewritten on Mother's electric typewriter, which she'd used when she worked with my dad in his dental office. Rewritten with far more difficulty than I'd had making those corrections in the hospital bathroom! I hate electric typewriters, and here I was trapped with actually having to write new material while that infernal motor whirred and the keys grabbed my fingers before my confused mind could spell "helmsman." But the changes were finally made, read aloud to Mother and Nance, and sent off to Tay, who called as soon as she'd read them to commend me upon my nautical expertise.

I stayed with Mother until mid-March, when she convinced me that I should get back home to my Island again. I did still have the Afterword to write, and I knew it would be a stilted affair if I tried to do it on that leaping electric! Anyway, she and Nancy and Mary Jane had such a beautiful routine worked out that I was simply not needed any longer. So, by March 17, I was back on St. Simons, hard at work on the Afterword and the map for the end sheets of the early editions of *Lighthouse*.

During the month of April, when the air is filled with the sharp, purposeful calls of peepers, flycatchers, peewees—and at sundown, the equally purposeful but plaintive call of the chuck-will's-widow—I did not feel purposeful at all. Oh, I was busy—every day of the month I labored over the piled-up mail to be typed, to be dictated, to be notated and sent to Lorrie Carlson in Chicago—but it was an interim month, without any particular focus. There was a pleasant visit with our long-time friend, Bill Schoenberg, who was then with Harper and Row but is now happily selling for us both at Lippincott; there was a speaking engagement in Atlanta and numerous long-distance calls to and from

Lippincott on jacket design, book design, and the continuing hard work —for me—on the end-sheet maps. But even with such duties and pleasures, I was slipping already into my now familiar fuzzy interim mood—I am as rudderless between books as James Gould's boat was the way I first wrote of it!

In May I went back to visit Mother for another week and spent three days en route home with one of my closest friends, Easter Straker, in Lima, Ohio. As usual, I thoroughly enjoyed myself in the often riotous company of Easter and her friends, and as always I appeared on her superior TV show. Easter has believed in me as a writer for all the many years of our friendship, and not once has she ever praised me insincerely. I am relieved to know that she likes my novels, and our relaxed, in-depth interviews together on the air are among my favorite things to do.

I had planned to spend the summer more or less resting, with as much time at Mother's as my usual round of desk work would allow, but one night, as we played an Ethel Waters recording, Joyce was struck with an idea that would not let go. An idea I certainly shared. For most of our lives, we had both—long before Mom Waters ever joined the Billy Graham Team—been at the woman's feet. I had met her once briefly on the West Coast on a speaking tour—had, in fact, appeared on the same program with her. When I learned that the great Ethel Waters was to sing before I spoke, I became almost tongue-tied. Now Joyce and I seemed unable to let go of the idea that the vast public who knew her as a Christian singer needed to know her—for Ethel's sake—as the truly great vocal and dramatic artist she'd been all her life.

The upshot, after many long-distance calls and a million laughs and upsets—Mom Waters was that kind of woman; in quick succession she could evoke both upsets and laughter—we ended up in Los Angeles, making daily visits to the Ethel Waters apartment for hours of tape recordings. Joyce and I edited *To Me It's Wonderful* for Harper and Row, the story, mostly in Mom Waters's own words, of this great lady's life from her conversion to that date—nearing her seventy-sixth birthday. Her book shot my summer's relaxation full of holes for sure, but neither Joyce nor I would take anything for the experience.

Ethel, bless her, came to the Island in August, and for three nights we read the manuscript to her. She surprised us by loving every word of it, and when we put her back on her plane, we both slept for ten hours! She had, at her age, kept us reading steadily each night until 2 A.M.

Her last night with us we will never, never forget. Since she had wholeheartedly approved of what we'd done with her book, that night we all planned to have some fun. Mom, attired as she was for all of her stay with us in a short white nightgown, gave a performance which will remain in the memories of the three people who witnessed it. We'd invited only Clara Marie Gould, also a rabid fan of Ethel's, and all evening we played Ethel's oldest recordings. Rare records which Mom herself had given us. Not, I might add, of a religious nature by any means! We sat enthralled—laughing and then wanting to weep—as Mom lounged on our sofa in her shortie nightie and pantomimed each well-remembered phrase of "Dinah," "Stormy Weather," "Bread 'n' Gravy," "Suppertime," "St. Louis Blues," and dozens more—many of which she'd either introduced or made famous in years past.

Although Mom Waters was still able to have fun when we were seeing her, even then she sometimes sighed for heaven. Since I've begun the writing of this book, she has gone at last, to be with the Lord she truly loved with all the vibrancy and stubbornness of her artist's heart. We miss her, but we still have those recordings and, because of the love we shared, we can only be glad for her now.

As I recall, it was at about this time that my friend and fellow novelist, Beth Engle, gave me what has become one of my dearest possessions. During a conversation one afternoon, I noticed an odd-looking object on her coffee table—something like a chunk of drift-wood and yet not. Wood it was, weathered and gray. It stood on one end, its upper portion rounded (except on one side), and appeared a bit charred. But there was a definite circular pattern cut into part of the strangely fascinating piece. Finally, I could no longer contain my curiosity. I picked it up and asked Beth what it was.

"Well, for one thing—it's yours," she said. "I found it a few months ago, walking in the woods near your property at Frederica. I honestly don't know what it is, but I felt you might like to have it."

I sat looking hard at the strange object, wheels spinning in my brain. After a few more questions, I was all but certain that I held in my hands some remnant of the house which Anson had built for Ellen, later the Dodge Home.

On my way home, I stopped at the architect's office, and Lamar

Webb confirmed that the piece was indeed hardwood. Knowing that Anson had imported all the hardwood from the North, I hurried from Lamar's office to Lorah Plemmons's house.

"Look at this, Lorah, and tell me what it is."

For two or three minutes, she held the weathered chunk in her hands, smoothing its circular whorls. Then, calmly but with great certainty, she said, "Why, Genie, this was Mrs. Dodge's stairway post. The top of it." And then she chuckled. "I should know. I've dusted it often enough."

I had been right. Lorah explained that debris from the old house, totally destroyed by fire in 1927, had been hauled away over an old road that once ran through the woods outside my gate. The partially charred newel-post ornament had evidently rolled off a wagon and lain in the woods since. Thanks to Beth Engle, I own the last weathered fragment of Anson Dodge's house.

The real highlight of that summer—one of the highlights of my entire life—was Tay's first and only visit to the Island. Actually, I had almost given up the long-cherished dream that she would ever visit me. She despised travel, and by then her sight was so dim she could not even read gate numbers in an airport. Visiting St. Simons had become a favorite thing for many of our other friends in the publishing world, but Tay had never come down.

One of the most lovable and contradictory things about her, if one saw deeply enough, was her pretended aversion for the South. Never mind that she had edited Harper Lee's *To Kill a Mockingbird* and my St. Simons trilogy. "I also hate Victorian buildings," she said, as I promised to show her Christ Church. I laughed. Spouting hyperboles was one of her endearing quirks. I loved it. She knew I did, and so we settled into a comfortable, accepting relationship—she accepting that she was proud of me, loved me, although she thought it ridiculous to mention it. By then, it was ridiculous, really, except that I enjoyed the rise I always got from her when I said, "I love you and you *are* the world's greatest editor."

Even with normal sight, it took some doing for a newcomer off a New York plane to find our little Island Bluebird in the huge Atlanta airport, so we had Tay fly nonstop to Jacksonville, a much easier drive from St. Simons then the drive to Atlanta. A friend could help Tay board her plane in New York, and Joyce and I could pick her up in Jacksonville no farther from the plane than the end of the ramp. For as long as I live, I will see her in my mind's eye as she looked that day —fragile, smartly dressed, her handsome gray head high as she walked far too rapidly for safety toward me down the enclosed ramp. It was plain that she could not spot me at a normal distance; her hand didn't come out toward me until I began to run toward her. But she was in the South at last, and I was elated. She arrived on Friday afternoon, June 4, and stayed until Monday, June 7.

My (un)sentimental editor had remembered my June birthday and brought me the most sentimental gift she could devise—her very own pin reproducing the overlapping TH that was her famous signature —known all over the publishing world—done in German silver for her by a World War II GI she'd befriended. To this day, it is the only piece of jewelry I wear with any regularity. It told me all she meant it to tell me.

We showed her the Island and she seemed to enjoy every minute, although I was never sure how much she was able to see. I was accosted by tourists four times during our brief walk through the churchyard, and she fussed but seemed secretly proud when her author was recognized. Our local historical society was in the process of restoring the present lighthouse keeper's cottage—not the one in which James Gould had lived—and I was deeply involved in the restoration, so we went there. The recently excavated site of James's original lighthouse interested her keenly.

We ate every meal at The Dodge, because that was where she seemed most at ease and happiest.

Her love for Joyce has always been one of my deep satisfactions, and because music meant life to them both, the house was filled with music for almost the entire time she was here. Tay was a Mozart woman, and our collection of Mozart, Bach, Vivaldi, and Beethoven pleased her enormously. She lived only two and a half more years, and since our first sight of her in the Jacksonville airport, we had been struck with how frail she was. But there was little or no sign of the frailty when our downstairs filled with the first strains of a Beethoven Quartet. Tay seemed almost young again, and we sensed still more deeply why she was able to enter into the minds and spirits of authors and of their books. Editors work so behind the scenes that their compensation *must* come from within. My "editor, dear" showed us some of that "within" during those long, elevating afternoons and evenings of music.

Tay had been sent down by the company, I knew, to sign me to another contract. The St. Simons trilogy was finished. *Lighthouse* would be published that fall. Until her last night here, she had said nothing about a contract. In fact, she hadn't talked books with me except to urge me sometime to write the book I'm writing now—the story of our finding St. Simons Island. "Your readers, who are so loyal, deserve that book," she said. "It will be a nice change for you from these difficult novels. I want you to write it while I can still edit it. It must be done . . . just right."

But when I told her that I still felt too close to the whole St. Simons scene, that I didn't feel I could get the needed objectivity for a personal memoir about the Island, she agreed. We let the matter drop and returned to Mozart.

Joyce went to bed about eleven that night. It was nearly 4 A.M. when I finally climbed the stairs to my room. Tay was a night person, her lasting power far greater than mine. For a long time we talked about novels in general. About whether I should go on writing about people who actually lived or whether I should do what I often want to do— a purely fictional novel based in an accurately researched period. "You can write novels," she said finally. "Whether they're based on real people or not seems beside the point to me. The only thing I need to know is that you *will* go on writing them. You must."

I knew by then that I had to do just that. Nothing I had ever tried fulfilled or absorbed me as did the agonizing business of putting together a big novel. For a period of from two to three years, each one drained me, made it almost impossible at times to function in the twentieth century. Writing novels caused me to forget important things expected of me unless written down, to neglect my friends everywhere, or to let my mind wander while I was with folk dear to me —because at best I'm weak on small talk. Writing novels does more for the growth of my inner self than anything else I've ever tried, but with work in progress I want to do nothing but think or write or talk about that. (To the utter boredom, I'm sure, of those with other interests.) And yet the learned discipline of remaining a social creature is one of the enormous assets. After all, only I am "into" that book. My sense of Christian courtesy reminds me to be kind when I don't feel kind, to entertain when I don't want anybody around, and constantly to readjust my perspective so that everything but the work at hand does not seem like sheer waste of time.

Tay's thinking, I knew, had to do with the fact that even the first novel had sold well. As an editor, she owed it to her company to sign me to still another contract. She also let me know again on that memorable night that she believed in me as a writer, no matter who my future editors might be. We both knew that her retirement was inevitable, but we did not talk of it, which is probably why she did not tell me that night that she had already selected Carolyn Blakemore for me, then a colleague of hers at Lippincott and a dear friend. Her sure judgment was that Carolyn and I would have a fine editor-author rapport, and I believe we would have had just that—we later met and became friends—but by the time Tay left us, Carolyn was with another publisher.

At about 3 A.M., our talk veered to Walter Hartridge, and I told Tay about how much I depended upon his expertise as a historian and upon his genuine, everlasting enthusiasm. "He's been working in Georgia and Florida history since he graduated from Princeton," I said. "I think he was only in his early twenties when he edited a marvelous collection of Don Juan McQueen's letters to his family."

Tay jumped to her feet. "Well, you finally said it!"

A little bleary-eyed by then, I asked, "Said what?"

"The name of Don Juan McQueen, silly! When I came down here I was determined that I'd wait to see if *you* brought up his name. After all, it's you who will have to sit at that typewriter for all those months—living with the man."

My mind was a rag by then. Once a night person too, I'd begun going to bed early almost as soon as we moved to St. Simons Island because I so loved the morning here. I mumbled something like "Live with Don Juan McQueen?"

"Genie, don't you agree he should be your next novel?"

I didn't know whether I agreed or not. The idea had never occurred to me. I loved Don Juan—wrote him purposely into the East Florida sequence of *Lighthouse*—but an entire novel about him? "I suppose Walter *must* have vast amounts of information on McQueen," I offered weakly. "But what makes you think I could handle a complex character like that?"

"Simple. You could so easily have made him a buffoon in *Lighthouse* and you definitely did not. I cared about him exactly as you wrote him—even in that minor role."

"I see."

"No, you don't. But go to bed now. We can talk more tomorrow.

I've been selfish, but I had to hear you mention his name."

We didn't go to bed. The lightning of the idea struck me suddenly and I came wide awake. And for at least another hour we talked—as though we'd both had a night's sleep—about the man with whom I would indeed live long after Tay had left me.

Almost every year at The Dodge, we've had a family of raccoons —three little ones and mother, I presume, judging by the way she herds them around. Almost any night I can step out onto the back porch and hear a soft rustle on the wall that tells me our opossum is there, feasting on birdseed left when darkness overtook our feathered friends. (Which we call FF's.) And especially on a moonlit night, it isn't unusual—but it's always thrilling—to look out the front window and find from three to five deer grazing in our yard. But in the late summer of 1971, we had a fascinating visitor who has never again returned.

Her name was Lucretia, and she was a giant yellow and black spider, at least three inches from leg tip to leg tip and three quarters of an inch or more across her brilliant body. Lucretia built a masterful golden web all the way across our powder-room window, which looks out across the porch and over the front yard. She took up her abode in a safe spot—we seldom use our front porch—and neither of us would have disturbed her for anything. Johnnie thought us a touch mad, but invariably he humored us. We checked on Lucretia every day for the month of August, and one day there was an offspring, whose name came at once—Sis Lu. Sis Lu grew rapidly, and in one week, Lucretia was gone. Did Sis Lu eat her mother? Did Lucretia simply walk away and die because her life's work was finished? We'll never know, but neither will we ever forget her or her sheer, perfectly woven web across our window.

Joyce and I (mostly Joyce!) have killed a few snakes since we've lived at The Dodge, although now that the Island is being so devastated by overdevelopment, not only our deer are diminished in numbers every year, but our snakes too. Joyce shot a rattler in an overhanging branch of an oak tree once, but most of our snakes are only beautiful —not poisonous. Notably, there is Blackie, a constant and welcome resident. Blackie is of course a common black snake, and he (or she) keeps us reasonably free of marsh mice and rats, always attracted by our birdseed.

When we first moved in, we spent half our back-porch relaxing time batting little harmless green lizards out the door. Now, that seems utterly foolish to us. Adam, a fine specimen, whose pink mating bubble is pinker than pink, relaxes with us on the porch and keeps us free (almost) of spiders.

The only point of disagreement which Joyce and I continually have (and it has turned into a joke) is her segregationist impulses where the birds are concerned. Our songbirds are fewer than when we moved in in 1967, also, the experts tell us, because of the overdevelopment around us, and Joyce fights for their remaining rights at our feeders. As they lessen, it seems that the fittest survive and increase; we have greater and greater numbers of red-winged blackbirds and doves—from twenty-five to fifty to a hundred at once. Even a stray grackle or two this year. Joyce portions out seeds, according to type of seed and type of beak. I? I'd simply buy more and cover the entire wall, every feeder, and a stretch of our lane as many times a day as necessary. Solution? We take turns putting our separate "plans" into effect. Which plan works better? I can tell no difference.

One of the most difficult things I face in my own life is containing myself between books. Once I have approved the copy editing and proofs and the book is forever out of my hands, I'm used up. I know I *need* to call a halt. I dread tackling the usual mountain of mail left to grow during the final days of blitzing a manuscript, but I think it's good that I invariably have the mountain to move. I need my mail for more reasons than one. There is only one way to describe me when a book is finished: *I'm lost.*

By August 1971, *Lighthouse* was gone. My loneliness, especially after that one, was acute. *Don Juan McQueen* was up ahead, but so was the *Lighthouse* tour and all the piled-up desk work. What to do? As usual when she senses my helplessness, Joyce took charge.

"We're taking a trip," she said. "We'll go somewhere in north Florida—to Don Juan country. You can rest, but if you get too fidgety, we can always run down to St. Augustine, where he lived."

It sounded perfect, and we did just that. Get me away from my desk and I do rest. Rest, to me, is about nine hours' sleep a night and a book a day to read. I loathe exercise, but in our comfortable beach motel near Jacksonville, I made myself walk for an hour or so up and down the sandy shore each morning. I also dieted, a thing I have to do *every time* I finish a book. I felt great. But in about five days, I wanted to "run down to St. Augustine." The most exciting part of that trip was the day Joyce discovered—again in our Triple A guidebook— that Don Juan McQueen had built a house on Fort George Island which still stood! Of course, we went there about six times during my "rest" period.

Back home in September, with the yellow air full of sulfur butter-flies and monarchs and with mud daubers busily building their "apart-ments" for winter, the wires began to hum between St. Simons Island and New York and Philadelphia concerning what kind of tour I'd make for *Lighthouse*. Tay agreed with me that it was far more important for me to do a light tour—nice and short—so as to begin as soon as possible on the research for *Don Juan McQueen.* (I had signed a two-book contract with Tay this time: Don Juan and one more "untitled novel," which turned out to be *Maria.* With not one but two new novels to anticipate, it would have been hard to hold me to a long, exhausting tour anyway.) I went, of course, to Rich's in Atlanta, where Faith Brunson and her fine staff crippled my right hand by selling eight hundred copies in one day. I then spent a week with Mother and autographed successfully again for Elaine Howell at the Diamond, my hometown's large department store. And as far as traveling away from the Island was concerned, that was it. The book sold just as well as if I'd worn myself to a frazzle, as I had with *New Moon Rising.*

But before all that—*this.* Although October 11 at Rich's was national publication date, Lippincott and Faith Brunson had agreed enthusiastically to an early pub date just for St. Simons. And in mid-September, a huge banner had gone up across the St. Simons causeway bridge, above the toll station:

EUGENIA PRICE DAY!
at the Lighthouse, October 2

During the years in which I had lived in Georgia, awards of various kinds had been generously bestowed; I had, at times, been almost overwhelmingly "recognized." But bright and forever shining in my memory will be October 2, 1971, when, by arrangement of the joint Chambers of Commerce of St. Simons and Brunswick, the people who had become my people gave me my very own Day. Earlier, the Glynn-Brunswick Chamber had kindly made Joyce and me honorary members, and the small, cheerful office of the St. Simons Chamber in Neptune Park by the ocean had come to be a favorite stop for us both. I don't need to suspect, I *know* that our friend Jean Alexander, who runs the St. Simons Chamber office, was the motivating force behind my Day. I hope she has a small notion of what it meant to me.

Actually, I had gone to Jean, a thorough diplomat, in a bit of a dilemma about the launching of *Lighthouse*. For *Invader* and *New Moon*, the dear ones at the St. Simons Library had given me beautiful teas. As I recall, the two local bookstores sold at those events. But by the time *Lighthouse* was due, my novels were even on sale at the airport, and other outlets had sprung up. The library would be just too small. People had begun coming in numbers to the Island because of my novels. Also because of Joyce's *Oglethorpe* and her children's book *Suki and the Magic Sand Dollar*, set on East Beach and at the Ship House.

It is a never-failing source of encouragement to us when readers single out Georgia and the Golden Isles because something we've set down on paper enchanted them. But we confess to mixed reactions. We love living here and we wish everyone on earth could share it— and yet, because of uncontrolled growth, the difference already in the quality of life from that of our early days on the Island is frightening. Many of the arching trees and much of the grapevine and smilax and the sumac and palmetto and wild sweet peas and morning glories— which once crowded to the very edge of our beloved, narrow Frederica Road—have been whacked down—so that the shadowy, romantic lane could be widened to accommodate ever larger equipment and the heavy increase in population. A population which has jumped from under 3,000 when we found it in 1961 to more than 12,000 now!

At any rate, somehow I knew that Jean Alexander at the St. Simons Chamber of Commerce would have a solution to my dilemma about how to cope with all the book outlets. Should I simply skip the Island and do no local promotion? Was I damaging it by too much publicity already? Even as Jean Alexander and her associate, gracious Dot Raulerson, greet all visitors with genuine warmth and hospitality, they do keep trying, along with some of the rest of us, to protect the eroding charm and beauty which still remain—the Island's main attractions. Without our natural beauty and the small-town charm, tourists might just as well visit any bustling, condominium-choked beach. So, knowing Jean's balance and tact, I stated my case.

"I see no problem," she said calmly. "And you must not deprive us of doing something for you! We love you and Joyce too much. Just leave it all to me."

Jean not only got the immediate cooperation of the joint St. Simons-Brunswick Chambers; she hit upon the significant plan to have my party in the recently vacated keeper's house beside the present St. Simons light.

The idea couldn't have been more appropriate! After all, my book was titled *Lighthouse*—and the year, 1971, was the one hundredth anniversary of the commissioning of the present light. Beyond that, the keeper's house had been granted only days before to our Coastal Georgia Historical Society, of which I was a charter member. We were going to raise funds to restore the keeper's house, which had been used by the Federal government as offices. The building itself was a fine example of the work of a famous Savannah architect and builder, Charles Cluskey. It needed everything done for it, but Walter Hartridge had assured me that it was well worth the effort. Holding my Day there would not only delight me; it should, I reasoned, arouse community interest in the old building (which now, completely restored, houses our Museum of Coastal History).

But on my Day, October 2, 1971, the weathered red-brick house stood, its windows open to the sea, right beside the spot where I was sure James Gould had built the first lighthouse. (Later excavations and a picture found by Burnette Vanstory proved my guess to be correct. We have been forced to cover over the ruins, but during the digs I saw with my own eyes the carefully constructed octagonal remains of the Gould tower foundation.)

On account of her accident, Mother would be unable to come, but Joe was flying over from Nashville and Nancy from Charleston—and I knew that every living Gould would be there to cheer me on as they'd done from the beginning. Eugenia Price Day was planned as an honor for me, but it was far more. To me, personally, the very choice of the date was significant. On October 2, 1949, twenty-two years earlier, I had become a follower of Jesus Christ. Words grow stubborn when I try to express the depth of emotion which filled me through every hour of every day that led up to my Day. I felt far less honored than melted. The big banner across the causeway bridge was dwarfed beside the inward banners waving in me.

All the local booksellers were pleased with the idea; they would sell books on the front porch of the keeper's house and in the front room to the right of the entrance. In the room to the left, the one with the view of St. Simons Sound, I would be seated at a table placed under a handsome portrait of James Gould himself, loaned to us by the Alfred Hartridges (Walter's cousins) who had also just succumbed to the charms of St. Simons and built their home on the old Black Banks tract. In those days, there was no air conditioning in the keeper's house, but my table for signing and greeting the people was to be set up beside a window open to catch every sea breeze.

Nancy called to say she'd be arriving on September 29, and my brother announced his arrival date, October 1. My heart sang when Fé Gould Powell, Mary's and Berta's youngest sister, whom I loved so much, called to say that in spite of her recent heart surgery, she was packing to join us from Albany for Eugenia Price Day! This, none of us had dared hope for. Fé was everyone's tender favorite, and my cup was so full of joy and excitement it splashed over. Plans were for the women members of the Gould family to dress in period costumes and act as my hostesses. Fé had her dress ready. Virginia Gould, wife of Potter's son David, and her daughter, Debby, would be there from Brunswick to attend one of the refreshment tables set with family silver. Present among my Island Goulds were Berta's daughter, Kitty Grider; Mary's daughter, Mary Jane Howe, and her daughter, Beth; Mary Frances Gould; Ju-ju Shelfer—all dressed in their beautiful period gowns—and Clara Marie, who had opted for just a dress. Joyce and I too would wear dresses, but I was still pleased that most of the Gould cousins would be so distinguished from the rest of the crowd.

On the night before the big Day, with Joe and Nancy here, The Dodge was rocking with laughter and good spirits when the telephone rang.

I answered. It was Kitty Grider. "Darlin', I almost can't bring myself to tell you—but precious little Fé died this afternoon."

My long silence gave my heart and Kitty's a chance to meld still more—and then to break. Kitty and Fé had been closer than most sisters. My heart broke especially for Kitty—and then for Dutch. Fé had planned to move soon to St. Simons to share the Everett house with Dutch and his little dog, Ginger. I don't remember what I said to Kitty then, nor she to me. Love words, because only love was there to comfort us both. But I do remember that one of us mentioned Dutch and how much he loved Fé. Finally, Kitty managed to tell me that Fé had her costume ready and her bag packed, and was about to carry it out to her car when her heart failed. Then I said something about calling off the party.

"It's not going to be called off!" Kitty's voice was suddenly firm and strong. "What's more, we're all coming in our pretty long dresses. We made them for *your* Day. Fé would have a fit if we didn't go through with it. She loved you, Genie."

All I could make myself say was, "She still loves us, Kitty. And she'll know about everything that goes on tomorrow—beside James Gould's light."

Dutch was among my first callers at the autographing table beside the window open to the sea, his gentle face wreathed in smiles, his eyes brimming with tears. But he was there, as were all the living Goulds and their families. The thermometer hit 103 that afternoon, but this prophet was *not* without honor in her hometown.

For over three hours, the line of people waiting to greet me stretched out the front door of the keeper's house, down the front steps, along the walkway to the sandy road, and out the sandy road to the paved street almost a block away. Any author would be overjoyed at a turnout like that, anywhere. This author's joy—in the midst of grief— knew no bounds. Some in the crowd were, of course, my readers from other parts of the country, who happened to be visiting St. Simons that autumn afternoon, but Joyce assured me that the majority were from Glynn County. Not there to see what the book trade calls a "name author"—blessedly, they did not think of me that way. Most of them saw me often buying groceries or in the drugstore. They had come, I chose to believe, for love's sake. I know Elsie Goodwillie was there for that reason. Her beloved Walter had just suffered a crippling stroke; overnight she had become a full-time nurse. But she was there that day for a few minutes—for love's sake. Many had come for love of me, yes, but mostly to share our *mutual love* of St. Simons Island and its history.

My picture must have been snapped a hundred or more times under James Gould's portrait, and I didn't get cramped or tired from sitting because I kept getting up to go around the big table—graced by a bouquet of roses from Mother—to hug people. To thank them for standing so long under that broiling Island sun, to thank them for caring, to thank them for being my people.

222

The local brass were there, along with my friend Bill Stuckey, then our United States congressman. But no one was really "brass" that day. Least of all the guest of honor, whose heart turned child and stayed that way as Joe drove Nancy and Joyce and me back to The Dodge with the haunting, primitive sound of bagpipes still ringing in our ears.

My big surprise of the day had been arranged in total secrecy by Joyce and Emmy Minor, owner of the Clapper Rail, whose ingenious husband, Al, and his friend Gerald Buchan had built a scale model of James Gould's lighthouse for the front porch of Emmy's shop. There is a scene in *Lighthouse* which Joyce loved—the high, exhilarating moment when James Gould, the assembled Islanders watching, lighted his lamps for the first time. To honor this moment, his longtime friend, John Couper of Cannon's Point, had brought along his servant, Johnson, to play the bagpipes.

The scene from *Lighthouse* which inspired Joyce and Emmy that day in 1971 went like this:

"Haven't we had enough entertainment, Jock?" James asked. "By the time I climb the tower, the sky will be nearly dark. I want to get on with it."

In answer, Couper leaped onto one of the empty tables.

"Friends and neighbors," he began, "the moment for which Mr. James Gould has worked, the moment for which we have all waited, is almost upon us. The Almighty has seen fit to begin to lower the light in the sky, and our beloved and respected friend and neighbor will climb to the top of his magnificent tower and officially light the full set of lamps in the lantern of the St. Simons lighthouse!" Couper permitted a moment's applause, then held up his hand. "I have planned what I hope is an appropriate accompaniment. My Johnson, known to you all, has, at my request, brought his pipes and even now stands ready, on a signal from me, to herald this glorious occasion—as James Gould, the builder of the light, proceeds to his tower."

The last thing James wanted was all this fanfare. The lighthouse itself would be its own announcement. He had intended simply to slip up the stair and light the lamps, but when he glanced toward the grinning Johnson, then at John Couper, he saluted.

A murmur of anticipation rose from the crowd. John Couper gave his signal, and after one sustained blast from the drone under Johnson's arm, the air was split by the ancient skirl of the bagpipes, as James, carrying his tin lantern, walked toward the lighthouse, pushed open its heavy door, and began the climb.

From the top of the tower, in the glow of the beach fire, he could see Couper urging Johnson to keep playing. With fire from his lantern, he lit first one lamp and then another.

When the full set of lamps flared and the big lantern began to revolve, the pipes were drowned by cheers and applause.

Joyce was not the only one stirred by James Gould's moment of triumph. Many readers have told me that it is one of their favorite passages.

The sun had just begun to lower in the high, southern sky that perfect afternoon and the crowd was drifting away when, feeling my first small wave of weariness, the Island air was once more split with the ancient skirl of bagpipes! Joyce and Emmy had arranged for fellow writer Bob Green to surprise me with the spine-tingling, primitive sound which has always set my strain of Scottish blood racing.

I rushed to the open window, and there was versatile Bob, blowing away in all that heat, silhouetted against the burning sunset—and walking sturdily up and down over the very spot where James Gould's light had stood.

The piped marches and reels echoed across the water in ancient cadences as they had done when James Gould lit his lamps publicly for the first time—and on this day the Islanders had come out for me too.

Even more than during the writing of his story, I understood how James Gould felt.

The following afternoon we buried dear Fé in the churchyard at Frederica, and the memory of our day spent with loved ones at the site of her great-grandfather's lighthouse helped us all.

It helps me still.

Printed in the USA
CPSIA information can be obtained
at www.ICGtesting.com
JSHW022325140824
68134JS00019B/1303

9 781684 427123